Markus Groß

Managing IT in the Age of BYOD and Remote Work

An Information Model for Managing Performance with the Balanced Scorecard, COBIT19, and BYOD

Springer Gabler

Markus Groß
University of Library Studies
and Information Technologies Sofia
Sofia, Bulgaria

This book is based on the author's PhD dissertation accepted by the University of Library Studies and Information Technologies (UNIBIT), Faculty of Information Sciences, Sofia, Bulgaria.

ISBN 978-3-658-51215-6 ISBN 978-3-658-51216-3 (eBook)
https://doi.org/10.1007/978-3-658-51216-3

This Springer Gabler imprint is published by the registered company Springer Fachmedien Wiesbaden GmbH, part of Springer Nature.
The registered company address is: Abraham-Lincoln-Str. 46, 65189 Wiesbaden, Germany

Abstract

Groß, M.: "Information model in the system for measuring and managing the performance of the balanced scorecard". Scientific advisor: Prof. D.Sc. Stoyan Georgiev Denchev. National Security and International Department to the Faculty of Information Sciences. Doctoral Programme: "Organization and Management of Information Processes". ULSIT, Sofia, 2025. 339 pages; 167 information sources; 30 figures; 90 tables.

Since its introduction in 2004, the 'consumerization of IT' and 'Bring Your Own Device' (BYOD) have gained considerable attention, further accelerated by the COVID-19 pandemic and the rise of remote work. This research provides an integrated overview of BYOD, remote work, the Balanced Scorecard (BSC), the COBIT 2019 framework, and their embedding into a structured Information Process Management (IPM) approach.

The study addresses the challenge of aligning employee satisfaction, cost efficiency, and regulatory compliance. An empirical analysis combining quantitative and qualitative methods was conducted to evaluate the current implementation of BYOD, IT-BSC, and COBIT, considering both organizational structures and user perspectives.

Based on the findings, a comprehensive implementation model grounded in IPM and aligned with international best practices from IT-BSC and CO-BIT is proposed. It defines key processes and performance indicators (KPIs) to help organizations manage information flows, ensure strategic alignment, and optimize performance. The research contributes to both academic discourse and applied practice in this dynamic and complex field.

Keywords: IPM · BYOD · BSC · IT-BSC · COBIT

Introduction

The IT department is constantly confronted with new requirements and data processing procedures. Nevertheless, it rarely receives recognition in companies because it is merely seen as an internal service provider. Consistently positive performance is rarely noticed, while individual disruptions remain in the memory of the specialist departments for a long time (cf. Blankenhorn, 2005, p. 2). Not only the availability of IT systems is of crucial importance for companies today, but above all the support of the core business through the use of information technology. An IT department should help to achieve a company's goals and must be able to react flexibly to changes (cf. van Bon, 2005, pp. 7 f.). To fulfil this requirement, the IT strategy must be in line with the company's strategy (cf. Kamleitner and Langer, 2006, p. 12).

> "The degree to which you can express something in numbers is the degree to which you really understand it."[1]

The central message of the british physicist William Thomson illustrates the importance of continuous performance measurement in today's economic climate. Without constant optimisation and adaptation, companies cannot survive in international competition. Nevertheless, the benefits and value contribution of the IT sector for the company are often the subject of discussion between company management and IT management (cf. Gartner, 2020, pp. 25 ff.). The increasing intensity of information, the high complexity of the IT landscape and the

[1] William Thomson, Lord Kelvin (*1824–†1907), professor of theoretical physics

high speed of innovation inevitably lead to high budgets. However, a one-sided orientation towards financial key figures is not enough. A company's financial performance is based on the past and provides no information about the extent to which a strategy decided by management is promising and what measures need to be taken to achieve the strategic goals (cf. Wiedemann, 2012, pp. 2 f.).

Therefore, controlling within information technology must also be seen in a holistic context. The internationally recognised concept of ROBERT S. KAPLAN and EDWARD NORTON, which was published in the 1992 essay 'The Balanced Scorecard—Measures that Drive Performance', provides a company-wide orientation (cf. Kaplan and Norton, 1992, pp. 24 f.). This integrative management concept makes it clear at all levels of the organisation that focusing exclusively on financial key figures is insufficient. As a result, the investments necessary for long-term business success in employee training, new product development, optimisation of internal processes and improvement of customer relations are either neglected or only implemented in a rudimentary fashion (cf. Wiedemann, 2012, p. 4).

The current BYOD trend, i.e. bringing and using private mobile devices in a business context, promises a variety of approaches to integrate the internal process perspective, which is often neglected in the IT area, the further development of employees and the external view of customers into IT controlling. However, it also brings previously unresolved and complex problems in the legal and technical areas for companies. In particular, data protection issues, such as the differentiation between private and business questions, while at the same time ensuring information security in the company, are comprehensive challenges (cf. Buckley, 2012, pp. 10 f.; cf. Fischer, 2012, pp. 60 f.).

With the onset of the COVID-19 pandemic, the world of work was reorganised practically overnight, as companies worldwide switched to remote working to ensure business continuity (cf. Kumar and Rahman, 2020, p. 12). During this unprecedented change, the concept of BYOD has received a significant boost. BYOD allows employees to use their own devices—be it laptops, tablets or smartphones—for work purposes, which is particularly helpful in a world that is rapidly turning to remote working (cf. Cisco, 2021, p. 2).

In the pre-COVID era, BYOD was already an emerging trend as it provided benefits to both employees and companies. For employees, it increases flexibility and satisfaction by allowing them to use their preferred devices. For companies, it reduces the cost of hardware procurement and maintenance (cf. Gartner, 2020, p. 2). However, the COVID-19 pandemic has significantly increased the relevance of BYOD. With the strict lockdown measures, most employees suddenly had to work from home, with many companies not having sufficiently equipped IT infrastructures to support this. BYOD has become a necessity to ensure business continuity while maintaining employee satisfaction (cf. McAfee, 2020, p. 10).

Furthermore, the COVID-19 pandemic has demonstrated the advantages of home office and could lead to a permanent shift towards more teleworking (cf. Gartner, 2020, pp. 2–5). The necessity of working from home has shown that many tasks can be effectively done remotely. It has also encouraged many employees and companies to recognise the advantages of more flexible working arrangements (cf. Eurofound, 2020, pp. 12 ff.). In this new era of work, BYOD plays a key role. It not only enables greater flexibility and adaptability in the way we work, but can also help to increase productivity and reduce operating costs (cf. Cisco, 2021, pp. 1 f.). Amid the challenges posed by the COVID-19 pandemic, the BYOD concept has proven its relevance and strength. With the increasing importance of home office, the BYOD trend is expected to continue even after the pandemic, as companies recognise the advantages and strive to create flexible and efficient working environments (cf. Microsoft, 2021, pp. 2–6).

Theme motivation

"Kein Bereich der Wirtschaft weist so hohe Zuwachsraten und so kurze Innovationszyklen auf wie die Informationstechnologie, insbesondere, wenn es um Mobile Computing geht." (Kersten and Klett, 2008, p. 13) ["No other sector of the economy has such high growth rates and such short innovation cycles as information technology, especially when it comes to mobile computing." (author's translation)] Nevertheless, information technology is still often seen as a separate support process in companies that does not contribute to increasing the value of the business. Therefore, the IT department usually has a strategy that is independent of the company's goals (cf. Kamleitner and Langer, 2006, p. 12). However, the IT department nowadays makes a significant contribution to achieving corporate goals, as it supports all value-creating business processes and these could no longer be provided without it. Carr already put forward the following thesis in the Havard Business Magazine in 2003: 'Today, no one would dispute that information technology has become the backbone of commerce.' (Carr, 2003, p. 12). This thesis was supported by Sury in an article in Informatik Spektrum in 2005: "In the information society the use of information technology is the base and instrument of all entrepreneurial activity." (Sury, 2005, p. 69) These statements illustrate the importance of IT for a company, since all business-relevant information is managed and stored with IT systems. This does not only affect large corporations; without functioning IT, even a medium-sized or small company is almost incapable of acting (cf. Kütz, 2002, pp. 119–124).

Therefore, organisations that want to survive economically in the long term must map all the functions of integrated, value-creating IT controlling. According to Schmidt-Kleemann, IT controlling encompasses the totality of all institutions, processes and instruments with which the planning, management and control of IT deployment and service provision are coordinated (cf. Schmid-Kleemann, 2003, pp. 27 f.). Whereby controlling, according to Horvarth's definition, focuses on the objects of IT deployment and IT service provision. IT deployment reflects the perspective of the customers (IT users in the company) and IT service provision embodies the perspective of the company. The effectiveness and efficiency of the use of IT services can be measured primarily in terms of customer satisfaction. This satisfaction represents the perceived benefit of computer-based systems for IT customers and other service recipients (such as suppliers and external customers) (cf. Horváth, 1997, pp. 25 f.).

Controlling in the field of IT is still not really anchored in the company, since the principle of economic efficiency also applies to key figure systems, i.e. the benefits of the control that is made possible must be greater than the effort required for setting up and operating (cf. Kütz, 2009, p. 35). According to Brun, in many IT departments neither the costs nor their distribution are transparent and there is often no allocation of IT costs to business processes. The traditional approach to planning IT deployment starts from a corporate strategy that defines the requirements for the company organisation and the design of business processes. From this, the requirements for information technology support are then defined. By using the Balanced Scorecard for the IT area, this traditional approach is complemented by the use of the potential of information technology for the design of business management (cf. Brun, 2008, p. 62).

The trend of consumerisation of IT, which has only 'recently' begun, i.e. the ubiquitous use of one's own digital devices in both one's private and business life, represents a further challenge for corporate IT. Even though the term 'Bring your own Device (BYOD)' was first coined by Ballgas in a conference paper as early as 2004, it was not used in the business context in which it is used today for mobile devices. In a business environment, it is understood to mean the extensive use of private IT services that are also introduced into a commercial context due to their uniformity, convenience or familiarity. Companies expect a wide range of cost savings from this, due to the reduction of investment costs, as well as higher sales through more flexible business processes, since almost every employee can be reached at any time and has access to professional information. Often, the technical and legal implications are overlooked in the first step or BYOD initiatives are stopped early for precisely these reasons. Management lacks a holistic view of the effects and a beneficial integration into the company's performance measurement system to be able to compare the risks with the benefits (cf. Ballgas, 2004, pp. 1 ff.).

The BYOD concept, i.e. bringing your own devices, and home office are two aspects of mobile working that have become significantly more important in recent years. This development has been accelerated by the COVID-19 pandemic, which has forced a rapid shift to home office (cf. Eurofound and the International Labour Office, 2020, p. 12). The advantages of BYOD and home office are manifold. They can increase employee flexibility and satisfaction, reduce travel costs and times, and contribute to an improved work-life balance (cf. Andriessen, 2013, pp. 113–116; cf. Delloitte, 2016, p. 14).

In the context of the COVID-19 pandemic in particular, the option of working from home has saved many companies and their employees from major disruptions. It has made it possible to maintain business operations despite the restrictions imposed by the pandemic, while protecting the health and safety of employees (cp. Bartik et al., 2020, p. 12). However, there are also challenges and risks. These include, in particular, data security and data protection issues. With BYOD, companies must ensure that they implement appropriate security measures and that they can ensure compliance with data protection regulations even when employees use their own devices for work (cf. K. W. Miller et al., 2012, pp. 8 ff.).

Due to the lack of synchronisation of IT costs with traditional business processes, which are often already integrated into a performance measurement system, it is difficult to systematically identify potential savings and synergies (cf. Baschin, 2001, pp. 99–103). According to various studies, the consumerisation of IT in particular promises a wide range of potential savings and process optimisation. Therefore, an effective IT controlling is in demand as part of the corporate controlling, which optimises the operational costs and strategically controls the IT in line with the corporate vision. The Balanced Scorecard is a strategic controlling instrument that is particularly successful in complex topics and not only in financial key figures (cf. K. W. Miller et al., 2012, pp. 12–15).

State of research

In the United States, the use of personal devices such as smartphones or tablets in a professional environment is already well advanced. The IBSG-Horizon study found that 95 per cent of companies in the US allow their employees to use their own hardware. What's more, 84 per cent of companies even provide special IT support for private devices. Even though these figures suggest that the BYOD trend is already highly prevalent in the market, the driver is more likely to be seen in the Asian region. According to a study by the management consultancy Deloitte, the origin lies primarily in the Asia-Pacific region, 'where' high-performance network infrastructures, the high importance of mobile communication and a strong commitment to the job are drivers of BYOD development. In South Korea, Singapore and Taiwan, this topic is part of employees' everyday lives (Deloitte, 2016, p. 15).

In contrast, the European region is just at the beginning of this industry trend. In Germany, BYOD initiatives are slowly gaining momentum. However, in direct comparison with the US, private devices are used much less frequently for professional purposes. A 2011 survey of German companies conducted by management consultants A.T. Kearney indicates that the figure is only around 40 per cent (cf. Kearny, 2011, p. 12). A study by the management consultancy Morgan Stanley shows that in 2013, more than half of the network devices delivered were wireless, with the vast majority of these being used in the workplace (cf. Stanley, 2013, pp. 5 f.). In a study conducted by the market research company IDC in September 2012, 58 per cent of companies allowed employees with company-owned mobile devices to access business applications, but only 33 per cent allowed mobile application access with private tablets or smartphones (cf. IDC, 2012, p. 14). The survey conducted by Avanade during the same period shows that 61 per cent of the companies surveyed stated that the majority of their employees are now allowed to use private devices at work (cf. Avanade, 2012, p. 16). The latest studies by the German IT industry association Bitkom and the global management consultancy Gartner confirm the trend. The central statement of the Bitkom study is that '(...) almost three quarters of all employees use private devices at work' (BITKOM, 2013, p. 12). According to Gartner, over 38 per cent of respondents expect that by 2016 they will no longer have to procure (mobile) devices for their employees. 86 per cent of respondents state that they use their private devices for work day and night (cf. Gartner, 2013, p. 1). Even if these studies do not show a consistent picture of the implementation and prevalence of BYOD initiatives in Europe, there is still a clear upward trend. More and more companies are dealing with the topic of BYOD and integrating it into their IT strategy (cf. Wiedemann, 2012, pp. 18 f.).

The fundamental idea behind the Balanced Scorecard (BSC) concept is that the economic success of an organisation is based primarily on influencing factors that lie behind the financial target values and originally determine the achievement of objectives. In particular, companies that depend heavily on functioning information technology and require intangible goods to create value rely on the BSC approach to assess their economic success. According to Silk, 60% of Fortune 1000 companies in the United States had already experienced the BSC, and according to a study by Marr, more than 50% of the largest U.S. use a BSC or a similar performance measurement system (cf. Silk, 1998, pp. 13–19; cf. Marr, 2010, p. 4). Williams showed that more than 60% of the Fortune 500 actively use a BSC and Risby calculated a BSC user rate of 44% (cf. Risby, 2004, p. 11; cf. Williams, 2005, pp. 4–9).

All these studies and a large number of scientific publications prove the importance and popularity of the BSC as a strategic controlling instrument. However, the BSC is not the only management concept that has caused a rethink in IT management in recent years (cf. Haeseler and Hörmann, 2005, pp. 54–57). In the context of information technology and information management, controlling has increasingly become the focus of interest and a wealth of comprehensive monographs and technical papers on key figures in IT have been written in recent years (cf. Zumstein, 2005, p. 3). Nevertheless, there is still little literature on the application of the BSC concept to support IT controlling (cf. Kütz, 2009, pp. 77 f.). The IT Balanced Scorecard (IT-BSC) is a goal- and value-oriented planning, communication and control instrument. One of its important tasks is to consistently link the IT strategy with operational actions by systematically breaking down IT goals to the employee level. The IT-BSC aims to achieve a balance between different elements, in particular the IT objectives and the resulting key figures. These include strategic and operational metrics, short- and long-term goals, financial and non-financial key figures, qualitative and quantitative metrics, internal and external influencing factors, as well as performance drivers and key performance indicators for the IT area. Another core idea is to link the strategic goals using perspectives and strategic topics through a cause-and-effect chain (cf. Keyes, 2013, p. 47).

In the context of the dynamic developments in the IT landscape, the question of how to effectively integrate IT strategies into corporate management is increasingly becoming the focus of scientific discussion. In this context, the Control Objectives for Information and Related Technology (CO-BIT) framework, particularly in its latest edition COBIT 2019, provides a potentially effective interface for integrating BSC principles into IT governance and management processes to promote a harmonious alignment of business and IT goals (cf. ISACA, 2019c, pp. 22 f.).

For future research, it is therefore important to identify and analyse the specific pathways and mechanisms through which BSC can be integrated into the COBIT framework to not only increase the efficiency and effectiveness of IT organisations, but also to enable a better strategic alignment (cf. ISACA, 2019a, pp. 25 f.), and to assess the possible effects of a successful integration of BYOD into the management systems in the context of CO-BIT. The continuous increase in the worldwide use of COBIT in companies is regularly examined by the IT Governance Institute and indicates a prevalence of approximately 75% in the last study in 2023, although no level of implementation maturity is surveyed (Fig. 1).

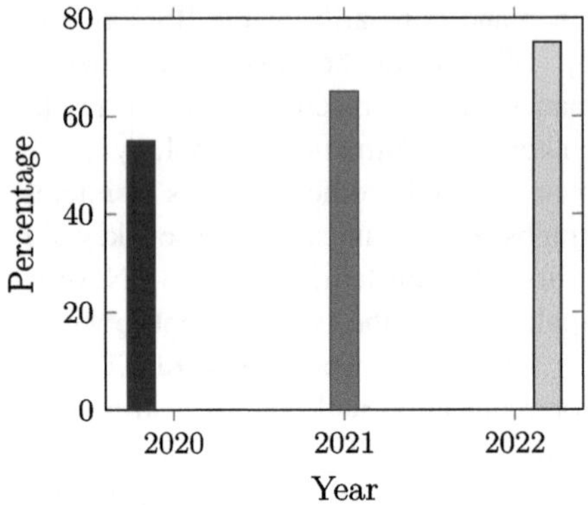

Fig. 1 Global Adoption of COBIT 2019 (adopted from (ILO) (2023))

A first approach to linking the BSC with the concepts behind the consumerisation of IT trend has been provided by Keys in the ‘Bring Your Own Device (BYOD) Survival Guide’. In the monograph published in 2013, Keys postulates “Whatever the organisation size, it is important that BYOD be carefully measured for its impact on performance. To do this requires just a bit of tweaking to the organization’s performance measurement and management systems. BYOD is definitely a strategy.” (Keyes, 2013, p. 54)

The trends of mobile working, especially BYOD and home office, have been steadily increasing in recent years, with the COVID-19 pandemic accelerating this development. In the context of BYOD, a study by Cisco (2016) prior to the pandemic showed that 69% of IT decision-makers in the US viewed BYOD positively as it increased productivity, satisfaction and morale. Similarly, a study by Syntonic (2016) found that 81% of companies had implemented BYOD policies, demonstrating the prevalence of this practice. For remote working, statistics show a similar growth trend. Before the COVID-19 pandemic, about 5% of employees in Germany worked mainly from home, according to the Federal Statistical Office (cf. Destatis, 2019, n. pag.). However, with the onset of the COVID-19 pandemic and the resulting restrictions, the use of remote working and BYOD increased sharply. A study by Eurofound and the International Labour Office (2020) found that nearly 40% of workers in the EU worked from home during the pandemic.

It is evident that the COVID-19 pandemic has significantly accelerated the adoption of BYOD and home office models. Surveys by Pew Research Center and Gallup from 2020 to 2024 confirm persistently elevated remote work levels in the US, while Eurostat and Destatis report similar trends for the EU and Germany. The International Labour Organization predicts that 30% of the global workforce will work remotely on a permanent basis by 2023 (cf. (ILO), 2023; Eurostat, 2023; Federal Statistical Office of Germany (Destatis), 2024; Pew Research Center, 2020). Fig. 2 visualizes these developments by region from 2017 to 2025, including a 2025 estimate extrapolated from consistent trend data in the cited sources.

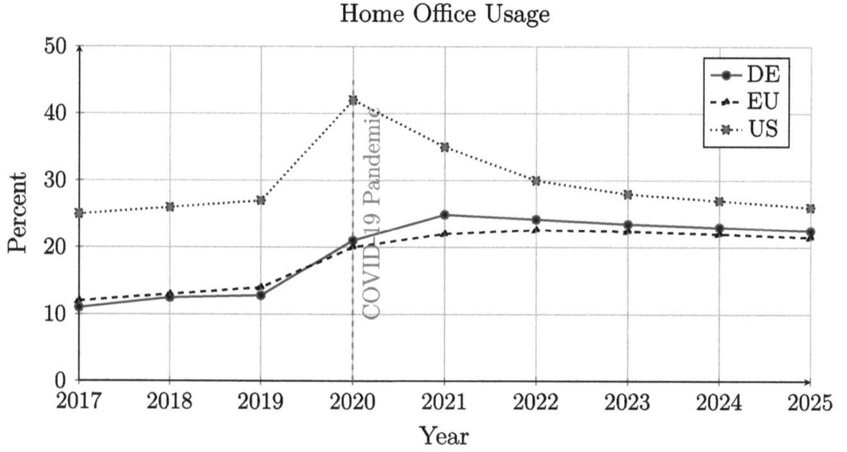

Fig. 2 Home office usage by region from 2017 to 2025. (Own illustration, 2025; data for 2025 is extrapolated based on trends and public sources including ILO, DeStatis, Pew Research and Gallup (2017–2024))

Research approach model

The author intends to develop a comprehensive methodology for the design and implementation of a IT-BSC that is based on the COBIT framework and specifically designed for BYOD initiatives. This methodology should be designed to provide high-quality and rational solutions for organisations of all sizes.

Research Object

The primary **research object** of this study is the comprehensive analysis and integration of IT management systems, focusing on the IT-BSC framework and its interplay with BYOD policies, particularly in the context of the governance and strategic alignment provided by the COBIT framework. This research explores the crucial role of the IT-BSC in aligning IT objectives with broader business strategies to enhance efficiency, effectiveness, and strategic alignment of IT structures in companies, ensuring that IT operations contribute significantly to the overall success of the organization. The IT-BSC framework is utilized as a pivotal tool to evaluate the effectiveness of BYOD implementations within organizational IT environments, incorporating multiple dimensions of IT performance measurement such as financial performance, customer satisfaction, internal processes, and learning and growth perspectives. In light of the COVID-19 pandemic, which has accentuated the importance of the BYOD approach, this study delves into how the structured approach of the IT-BSC can integrate specific KPIs related to BYOD, enabling organizations to assess how the use of personal devices impacts IT performance and aligns with strategic goals.

Additionally, the integration of BYOD into the IT-BSC framework necessitates a reassessment of traditional IT governance models. Personal devices introduce new risks and challenges, such as data security and compliance with regulatory standards, which are addressed under the COBIT framework. COBIT provides a comprehensive governance structure that assists organizations in managing IT risks and ensuring compliance with indus-try standards. The research examines the relationship between the IT-BSC and COBIT governance frameworks in managing BYOD, exploring how organizations can leverage COBIT's governance processes to mitigate risks while maximizing the benefits of BYOD, including increased flexibility, cost sav-ings, and employee satisfaction.

Furthermore, this research includes an exploration of the operational challenges and opportunities that arise from the implementation of BYOD. It investigates the impact on IT infrastructure, the need for continuous monitoring of security protocols, and the importance of compliance with data protection regulations. By integrating BYOD into the IT-BSC and COBIT frameworks, the study proposes a holistic approach to IT governance that ensures personal devices are used effectively and securely, without compromising the organization's strategic objectives.

In summary, the **research object** of this work is to investigate how the IT-BSC framework, combined with COBIT governance principles, can be utilized to optimize the management of BYOD strategies in companies. This study aims to provide insights into how organizations can align their IT systems with business goals while addressing the complexities introduced by the use of personal devices in corporate environments.

Research Subject

The **research subject** of this study encompasses IT departments of companies that are keen on designing and optimizing their IT strategy in line with overarching corporate goals, with a specific focus on the strategic integration of BYOD initiatives within established IT governance frameworks such as IT-BSC and COBIT. The study investigates how BYOD strategies can be effectively embedded into these IT management systems to control IT services and processes in alignment with the COBIT framework, thereby ensuring that personal devices are leveraged in ways that align with organizational goals without compromising security, compliance, or operational efficiency.

The IT-BSC is utilized as a performance measurement tool within this research, allowing organizations to evaluate the success of their IT systems based on various KPIs, such as financial performance, customer satisfaction, internal processes, and organizational learning. The inclusion of BYOD into this framework introduces additional complexities to the management of IT resources, given the unique challenges posed by personal devices in terms of data security, device control, and user autonomy. Consequently, the research subject is primarily concerned with how organizations can modify or enhance their IT-BSC systems to accommodate the distinctive aspects of BYOD, while still maintaining alignment with strategic business objectives. Furthermore, this research delves into the role of COBIT as a governance framework that provides the necessary structure to manage BYOD-associated risks, such as data breaches and non-compliance with regulatory requirements. COBIT's comprehensive set of governance and management objectives offers a structured approach to mitigating these risks while ensuring that IT operations, including BYOD initiatives, contribute effectively to organizational performance. By integrating COBIT's risk management processes with the performance measurement tools of the IT-BSC, this research aims to provide a framework for aligning IT governance with the dynamic and flexible nature of BYOD, ensuring that personal devices are used securely and productively within corporate environments.

This study, therefore, limits its scope to the intersection of BYOD, IT-BSC, and COBIT, examining how these frameworks can be adapted to manage the complexities of modern IT environments where personal devices are increasingly prevalent. The research subject is particularly relevant in the context of the evolving work environment, where remote work and mobile device usage have become integral to business operations, necessitating a re-evaluation of traditional

IT governance models to ensure they remain effective and aligned with current trends.

Research Aim

The **research aim** of this study is to develop a robust framework that strategically integrates BYOD policies into IT governance systems, leveraging both the IT-BSC model and COBIT governance principles. This framework is designed to enhance IT performance and strategic alignment by providing a structured method for managing the complexities introduced by BYOD, such as data security, compliance, and operational efficiency, while ensuring the performance and value creation of the IT department are measurable and align with the overarching corporate goals.

The IT-BSC framework is utilized as a performance management tool designed to closely align IT systems with broader business objectives. By incorporating BYOD into this framework, the research intends to devise tailored KPIs that measure the impact of personal device usage on IT performance, cost savings, and employee productivity, ensuring that the integration of BYOD initiatives into IT controlling systems meets the requirements for security, data protection, and resource optimization.

Moreover, the research aims to harness the COBIT framework's governance processes to address the risks associated with BYOD, such as data breaches, unauthorized access, and regulatory non-compliance. COBIT's structured approach to IT governance includes continuous monitoring, risk management, and the alignment of IT operations with business goals. By amalgamating these principles with the IT-BSC, the research aspires to forge a governance model that guarantees the secure and efficient utilization of personal devices within corporate IT environments.

The framework developed through this research will equip organizations with the necessary tools to balance the benefits of BYOD—such as increased flexibility, enhanced employee satisfaction, and reduced hardware costs—with the imperatives of robust IT governance. The research will investigate how the alignment of the IT-BSC and COBIT frameworks can amplify strategic alignment, elevate IT performance, and ensure that BYOD policies contribute positively to the overall success of the organization.

In conclusion, the **research aim** is to forge a governance model that effectively integrates BYOD into the IT-BSC and COBIT frameworks, optimizing IT performance while safeguarding security, compliance, and alignment with business objectives.

Research Tasks

The **research task** of this study is to develop a conceptual model that effectively enables the implementation and integration of BYOD into IT management systems, with the aim of improving resource utilization, making IT services more efficient, and optimizing strategic alignment between IT and management. This will be achieved by linking the IT-BSC with the COBIT framework to ensure holistic and long-term IT governance. To address this comprehensive task, the research is structured around four main objectives:

1. **Evaluate the current state of BYOD adoption and challenges:** The first task is to assess the global adoption of BYOD strategies, focusing particularly on industries that have actively integrated personal devices into their corporate environments. This evaluation will explore how BYOD adoption varies across different sectors, identifying key drivers, and delineating the prevalent challenges such as data security, regulatory compliance, and balancing employee autonomy with corporate control. This analysis will draw upon existing literature, industry reports, and empirical studies to establish a foundation for understanding the dynamics and implications of BYOD within contemporary IT landscapes.
2. **Analyze BYOD integration with IT-BSC and COBIT:** The second task will investigate how BYOD initiatives can be synergistically integrated with the IT-BSC and COBIT frameworks to enhance strategic IT governance. This involves exploring how the IT-BSC can be tailored to accommodate BYOD, thereby ensuring that personal device usage aligns with and supports strategic business objectives. Additionally, this task will explore how COBIT's governance and risk management processes can be adapted to address the specific challenges posed by BYOD, such as securing personal devices and ensuring compliance with relevant laws and policies.
3. **Develop a conceptual model:** Based on insights gathered from the initial tasks, the third task involves developing a conceptual model that encapsulates the integration of BYOD within IT governance frameworks. This model will combine elements from both IT-BSC and COBIT, outlining a structured approach to manage the complexities introduced by BYOD. The model will aim to optimize IT performance, enhance data security, and ensure regulatory

compliance, while also addressing how organizations can measure the impact and effectiveness of BYOD through relevant KPIs.

4. **Provide guidelines for BYOD implementation:** The final task focuses on formulating practical guidelines for the implementation of BYOD strategies based on the developed conceptual model. These guidelines will provide detailed, step-by-step instructions for organizations looking to integrate BYOD into their IT governance systems effectively. They will cover critical aspects such as policy development, risk assessment, and the continuous monitoring of BYOD impacts on IT and business performance.

Each of these tasks is designed to contribute to the overarching goal of the research: to establish a robust framework for integrating BYOD into IT management that supports efficient service delivery and aligns IT operations with broader business strategies, while maintaining high standards of security and compliance.

The intended scientific work is divided into three main areas in terms of content: a theoretical-scientific area, an empirical area and an analytical area (Fig. 3). The main focus of this work is on the targeted linking of primary research, i.e. the evaluation of new original data to be collected, and secondary research, which includes previously published results. The purpose of this linking is to develop precise and practical recommendations for specific key figures and operational processes. These should serve as a set of instruments for the successful implementation and management of an IT-BSC. It is important that this scorecard is aligned with the principles of the COBIT framework and also enables the integration of BYOD strategies. In this context, a comprehensive risk and opportunity analysis is also carried out. This will explore the potential implications, both positive and negative, that may arise from the introduction of BYOD initiatives in companies. The analysis covers various aspects of the company, such as IT security, cost-benefit ratio and strategic direction. The aim is not only to point out the possible challenges that a BYOD strategy could bring, but also to highlight the potential benefits that such an initiative could have for the company.

In the theoretical-scientific section, an in-depth look is taken at current methods and trends in the field of IT consumerisation and in particular BYOD. A comprehensive evaluation of these approaches is undertaken, whereby both general implementation issues and specific questions directly related to the focus of this work are examined. These issues are then embedded in the previously developed theoretical framework.

After this detailed theoretical discussion, the following section will develop a basic concept that shows how IT controlling based on COBIT can be used effectively in conjunction with an enterprise BSC. The aim of this approach is

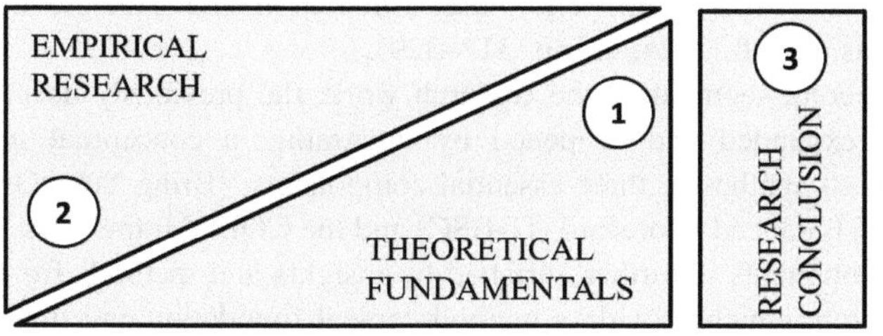

Fig. 3 Research Model. (Own illustration, 2023)

to provide companies with a clear and practical guide for integrating BYOD initiatives, taking into account efficient and effective IT control methods. The COVID-19 pandemic has led to profound changes in the business world, particularly through the widespread adoption of the home office model. These changes have increased the importance of IT management systems to measure and control IT performance.

Working Hypotheses

Based on these findings, the overarching research hypothesis is formulated as follows: 'The systematic integration of BYOD into the IT-BSC management system significantly improves the efficiency, effectiveness and strategic coherence of IT structures within the COBIT framework in the context of the organisation and management of information processes.' In addition, the following more precise sub-hypotheses can be derived:

1. 'The integration of BYOD strategies into IT management systems promotes optimised resource utilisation and contributes to a significant reduction in operating costs within the COBIT framework.'
2. 'Implementing BYOD methodologies in the IT-BSC system results in more effective control of IT services and processes, thereby meeting end-user requirements more efficiently and in accordance with COBIT guidelines.'
3. 'The integration of BYOD contributes to a better strategic alignment between business and IT objectives and strengthens the IT department's ability to adapt to external changes.'

These hypotheses focus on the link between BYOD integration and the optimisation of IT process control within the COBIT framework, emphasising their contribution to resource efficiency, user orientation and strategic flexibility in organisations. (Groß, 2024, cf. pp. 312–329).

In the second segment of the research work, the previously developed basic concept is expanded and deepened by integrating a conceptual model. This model aims to synthesise three essential components: 'Bring Your Own Device' (BYOD), IT-Balanced Scorecard (IT-BSC) and the COBIT framework. The fusion of these components is further enriched by insights and methods from empirical social research, which provide a methodological foundation and thus ensure the scientific robustness of the model.

Furthermore, a detailed description of the chosen research design is presented in the context of this segment. This includes, in particular, an explanation of the criteria for sample selection, the methodologies used for statistical data analysis, and the subsequent data interpretation. The analysis aims to generate an in-depth understanding of the current level of implementation, the problem areas that arise, and the general prevalence of BYOD initiatives in the target group. In addition, a critical examination of the applied methods and processes in relation to practical realisation using COBIT is to be carried out. This part of the work thus offers a comprehensive reflection of the current state as well as the challenges and best practices regarding the integration of BYOD in the context of the COBIT framework and the IT-BSC.

In the third and final segment of the present work, the synthesis of the methodologies and concepts developed in the first two parts is in the foreground. In doing so, a comprehensive and detailed IT-BSC is developed that is not only based on the previous findings, but also integrates selected and practice-relevant methods for its implementation. This should provide companies with a well-founded, action-oriented guide to profitably apply the principles of the IT-BSC in the context of BYOD initiatives.

Finally, based on the current COBIT 2019 framework, extensive Key Performance Indicators (KPI) and complementary measurement systems are presented. These serve to objectively evaluate the quality and effectiveness of BYOD implementations. In addition, they provide strategic control options that can be used to seamlessly integrate and continuously optimise such measures into a company's comprehensive IT BSC.

Contents

Abbreviations

AI	Artificial Intelligence
API	Application Programming Interface
APO	Align, Plan and Organize
BAI	Build, Acquire and Implement
BI	Business Intelligence
BPM	Business Process Management
BPO	Business Process Optimization
BSC	Balanced Scorecard
BYOD	Bring Your Own Device
CASB	Cloud Access Security Brokers
cf	confer
CLEO	Corporate Liable Employee Owned
CMMI	Capability Maturity Model Integration
CMS	Compliance-Management-System
COBIT	Control Objectives for Information and Related Technology
COPE	Corporate Owned, Personally Enabled
COVID	Coronavirus deseas
CPM	COBIT Performance Management
CRM	Customer Relationship Management
CYOD	Choose Your Own Device
DFD	Data Flow Diagrams
DSS	Deliver, Service and Support
EDM	Evaluate, Direct and Monitor
EDR	Endpoint Detection and Response

ER-Modelle	Entity-Relationship-Model
ERP	Enterprise Resource Planning
et al.	et alia
ETL	Extract, Transform and Load
EVA	Economic Value Added
GCD	Greatest Common Divisor
GDPR	General Data Protection Regulation
GEIT	Governance of Enterprise IT
IEC	International Electrotechnical Commission
IoT	Internet of Things
IPM	Information Process Management
IS	Information Systems
ISACA	Information Systems Audit and Control Association
ISO	International Organization for Standardization
IT	Information Technologie
IT-BSC	IT-Balanced Scorecard
ITIL	Information Technology Infrastructure Library
JSON	JavaScript Object Notation
KPI	Key Performance Indicators
MAM	Mobile Application Management
MDM	Mobile Device Management
MEA	Monitor, Evaluate and Assess
n. pag.	non paginated
NPV	Net Present Value
OECD	Organisation for Economic Co-operation and Development
p	page
PMBOK	Project Management Body of Knowledge
pp	pages
REST	Representational State Transfer
ROIC	Return on Invested Capital
SLA	Service Level Agreements
SME	Small and Medium Enterprise
SOAP	Simple Object Access Protocol
SPSS	Statistical Package for the Social Sciences
ROI	Return on Investment
UEM	Unified Endpoint Management
UML	Unified Modeling Language

UN	United Nations
URL	Uniform Ressource Locator
VPN	Virtual Private Networks
WTO	World Trade Organization
XML	eXtensible Markup Language

List of Figures

List of Tables

1 Theoretical Foundation in Information Process Management

The topic 'Information model in the system for measuring and the performance of the balanced scorecard' deals with the development and application of information models that are specifically designed to optimise the performance evaluation and control of organisations. Information models serve as structured representations of the relevant information and its relationships within a system. They are crucial for the efficient collection, processing and analysis of data required for informed management decisions.

In an academic context, this topic is particularly relevant as it addresses a variety of theoretical and practical challenges. On the one hand, it provides an opportunity to deepen the theoretical foundations of information management and systems theory. Information management is an interdisciplinary field that integrates insights from computer science, business administration, and management science to optimise the collection, processing, storage, and delivery of information (cf. Krcmar, 2003, pp. 45–48). Systems theory, as a further theoretical basis, provides a framework for analysing and modelling complex systems and their interactions. These two theoretical areas are central to understanding and developing effective information models (cf. Tarantino, 2012, pp. 35–39).

On the other hand, the topic has significant practical implications for organisational management and performance evaluation. In practice, organisations need reliable and comprehensive information systems to achieve their strategic goals and improve their operational efficiency. Information models support the identification and measurement of relevant performance indicators, which are essential for managing and controlling business processes. By applying these models, organisations can continuously monitor their performance, identify weaknesses and initiate targeted improvement measures (cf. Applegate et al., 2002, pp. 210–213).

M. Groß, *Managing IT in the Age of BYOD and Remote Work*,
https://doi.org/10.1007/978-3-658-51216-3_1

Another practical aspect is the implementation and integration of information models into existing IT systems and business processes. This requires not only technical know-how but also a deep understanding of organisational structures and processes. The successful implementation of an information model can improve data quality, accelerate decision-making and increase the overall performance of the organisation (cf. Ward and Peppard, 2002, pp. 160–165).

1.1 Significance of the Topic

Information management is at the core of the topic under consideration, as it deals with the systematic collection, processing, storage and provision of information that is of central importance for supporting decision-making processes in organisations. In a scientific context, information management is considered an interdisciplinary field that integrates findings from computer science, business administration and management theory (cf. Krcmar, 2003, pp. 18–25).

The collection of information includes the identification and collection of relevant data from various internal and external sources. In a second step, this data must be processed, which involves cleansing, transforming and aggregating it in order to convert it into a format that is useful for decision-making. The information is stored in databases and other storage systems that enable the efficient and secure management of large amounts of data. Finally, the provision of information is of central importance, as this is the only way to ensure that the right information is available to decision-makers at the right time and in the right format (cf. Applegate et al., 2002, pp. 95–100).

Effective information management thus makes a decisive contribution to increasing an organisation's transparency, efficiency and responsiveness. It enables informed decision-making and supports strategic planning and operational control. In an increasingly digitalised and data-driven world, information management is therefore an indispensable basis for the sustainable success of organisations (cf. Krcmar, 2003, pp. 59–64).

The development of information models is largely based on system-theoretical approaches, which are deeply rooted in organisational theory. Systems theory provides a framework for understanding and analysing complex systems—such as organisations – in their entirety. It views organisations as open systems that consist of various interacting components and are in constant interaction with their environment (cf. Speckbacher et al., 2003, pp. 365–370).

A central concept of systems theory is the idea of interdependence of system components. This means that changes in one part of the system can affect other parts, which underlines the need for a holistic view and modelling of information systems. Systems theory also emphasises the importance of feedback loops and self-regulation mechanisms, which are essential for understanding dynamic processes in organisations (cf. Speckbacher et al., 2003, pp. 371–378).

In the context of developing information models, systems theory helps to structure and analyse the complexity of information flows and decision-making processes in organisations. It provides tools and methods for identifying relevant system components and their interactions, as well as for simulating and optimising information systems. By applying the principles of systems theory, information models can be developed that are robust, flexible and adaptable, thus meeting the requirements of modern, dynamic organisations (cf. Krcmar, 2003, pp. 69–75).

1.2 Practical Relevance

A key objective of the information model is to significantly improve performance evaluation within organisations. Performance evaluation is a critical process that enables the effectiveness and efficiency of business processes and organisational activities to be measured, analysed and optimised. A well-designed information model provides a structured and systematic basis for capturing the complex information flows and integrating the relevant performance data (cf. Bernhard, 2000, pp. 32–35).

Identifying performance data: Identifying performance data is the first and fundamental step in performance evaluation. It involves determining the relevant KPIs that reflect the various dimensions of organisational performance. These metrics can include both financial and non-financial aspects, such as sales, profit margins, customer satisfaction, employee productivity, and process quality. A robust information model supports the systematic collection of these KPIs and ensures that all relevant data sources are integrated (cf. Bernhard, 2000, pp. 41–45).

Performance data measurement: Performance data measurement requires precise and reliable methods for data collection and processing. Both qualitative and quantitative approaches play a role here. Quantitative methods involve the use of statistical and mathematical models to analyse numerical data, while qualitative methods focus on the collection and interpretation of non-numerical data, such as through interviews or observations. An effective information model ensures that the collected data is consistent, accurate and valid in order to provide a reliable basis for performance evaluation (cf. Applegate et al., 2002, pp. 97–101).

Analysis of performance data: The analysis of performance data is a crucial step that enables deeper insights into organisational processes and their results. By applying advanced data analysis techniques, such as data mining, predictive analytics and machine learning, patterns and trends in performance data can be identified. These analyses help to identify the causes of performance deviations, predict future developments, and develop targeted measures to improve performance. A comprehensive information model makes it possible to carry out these analyses efficiently and present the results in an understandable and actionable way (cf. Darvish et al., 2012, pp. 9 ff.).

Informed management decisions: A central goal of performance evaluation is to support informed management decisions. The information provided must therefore not only be accurate and comprehensive, but also timely and relevant. A well-thought-out information model ensures that decision-makers have access to current and accurate data that enables them to make informed decisions. This helps to increase transparency and accountability within the organisation and supports strategic and operational planning (cf. Bernhard, 2000, pp. 53 ff.).

1.3 Research Priorities and Methodological Approaches

The development of information models is a central aspect of information management that forms the basis for effective data management and use in organisations. Information models are used to abstract and visualise the complex relationships and structures of data within a system. They provide a methodical and systematic approach to structuring, analysing and optimising data flows. Two key aspects of developing information models are the application of appropriate modelling techniques and the integration of different data sources and formats (cf. Krcmar, 2003, pp. 132–135). **Modelling Techniques**: Investigating and applying various modelling techniques is crucial to creating a robust and adaptable information model. Common techniques include:

- **Entity-Relationship Models**: ER-Modelle are widely used to describe the logical relationships between the data entities of a system. They use concepts such as entities, attributes, and relationships to visualise the data structure. ER models are particularly useful for identifying a system's data requirements and creating a clear and understandable representation of data relationships (cf. Bernhard, 2000, pp. 42–45).
- **Unified Modelling Language**: UML is a versatile modelling language used for visualising, specifying, constructing, and documenting software systems. UML diagrams, such as class, use case, and activity diagrams, provide different perspectives on the system and help to model both the static and dynamic aspects

of data flows. UML is particularly suitable for modelling complex information systems, as it offers a comprehensive range of diagram types covering various aspects of the system (cf. Applegate et al., 2002, pp. 99–102).
- **Data Flow Diagrams**: DFD represent the data flows within a system and show how data is moved between processes, data stores, and external entities. They are helpful for analysing the functional requirements of a system and for visualising the interactions between system components (cf. Speckbacher et al., 2003, pp. 361 f.).

The selection of the appropriate modelling technique depends on the specific requirements and objectives of the information model. A robust information model should be flexible enough to adapt to changing conditions and requirements, while also being sufficiently detailed to provide an accurate and comprehensive representation of the data structure and relationships. (cf. Krcmar, 2003, pp. 151–155). **Data integration**: The integration of different data sources and formats is a major challenge in the development of information models. A holistic and consistent database is crucial to ensure the quality and reliability of the information. The following strategies are central to data integration:

- **Data consolidation**: Data from different sources is merged into a central repository. This requires the harmonisation of data formats and structures to avoid inconsistencies. Consolidation enables centralised data management and control, and facilitates access and analysis (cf. Applegate et al., 2002, pp. 155–158).
- **Data cleansing and transformation**: Before integration, data must be cleansed and transformed to eliminate errors and inconsistencies. Data cleansing processes identify and correct inaccurate or incomplete data, while transformation processes convert the data into a unified format (cf. Krcmar, 2003, pp. 160–163).
- **Middleware and ETL processes**: Middleware solutions and ETL processes Extract, Transform and Load play an important role in data integration. They enable the automated flow of data between different systems and support the extraction, transformation and loading of data into the central information model. ETL tools provide functionality to extract data from various sources, apply transformations to harmonise data, and load the transformed data into the target system (cf. Ward and Peppard, 2002, pp. 151–155).
- **Data Quality Assurance**: Ensuring data quality is an ongoing process that involves monitoring and maintaining data. Data quality metrics and tools help to check the consistency, accuracy and completeness of the data and ensure that the database meets the requirements of the organisation (cf. Applegate et al., 2002, pp. 158 ff.).

1.4 Performance Evaluation and Management

The evaluation and management of organisational performance require comprehensive systems that capture and analyse diverse performance metrics. This chapter focuses on the development, validation, and application of performance measurement systems, highlighting their role in providing a holistic and multidimensional understanding of organisational success.

Performance measurement systems: The development and validation of performance measurement systems is a central task in the performance evaluation and management of organisations. Performance measurement systems serve to map an organisation's performance holistically and multidimensionally by integrating a variety of metrics that reflect different aspects of organisational performance (cf. Speckbacher et al., 2003, pp. 366 f.).

- **Holistic mapping**: A comprehensive system of key figures must capture the many facets of an organisation's performance, including financial and non-financial indicators. Financial metrics such as revenue, profit andReturn on Investment (ROI) provide insights into economic performance, while non-financial metrics such as customer satisfaction, employee engagement and process quality provide additional perspectives. Combining these indicators provides a holistic picture of organisational performance (cf. Bernhard, 2000, pp. 41–45).
- **Multidimensional mapping**: Multidimensional performance measurement systems take into account the various dimensions of performance, such as temporal aspects (past, present and future perspectives), functional aspects (different business units and departments) and strategic aspects (short-term operational and long-term strategic goals). This enables a differentiated analysis and control of the organisation at different levels (cf. Speckbacher et al., 2003, pp. 367 ff.).
- **Development and validation**: Developing a KPI system requires a careful selection of relevant indicators that take into account both the strategic goals of the organisation and the specific requirements of the various stakeholders. The validation process includes checking the relevance, reliability and validity of the selected indicators. This can be done through statistical analysis, benchmarking and the inclusion of expert opinions. A validated KPI system ensures that the collected data provides an accurate and reliable basis for performance evaluation (cf. Speckbacher et al., 2003, pp. 369 f.).

Data Analysis: The application of advanced analytical techniques is essential to interpret the performance data captured in the performance measurement systems and to support informed management decisions. The most important analytical techniques include:

- **Data Mining**: Data Mining involves the exploration and analysis of large amounts of data to identify hidden patterns, relationships and anomalies. By using algorithms and statistical methods, valuable insights can be gained that help improve business processes and optimise organisational performance. Data mining techniques such as cluster analysis, association analysis and decision trees are particularly useful for penetrating complex data structures and generating actionable insights (cf. Darvish et al., 2012, pp. 16 ff.).
- **Predictive Analytics**: Predictive analytics uses historical data and statistical models to forecast future events and developments. This technique helps organisations to proactively respond to potential challenges and opportunities by providing informed forecasts of future trends and behaviours. Common methods of predictive analytics include regression analysis, time series analysis, and machine learning. By applying these methods, organisations can estimate the probability of certain events and plan appropriate measures (cf. Applegate et al., 2002, pp. 150–153).
- **Prognostic Models**: Developing prognostic models is an integral part of data analysis. These models are based on advanced algorithms and machine learning to make accurate predictions. For example, prognostic models can be used to create sales forecasts, estimate the demand for products, or assess the risk of failures and disruptions. The validation of these models requires continuous review and adjustment to ensure their accuracy and reliability (cf. Bernhard, 2000, pp. 46–50).

1.5 Foundations of Information Process Management

Information Process Management forms the foundational pillar for effective governance and strategic management in the digital era. It ensures that the appropriate information is systematically captured, efficiently processed, securely delivered, and effectively utilized at the right time, thus underpinning both strategic planning and operational execution. The increasing dependence of organizations on information as a critical asset necessitates the development of robust information management infrastructures that transcend traditional data handling approaches (cf. Krcmar, 2003 pp. 45–48; cf. Verweire and Van den Berghe, 2004, pp. 95–100).

IPM encompasses the holistic design, seamless execution, continuous control, and dynamic optimization of information flows across all organizational levels. It integrates human resources, business processes, and technological infrastructures in a coherent and synergistic manner to transform disparate and often unstructured data into structured, valuable knowledge assets that directly drive business success (cf. Krcmar, 2003, pp. 45–48; cf. Bainey, 2016 pp. 23–29). Notably, IPM must be understood as a dynamic and evolutionary function, capable of adapting to ever-changing organizational objectives and volatile external environmental conditions (cf. Applegate et al., 2002, pp. 210–213).

Understanding information not merely as an operational tool but as a fundamental strategic asset necessitates a shift in management paradigms. High-quality, readily available, and securely managed information has become a prerequisite for achieving and sustaining strategic and operational excellence. This perspective gains particular relevance in light of increasing workplace decentralization trends, such as BYOD initiatives and remote working models, which introduce new complexities and heightened requirements for IT governance, data security, and regulatory compliance (cf. ISACA, 2019b, pp. 22–25).

The integration of IPM principles into established management frameworks, notably the BSC, enables a coherent alignment between information processes and broader strategic objectives. By embedding information governance mechanisms within the BSC framework, organizations can systematically link informational inputs and flows to performance measurement and strategic control (cf. Kaplan and Norton, 1992, pp. 71–79). Complementarily, governance models such as COBIT 2019 provide comprehensive normative structures that facilitate the efficient monitoring, management, and optimization of IT-enabled information processes, ensuring alignment with organizational goals and compliance with international standards (cf. ISACA, 2019c, pp. 22–25).

In practical application, IPM transcends purely technical considerations and must be approached as a multidisciplinary field. It requires not only sophisticated technological infrastructures but also the strategic coordination of human, procedural, and cultural dimensions within organizations. The successful operationalization of IPM thus demands close interdisciplinary collaboration among IT departments, business units, and executive leadership to foster transparency, accountability, and responsiveness across all information-centric activities (cf. Krcmar, 2003, pp. 151–155; cf. Tarantino, 2012, pp. 35–39).

1.5.1 Theoretical Foundations

The theoretical foundation of IPM is anchored in three fundamental disciplines that collectively provide a comprehensive conceptual framework for understanding and designing effective information systems within organizations.

First, the discipline of information management provides the foundational logic for treating data and information as strategic assets. It emphasizes the structured acquisition, processing, dissemination, and use of information to support decision-making, coordination, and control across the organization. Information management frameworks highlight the need for data quality, lifecycle control, metadata governance, and access management to ensure that information not only supports operational efficiency but also aligns with long-term strategic goals (cf. Applegate et al., 2002, pp. 210–213; cf. Otley and Emmanuel, 2013, pp. 23–28).

Second, systems theory offers a dynamic lens through which organizations are understood as open, adaptive systems embedded in constantly changing environments. This theory posits that successful organizations maintain internal coherence by responding to environmental stimuli through structured feedback loops and adaptive information flows. Information models—when grounded in systems thinking—do not merely represent data flows but function as adaptive architectures that maintain equilibrium between internal capabilities and external demands. They map interdependencies, feedback paths, and decision points that facilitate systemic learning and coordinated change (cf. Speckbacher et al., 2003, pp. 365–370; cf. Beynon-Davies, 2019, pp. 56–59).

Third, Business Process Management contributes a process-oriented framework that links strategic intent with operational execution. BPM is concerned with the identification, modeling, execution, monitoring, and continuous optimization of business processes. It provides a systematic approach to enhancing organizational performance through end-to-end process visibility, process standardization, and strategic alignment (cf. Krcmar, 2003, pp. 151–155; cf. Baltzan, 2023, pp. 112–117).

Integrating these three perspectives enables IPM to be positioned not merely as an operational necessity but as a strategic enabler of innovation, organizational agility, and sustained competitive advantage. Information is thus not just a passive input but a dynamic resource that, when properly managed, can drive transformative organizational change and foster long-term success (cf. Ward and Peppard, 2002, pp. 160–165; cf. Bourgeois et al., 2014, pp. 122–125).

This multidimensional theoretical basis supports the argument that IPM must be designed and implemented holistically, considering technological, human, and organizational factors in an integrated manner. The alignment of information processes with broader corporate strategies through frameworks such as the BSC and COBIT 2019 further underscores the strategic relevance of IPM in modern organizational contexts (cf. Kaplan and Norton, 1992, pp. 71–79; cf. ISACA, 2019c, pp. 22–25).

1.5.2 Core Elements of Information Process Management

An effective Information Process Management system is composed of several core elements, each of which plays a crucial role in ensuring that information serves both operational and strategic organizational needs. These elements are intricately interconnected and must function cohesively to achieve optimal performance.

- *Process Architecture:* This element represents the structural foundation of IPM. It involves the systematic mapping of information flows across end-to-end business processes, the definition of interfaces between functional units, and the assignment of roles and responsibilities for process ownership. A coherent process architecture eliminates information silos, streamlines communication, and supports horizontal integration across departments, thereby enhancing responsiveness and efficiency (cf. Applegate et al., 2002, pp. 95–100).
- *Data Governance:* Data governance serves as the regulatory and ethical framework for information management. It includes policies, standards, and control mechanisms for data quality, integrity, availability, and compliance. Effective governance ensures that data is used responsibly and in accordance with internal and external requirements, including legal mandates such as the General Data Protection Regulation (GDPR). Key components include data ownership models, stewardship structures, and monitoring mechanisms that safeguard data throughout its lifecycle (cf. Tarantino, 2012, pp. 35–39).
- *Technology Infrastructure:* The technological layer of IPM comprises the digital tools and platforms that facilitate information processing, storage, and retrieval. This includes integrated enterprise systems such as Enterprise Resource Planning (ERP), Customer Relationship Management (CRM), and Business Intelligence (BI) platforms, which together enable real-time data exchange and analytics. A robust infrastructure supports system interoperability, scalability, and adaptability—essential features in dynamic and growth-oriented environments (cf. Applegate et al., 2002, pp. 45 ff.).
- *Performance Monitoring:* Performance monitoring provides the feedback mechanism that connects strategy with execution. It encompasses the definition, measurement, and evaluation of KPIs that reflect the effectiveness and efficiency of

information processes. Tools such as dashboards, scorecards, and alerts provide visibility into process behavior, enabling timely interventions and continuous improvement (cf. Kaplan and Norton 1992, pp. 71–79).

- *Change and Risk Management:* The final element addresses the dynamic and uncertain nature of information environments. Change and risk management encompasses proactive strategies for anticipating disruptions, assessing vulnerabilities, and implementing safeguards. Particularly in distributed work settings shaped by BYOD practices and remote collaboration, resilient design and governance structures are vital to ensure the stability and security of information systems (cf. Kersten, Reuter, et al., 2011, pp. 98–102).

As visualized in Fig. 1.1, these five elements interact dynamically within an IPM framework. Their interdependencies highlight the importance of a system-oriented view in designing and implementing information management strategies. Each of these elements is indispensable for ensuring that information not only supports immediate operational needs but also contributes meaningfully to the organization's long-term strategic objectives.

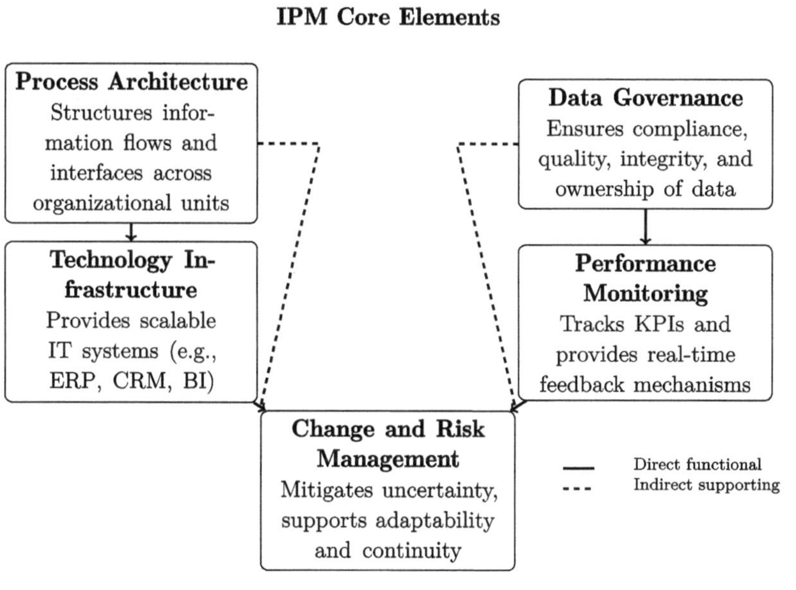

Fig. 1.1 Integrated Components of IPM and their functional linkages. (Own illustration, 2025)

1.5.3 Strategic Role of Information Process Management

The strategic role of IPM lies in its ability to align information flows with the overarching goals and ambitions of an organization. Rather than operating in isolation as a purely technical or operational function, IPM serves as a vital bridge that links strategic planning with operational execution, ensuring that information acts as an enabler of value creation across all organizational levels (cf. Krcmar, 2003, pp. 45–48).

A key contribution of IPM is the translation of strategic objectives into actionable information requirements. Through this mechanism, organizations ensure that strategic aspirations are operationalized by defining and structuring the necessary informational prerequisites. This alignment supports initiatives such as business development, market expansion, innovation management, and customer relationship optimization (cf. Applegate et al., 2002, pp. 210–213).

Moreover, IPM fosters transparency, accountability, and evidence-based decision-making by establishing integrated, timely, and accurate information channels. These information flows enable stakeholders across all organizational levels to access relevant data, thereby improving managerial oversight and facilitating real-time strategic adjustments (cf. Kaplan and Norton 1992, pp. 71–79; cf. Ward and Peppard, 2002, pp. 160–165).

In addition, IPM enhances business agility by promoting the development of flexible and adaptive information infrastructures. This capacity to dynamically adjust information systems is particularly critical in environments characterized by volatility and rapid technological change, such as the increased adoption of BYOD strategies and the widespread transition to remote work during the COVID-19 pandemic (cf. Eurofound, & the International Labour Office, 2020, pp. 12–15; cf. Bundesamt, 2022 pp. 10–13).

A well-implemented IPM system thus becomes a strategic lever, enhancing organizational resilience, fostering innovation, and ensuring sustained competitiveness even under conditions of profound uncertainty. The ability to integrate strategic vision with operational execution via optimized information processes not only strengthens immediate performance but also builds the structural and informational foundations for future growth and adaptability (cf. Krcmar, 2003, pp. 45–48; cf. Tarantino, 2012, pp. 35–39).

1.5.4 Integration of IPM with BSC and COBIT 2019

The integration of IPM with established governance and performance evaluation frameworks, such as the BSC and COBIT 2019, significantly enhances an organization's ability to achieve strategic coherence, operational excellence, and regulatory compliance.

The **BSC** provides a multidimensional framework that evaluates organizational success across four core perspectives: financial, customer, internal business processes, and learning and growth (cf. Ehrmann, 2007, pp. 45–50). IPM contributes to the operationalization of each perspective by enabling a structured and timely flow of information relevant to goal setting, performance monitoring, and feedback. For the financial and customer perspectives, IPM facilitates the integration of external and internal data, ensuring strategic decisions are data-informed. The internal process perspective, which focuses on the optimization and quality of key operational workflows, is directly strengthened through information process standardization and real-time visibility enabled by IPM. Furthermore, the learning and growth perspective is underpinned by IPM's ability to support knowledge management systems, skill development tracking, and innovation monitoring. By ensuring the traceability and validity of performance data across all perspectives, IPM acts as the informational backbone of an adaptive and strategically aligned BSC system (cf. Ehrmann, 2007, pp. 45–48; cf. Neely, 2007, pp. 312–316).

In parallel, **COBIT 2019** serves as a comprehensive governance and management framework that aligns enterprise IT with business objectives. It introduces governance components such as the Governance and Management Objectives (GMOs), focus areas, and design factors (cf. ISACA, 2019c, pp. 22–25). IPM supports the implementation of COBIT by mapping its principles—like value delivery, risk optimization, and compliance—onto operational information processes. In particular, IPM ensures that the information attributes required by COBIT, such as accuracy, confidentiality, integrity, and availability, are actively governed and continuously improved. The structured documentation of workflows and controls within IPM supports COBIT's enablers like policies, organizational structures, and culture, ethics, and behavior. Moreover, IPM contributes to audit readiness and compliance monitoring by enabling continuous assessment of information reliability and control performance. In doing so, it transforms abstract governance goals into actionable, traceable elements of operational management.

Figure 1.2 illustrates the integrative role of IPM in connecting the strategic logic of the Balanced Scorecard with the operational governance mechanisms defined in COBIT 2019. Integrating IPM with BSC and COBIT 2019 not only creates synergies between strategic planning and IT governance but also empowers organizations

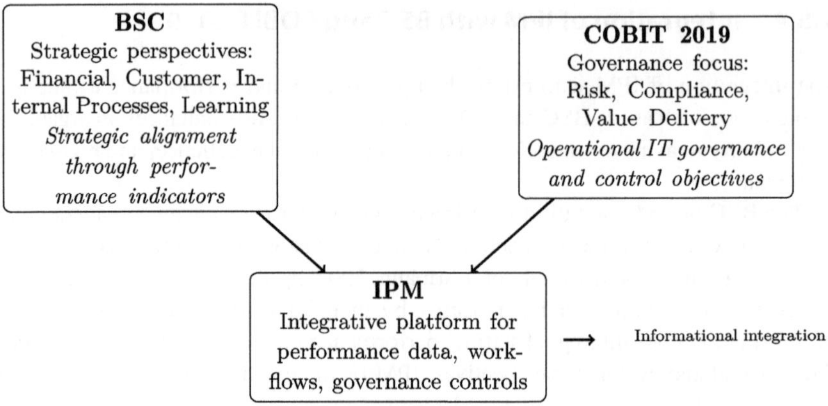

Fig. 1.2 Integrative Role of IPM in Bridging BSC and COBIT 2019. (Own illustration, 2025)

to proactively manage risks, optimize performance across multiple dimensions, and demonstrate regulatory compliance. Consequently, IPM evolves from a supportive administrative function to a critical strategic asset that drives organizational resilience, sustainability, and competitive advantage (cf. Ehrmann, 2007, pp. 48 ff.; cf. ISACA, 2019c, pp. 22–25).

1.5.5 Challenges and Future Trends in IPM

Despite its pivotal importance, IPM faces several ongoing challenges and emerging trends that will shape its future development. Organizations must proactively address these factors to ensure the continued relevance, effectiveness, and strategic value contribution of their IPM systems. One critical challenge is the exponential growth of data volumes and complexity, often referred to as "big data". Modern organizations must develop and deploy more sophisticated methods for data processing, integration, and analysis to cope with vast, heterogeneous datasets originating from multiple internal and external sources. Advanced data management technologies, including data lakes, real-time analytics, and machine learning algorithms, are increasingly required to transform raw data into actionable insights (cf. Darvish et al., 2012, pp. 9 ff.).

Simultaneously, the intensification of cybersecurity threats poses a significant risk to the integrity, confidentiality, and availability of information flows. As digitalization progresses, securing IPM systems against internal vulnerabilities and external attacks becomes paramount. Implementing comprehensive cybersecurity frameworks and fostering a culture of security awareness are essential measures to safeguard critical information assets (cf. Kersten, Reuter, et al., 2011, pp. 98–102).

Emerging technologies such as Artificial Intelligence (AI) and process automation present both opportunities and challenges for IPM. AI-driven solutions can enhance predictive analytics, automate routine information processing tasks, and support more informed and timely decision-making. However, the integration of such technologies requires careful governance to ensure transparency, accountability, and alignment with organizational objectives (cf. Applegate et al., 2002, pp. 158 ff.).

Moreover, sustainability and ethical considerations are gaining prominence in the realm of IPM. Organizations are increasingly required to address ethical dimensions of data collection, storage, usage, and privacy, particularly in a global context characterized by varying regulatory landscapes. Ensuring compliance with ethical standards and data protection regulations, such as the GDPR, is becoming a key aspect of responsible IPM practice (cf. Tarantino, 2012, pp. 35–39).

In conclusion, proactively engaging with these challenges and trends is crucial for organizations aiming to maintain the strategic relevance of their IPM initiatives. Future-oriented IPM systems must be designed to be not only efficient and secure but also ethically sound, adaptive, and capable of leveraging technological advancements to support sustained organizational success.

1.6 Governance, Communication, and Organizational Control in Information Systems

In an era defined by pervasive digitalization, increased regulatory scrutiny, and the rapid evolution of organizational IT landscapes, governance, communication, and organizational control in Information Systems have emerged as foundational constructs for securing sustainable organizational performance. These elements are no longer merely operational concerns but are essential levers of strategic alignment, risk mitigation, and value creation across modern enterprises (cf. Kaplan and Norton 1992, pp. 24 f.; cf. Neely, 2007, pp. 312–317). As organizations expand their reliance on complex, often decentralized, information systems, the integrative and proactive management of IS governance, communication structures, and control mechanisms has become critical to ensuring organizational resilience, regulatory compliance, and long-term competitiveness (cf. ISACA, 2019b, pp. 22 ff.; cf. Elmasri and Navathe, 2015, pp. 158–160).

IS Governance entails the development and execution of formalized processes that ensure IT decision-making aligns with strategic priorities. This includes defining accountability structures, evaluating performance outcomes, and embedding risk-aware decision processes at all organizational levels (cf. Krcmar, 2003, pp. 79–82). Governance frameworks such as COBIT 2019 provide structured methodologies to support this alignment, translating business needs into IT-enabled strategies.

Communication, in this context, serves as a multi-directional process of transmitting, interpreting, and contextualizing governance expectations across heterogeneous organizational units. Especially in the presence of remote work environments, BYOD policies, and cross-functional teams, effective IS communication frameworks are necessary to ensure transparency, reinforce behavioral norms, and institutionalize compliance practices (cf. Ehrmann, 2007, pp. 45–49).

Organizational Control mechanisms enable the operationalization of governance intent by translating abstract policies into actionable routines and measurable outcomes. These mechanisms encompass monitoring systems, performance evaluations, and real-time feedback loops, all of which are indispensable for adaptive management in dynamic IT environments (cf. Speckbacher et al., 2003, pp. 366–370).

The convergence of governance, communication, and control forms the conceptual and operational backbone of a robust IS management strategy. Their integration is particularly important in addressing emerging organizational challenges such as data sovereignty, regulatory fragmentation, and technological heterogeneity (cf. Verweire and Van den Berghe, 2004, pp. 95–100). Accordingly, this section explores these dimensions in depth and highlights the empirical and theoretical foundations that shape current best practices in digitally complex environments. Emphasis is placed on the implications of BYOD, remote work arrangements, the BSC, and the COBIT 2019 framework, all of which serve as representative anchors for designing and maintaining resilient and effective IS governance ecosystems (cf. Darvish et al., 2012, pp. 9 ff.).

1.6.1 Governance in Information Systems

Governance within IS is a cornerstone of organizational strategy and operational effectiveness in an increasingly digitalized and decentralized business environment. With the expansion of IT infrastructures and the adoption of flexible working models such as BYOD and remote work, the necessity for comprehensive and adaptable governance frameworks has intensified (cf. Ward and Peppard, 2002, pp. 65–67; cf. Krcmar, 2003, pp. 79–82). At the heart of IS governance lies strategic alignment, the process of systematically synchronizing IT initiatives with corporate strategies to enhance organizational value creation (cf. Ehrmann, 2007, pp. 45 ff.). This alignment ensures that IT investments are not isolated from broader business objectives but are integral to achieving strategic goals (cf. Kaplan and Norton, 1992, pp. 24 f.; cf. ISACA, 2019b, pp. 22 f.).

Risk management constitutes another pivotal dimension of IS governance. In decentralized IT environments, managing risks associated with cybersecurity threats, data protection, and regulatory compliance becomes increasingly complex. Frameworks such as COBIT 2019 advocate for a proactive, structured approach to identifying, assessing, and mitigating these risks (cf. Kersten, Reuter et al., 2011, pp. 98–102; cf. Pohlmann and Blumberg, 2006, pp. 45–48).

Resource optimization extends beyond traditional IT asset management to encompass the strategic use of human, infrastructural, and informational resources. Prioritization strategies and the establishment of clear performance indicators are necessary to ensure that resources contribute maximally to organizational objectives (cf. ISACA, 2019b, pp. 25 f.; cf. Ward and Peppard, 2002, pp. 148–150).

Performance measurement is a foundational pillar in evaluating the contribution of IT to organizational success. The adoption of frameworks like the IT-BSC enables a multidimensional analysis of IT performance, capturing financial outcomes, process efficiencies, and innovation capacities (cf. Bernhard, 2000, pp. 41–45). In light of BYOD and remote work developments, KPIs must also measure device compliance, data security, and user satisfaction (cf. Miller, 2012, pp. 53 ff.; cf. Hunt, 2012, pp. 69 ff.).

The shift toward BYOD and remote working models challenges traditional governance paradigms. Centralized frameworks must be recalibrated to address the decentralized, heterogeneous realities of modern IT environments (cf. Henderson, 2012, pp. 22–29). Organizations must implement robust policies for device management, secure data access, and regulatory compliance (cf. Fischer, 2012, pp. 60 ff.).

Thus, contemporary IS governance demands a dynamic, integrative approach. It must facilitate strategic alignment, ensure rigorous risk management, optimize resource utilization, and deliver transparent performance insights. Frameworks such as COBIT 2019 provide structured methodologies that guide organizations through this complexity, fostering resilience and strategic coherence in an evolving technological landscape (cf. Ward and Peppard, 2002, pp. 65 ff.; cf. Krcmar, 2003, pp. 79–82).

1.6.2 Communication in Information Systems

In the domain of IS, communication serves as the fundamental medium for transmitting governance principles, fostering compliance, and enabling strategic alignment across organizational structures. Effective communication ensures that governance policies, strategic priorities, and operational expectations are consistently disseminated and internalized within all organizational layers (cf. Applegate et al., 2002, pp. 121–125; cf. Ehrmann, 2007, pp. 45 ff.).

Central to IS communication is the structured dissemination of policies and guidelines. Formal communication channels, such as intranet portals, policy documents, and secured messaging platforms, are critical for ensuring that governance frameworks, particularly those addressing decentralized IT environments like BYOD, are understood and adhered to by all stakeholders. By systematically distributing information regarding security protocols, acceptable use policies, and device management standards, organizations mitigate risks associated with information asymmetry and policy noncompliance (cf. Pohlmann and Blumberg, 2006, pp. 45–48; cf. Ginovsky, 2012, pp. 24–27).

Training and awareness programs represent a proactive communication strategy aimed at fostering a security-conscious organizational culture. Regular training sessions, e-learning modules, and phishing simulations are increasingly utilized to equip employees with the knowledge and skills required to navigate complex IT environments securely (cf. Fischer, 2012, pp. 60 ff.). In particular, the context of remote work and BYOD demands heightened vigilance and continuous education to counter emerging threats (cf. Hunt, 2012, pp. 69 ff.). Beyond top-down dissemination, modern IS communication frameworks incorporate feedback mechanisms to enhance responsiveness and adaptability. Structured feedback channels such as incident reporting systems, surveys, and governance review forums enable employees to report security incidents, highlight usability challenges, and suggest process improvements. Such mechanisms not only facilitate early detection of governance issues but also promote a participatory governance culture, where users are active contributors to IS strategy refinement (cf. Golden and J. F. Veiga, 2005, pp. 301–308; cf. Rodham, 2012, pp. 12 ff.).

The technological landscape for IS communication has evolved to support the demands of distributed workforces. Secure collaboration tools, encrypted messaging applications, and virtual conferencing platforms enable seamless information exchange without compromising data security. These tools are indispensable for maintaining strategic cohesion and operational continuity, particularly as organizations increasingly embrace remote work models and cloud-based infrastructures (cf. Neely, 2007, pp. 312–317).

Overall, communication in IS transcends mere information transfer. It functions as an enabler of governance efficacy, a catalyst for cultural alignment, and a safeguard against operational risks. To sustain effective IS governance in decentralized and dynamic environments, organizations must prioritize structured, secure, and responsive communication strategies that integrate seamlessly with their governance and performance management frameworks (cf. Krcmar, 2003, pp. 79–82; cf. Ehrmann, 2007, pp. 45–49).

1.6.3 Organizational Control in Information Systems

Organizational control within IS comprises systematic frameworks, monitoring instruments, and corrective mechanisms that ensure IT activities are aligned with organizational objectives. Particularly in decentralized environments shaped by BYOD and remote work models, control systems must evolve to address new operational and security challenges (cf. Speckbacher et al., 2003, pp. 365–370; cf. Ehrmann, 2007, pp. 45 ff.).

Monitoring represents the continuous, automated acquisition and interpretation of operational data to provide transparency across IS processes. This includes not only the tracking of system availability and usage metrics but also the real-time detection of anomalies that may indicate security incidents or policy violations. Contemporary monitoring systems leverage advanced analytics and machine learning techniques to contextualize data streams and prioritize alerts based on threat severity and business impact. Effective monitoring requires the integration of centralized dashboards, event correlation platforms, and log management solutions that enable proactive oversight and timely intervention in both on-premises and cloud-based environments (cf. Applegate et al., 2002, pp. 158 ff.; cf. Speckbacher et al., 2003, pp. 373–376).

Evaluation builds upon monitoring by interpreting collected data in relation to normative benchmarks, strategic objectives, and performance expectations. It encompasses both formative and summative analyses, whereby IS activities are assessed in terms of efficiency, effectiveness, and compliance. Tools such as the IT-Balanced Scorecard (IT-BSC) provide structured models for translating technical indicators into management-relevant insights across financial, operational, and developmental domains (cf. Ehrmann, 2007, pp. 45–49). In environments characterized by BYOD and remote work, evaluation mechanisms must additionally address endpoint integrity, data sovereignty risks, and adherence to security baselines. The inclusion of qualitative indicators, such as user satisfaction and system usability, further supports a comprehensive understanding of IS performance (cf. Fischer, 2012, pp. 60 ff.).

Corrective actions are the operational responses triggered by deviations uncovered through monitoring and evaluation. These measures can range from automated responses—such as quarantining devices or revoking access—to managerial interventions like process redesign, retraining programs, or escalated incident resolution protocol. An effective corrective action framework integrates both technical and organizational dimensions, ensuring that remediation efforts are timely, proportionate, and aligned with strategic risk tolerance. Importantly, corrective mechanisms must be embedded within a continuous improvement loop, whereby insights from past incidents inform future policy development and system hardening (cf. Hunt, 2012, pp. 69 ff.; cf. Violino, 2012, pp. 29 ff.).

Advanced technological solutions significantly support modern control frameworks. Technologies such as Mobile Device Management (MDM), Cloud Access Security Brokers (CASB), and Endpoint Detection and Response (EDR) provide granular control over personal and corporate devices, enable comprehensive cloud activity monitoring, and enhance threat detection and response capabilities cf. Pohlmann and Blumberg, 2006, pp. 45–48; cf. Henderson, 2012, pp. 22–30. Organizational control must remain adaptive, integrating continuous monitoring, rigorous evaluation, and responsive corrective measures. Only by doing so can organizations ensure that IS activities comply with governance requirements while contributing actively to strategic objectives (cf. Ward and Peppard, 2002, pp. 148 ff.; cf. Krcmar, 2003, pp. 79–82).

1.6.4 Integration of Governance, Communication, and Control

The effective management of IS environments requires the seamless integration of governance, communication, and organizational control mechanisms. Rather than treating these elements in isolation, leading frameworks such as COBIT 2019 emphasize their interconnectedness as the foundation for a resilient and strategically aligned IT function (cf. ISACA, 2019b, pp. 22–26). Strategic transparency emerges when governance objectives are clearly communicated across the organization. Through structured dissemination channels, policy alignment is ensured, while transparent monitoring mechanisms provide real-time visibility into IS performance. Effective communication ensures that governance frameworks are not merely formal documents but are lived practices within the organization (cf. Ginovsky, 2012, pp. 24–27).

Accountability structures are established by linking clear governance roles with measurable outcomes derived from organizational control frameworks. Defined responsibilities, combined with the systematic evaluation of IS activities through KPIs, enhance compliance and foster a performance-driven culture (cf. Bernhard, 2000, pp. 41–45; cf. Ehrmann, 2007, pp. 45–49).

Feedback-driven adaptation plays a critical role in dynamic environments shaped by BYOD and remote work. Monitoring systems and feedback channels enable organizations to detect emerging issues rapidly and adjust policies and processes accordingly (cf. Hunt, 2012, pp. 69 ff.). Technologies such as MDM, CASB, and EDR not only reinforce control mechanisms but also provide the agility necessary to support evolving business models (cf. Pohlmann and Blumberg, 2006, pp. 45–48).

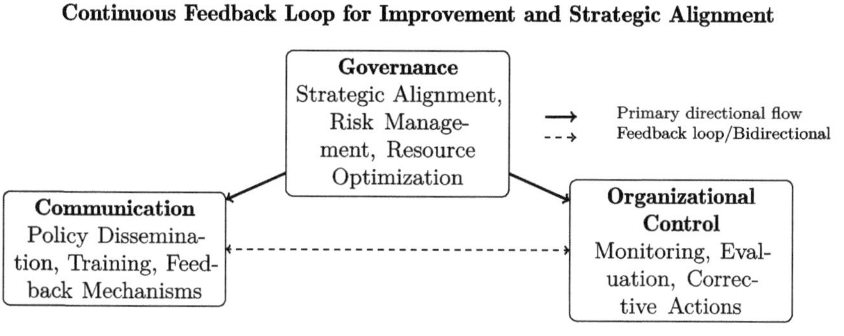

Fig. 1.3 Interaction of Governance, Communication, and Organizational Control in IS. (Own illustration, 2025)

Ultimately, the integration of governance, communication, and control fosters a resilient, adaptive, and strategically aligned IS environment. Organizations that operationalize this integration can enhance IT value creation, strengthen risk management capabilities, and ensure sustainable competitive advantage in increasingly complex digital ecosystems. The interplay between governance, communication, and organizational control can be conceptualized as a continuous feedback loop that fosters strategic alignment and organizational resilience, as illustrated in Fig. 1.3 (cf. Krcmar, 2003, pp. 79–82; cf. Ehrmann, 2007, pp. 45–47).

1.7 Information Modeling as a Tool for Strategic Performance Management

Information modeling is a central methodological and conceptual instrument in the strategic management of organizational performance. Its primary function lies in the structuring and systematization of information relevant to performance evaluation, enabling organizations to align operational activities with strategic objectives in a traceable, scalable, and responsive manner. In dynamic and complex business environments, the capability to model, adapt, and interpret performance-relevant data in real time constitutes a key enabler for sustainable value creation (cf. Ward and Peppard, 2002, pp. 65 ff.; cf. Verweire and Van den Berghe, 2004, pp. 95–99).

In this context, information models act as structured abstractions of organizational realities. They encapsulate entities, relationships, and rules that govern data flows and facilitate the operationalization of strategic control frameworks. This structural backbone supports the integration of strategic intent into day-to-day activities, while enabling multidimensional analysis, advanced diagnostics, and predictive evaluation. As such, information modeling is not merely a technical tool, but a strategic asset in performance management architectures (cf. Bourgeois et al., 2014, pp. 122–125; cf. Gallaugher, 2023, pp. 122–126).

Furthermore, information modeling enhances transparency and consistency across hierarchical levels and functional domains. It enables management to map KPIs to concrete organizational processes and to continuously refine decision-making based on empirical evidence. The integrative capacity of such models allows for a harmonized view of financial, operational, and developmental dimensions, which is particularly critical in governance-driven frameworks such as the IT-BSC or COBIT (cf. Otley and Emmanuel, 2013, pp. 23–28; cf. Elmasri and Navathe, 2015, pp. 158 ff.).

In sum, information modeling functions as a strategic infrastructure for performance-oriented governance. It enables the transformation of abstract goals into measurable actions and supports iterative refinement based on data-driven insights (cf. Bainey, 2016, pp. 158 ff.; cf. Neely, 2007, pp. 312–317). In the following subsections, this role is further elaborated through its contributions to alignment, advanced analytics, governance integration, BYOD-related structures, and practical implementation strategies.

1.7.1 Role of Information Modeling in Strategic Alignment

Strategic alignment represents a critical success factor in performance-driven organizations, as it ensures that operational decisions and resources are consistently oriented toward overarching corporate goals. In this context, information modeling functions not merely as a technical interface, but as a strategic coordination instrument that embeds organizational priorities into structural and process-oriented representations (cf. Kaplan and Norton, 1992, pp. 24 f.; cf. Ehrmann, 2007, pp. 45 ff.).

Unlike informal or ad hoc communication structures, formalized information models translate strategic priorities into standardized performance dimensions that can be operationalized through measurable indicators. This enables a continuous line of sight between abstract goals and process-level activities. Such alignment is particularly crucial in environments marked by high complexity, regulatory pressure, or rapid technological change (cf. Ward and Peppard, 2002, pp. 65 ff.). Three strategic alignment mechanisms enabled by information modeling include:

- *Goal-to-Indicator Mapping:* Through hierarchical decomposition, strategic goals are broken down into specific performance indicators (KPIs), enabling organizations to assign quantitative or qualitative metrics to otherwise abstract intentions. These indicators can then be linked to responsible units and timeframes, promoting ownership and accountability across levels (cf. Bernhard, 2000, pp. 42–45).
- *Cause-Effect Structuring:* Information models reveal the causal interrelations between different process domains, organizational layers, or outcome dimensions. This capability is vital for understanding how changes in one area (e.g., supply chain responsiveness) influence outcomes in another (e.g., customer satisfaction or financial return) (cf. Neely, 2007, pp. 312–315).
- *Alignment Simulation:* Using advanced modeling techniques, organizations can simulate how strategic initiatives would impact KPIs under various scenarios. This predictive functionality allows for anticipatory adjustments and improves the robustness of strategic planning (cf. Ehrmann, 2007, pp. 45 ff.).

Moreover, information modeling supports the mediation of conflicting priorities between departments by making dependencies and shared goals visible. In multi-business or matrix structures, such alignment tools reduce fragmentation and foster cross-functional integration. This becomes particularly effective when strategic objectives are embedded in enterprise-wide architectures such as Balanced Scorecards or strategy maps. Thus, information modeling in the context of strategic alignment is not only a descriptive tool but also a prescriptive and integrative mechanism.

It facilitates disciplined execution, transparency, and informed decision-making in support of long-term organizational coherence (cf. Kaplan and Norton, 1992, pp. 24 f.).

1.7.2 Advanced Applications in Performance Management

In contemporary organizations, performance management is increasingly expected to go beyond the static assessment of outcomes. It must enable dynamic steering capabilities, adaptive feedback cycles, and predictive insight into future developments. Information modeling serves as a critical enabler of this shift, offering methodological and technical means to transform traditional performance tracking into a proactive and learning-oriented system (cf. Speckbacher et al., 2003, pp. 373–376; cf. Ehrmann, 2007, pp. 45–49).

Rather than focusing solely on past-oriented indicators, information models integrate temporal, processual, and contextual data dimensions that allow organizations to:

- continuously update and recalibrate KPIs based on real-time inputs,
- simulate and anticipate the effects of managerial decisions,
- and systematically analyze deviations and failure patterns in key performance domains (cf. Bernhard, 2000, pp. 42–45).

To make these governance structures operable, organizations rely on specific modeling functions that embed control, accountability, and transparency requirements into their information landscapes. Information modeling enhances governance implementation by enabling organizations to define, coordinate, and evaluate complex rule systems in a traceable and transparent manner. This is achieved through several interrelated functions that form the methodological backbone of governance-oriented modeling:

- *Dynamic KPI Mapping:* KPI structures derived from static strategic documents risk becoming obsolete in volatile environments. Information models address this challenge by linking KPIs to data inputs that reflect shifting operational or market realities (cf. Ward and Peppard, 2002, pp. 65 ff.).
- *Real-Time Monitoring and Alerting:* Through integration with business intelligence systems and operational platforms, models enable real-time performance visualization, including early warning indicators and automated feedback loops (cf. Applegate et al., 2002, pp. 158 ff.).

- *Scenario Simulation and Sensitivity Analysis:* Organizations can experiment with hypothetical configurations or stress scenarios (e.g., supply chain disruption, sudden demand shifts) to assess their impact on performance outcomes. This improves strategic preparedness and investment decision-making (cf. Ehrmann, 2007, pp. 45 ff.).
- *Root Cause and Variance Analysis:* When expected outcomes are not achieved, structured models assist in drilling down through layered indicators and data sources to identify structural, behavioral, or contextual causes (cf. Bernhard, 2000, pp. 41–45).

Beyond these technical functions, information modeling in performance management also facilitates a cultural shift. Instead of viewing performance solely as a control mechanism, it enables performance to be understood as a dialogic process. When model outputs are made transparent and intelligible to stakeholders, they support participatory performance conversations and data-informed learning processes. As such, the contribution of information modeling extends beyond operational efficiency. It lays the foundation for an anticipatory, evidence-based, and reflexive performance management system, which are essential characteristics of organizations striving for resilience and sustainable competitiveness (cf. Beynon-Davies, 2019, pp. 56–59).

1.7.3 Interfacing with Governance Frameworks

Information modeling serves as a critical architectural element for embedding governance frameworks into operational and strategic management systems. In environments shaped by regulatory complexity, risk sensitivity, and the increasing formalization of IT governance, the capacity to map, monitor, and refine governance structures through structured models has become indispensable (cf. ISACA, 2019b, pp. 22–26).

Frameworks such as COBIT 2019 emphasize a comprehensive governance system that includes governance objectives, enablers, and performance management domains. Information modeling offers the tools to instantiate these abstract components into actionable system representations. It bridges the gap between normative governance principles and the everyday routines of IT and business operations (cf. Ehrmann, 2007, pp. 46–49).

To make these governance structures operable, organizations rely on specific modeling functions that embed control, accountability, and transparency requirements into their information landscapes. Information modeling enhances governance implementation by enabling organizations to define, coordinate, and evaluate complex rule systems in a traceable and transparent manner. This is achieved through the following functions:

- *Governance Structure Mapping:* Models provide a clear and structured visualization of roles, responsibilities, and decision rights across the governance architecture. This includes the mapping of process ownership, control responsibilities, and escalation paths within and across organizational units (cf. Ward and Peppard, 2002, pp. 148 ff.; cf. Krcmar, 2003, pp. 110–113).
- *Policy and Control Integration:* By linking policy rules with data structures and process logics, models support the enforcement of governance mechanisms through automated controls. This reduces manual intervention and increases consistency in control execution (cf. Kersten, Reuter, et al. 2011, pp. 98–102; cf. Ginovsky, 2012, pp. 24–27).
- *Audit Trail Formalization:* Information models capture the flow of data and decisions, creating a reproducible audit trail. This supports regulatory compliance, simplifies external audits, and enables internal reviews of governance maturity (cf. Bernhard, 2000, pp. 41–45; cf. Ward and Peppard, 2002, pp. 212–215).
- *Governance Adaptation and Simulation:* Dynamic modeling environments allow organizations to simulate governance changes (e.g., new regulatory requirements or organizational restructuring) and assess their operational and compliance impact prior to implementation (cf. Henderson, 2012, pp. 22–27; cf. Pohlmann and Blumberg, 2006, pp. 45–48).

As illustrated in Fig. 1.4, these core functions of information modeling translate governance requirements into actionable structures that promote accountability, traceability, and adaptive oversight. These modeling functions do not only enhance the transparency and efficiency of governance execution but also foster a governance culture that is integrated rather than imposed. By embedding control logic into models that are actively used for planning, execution, and review, governance becomes a living system rather than a static compliance artifact (cf. Ehrmann, 2007, pp. 47–50).

Furthermore, information models serve as a shared reference point for collaboration among compliance officers, IT architects, risk managers, and operational leaders. This integrative function facilitates cross-domain communication and the reconciliation of diverse governance expectations and risk tolerances (cf. Haeseler and Hörmann, 2005, pp. 54–57). Ultimately, the contribution of information modeling to governance lies in its capacity to operationalize principles of accountability, transparency, and control in a traceable, scalable, and adaptive manner, which are key attributes in achieving and sustaining governance excellence (cf. Speckbacher et al., 2003, pp. 373–377).

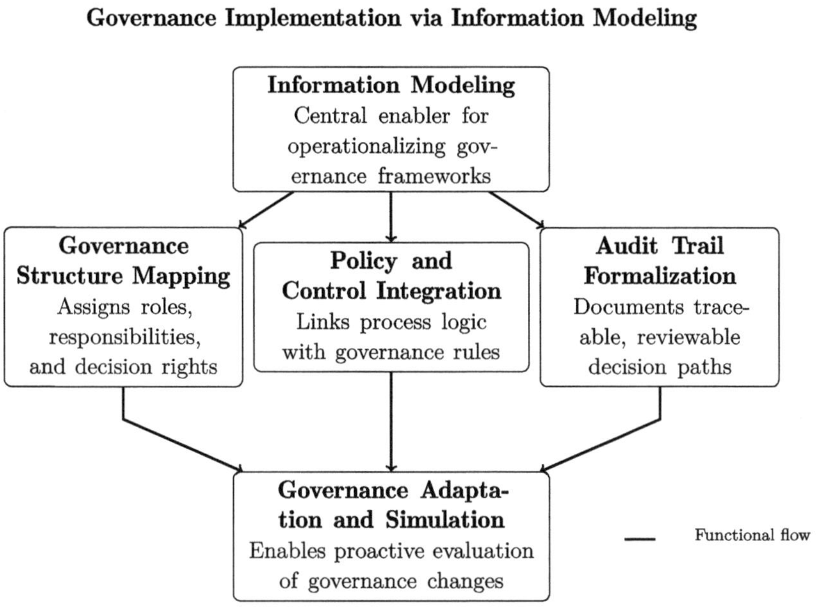

Fig. 1.4 Information Modeling Functions Supporting Governance Frameworks. (Own illustration, 2025)

1.7.4 Strategic Enhancement Through BYOD Integration

The increasing prevalence of BYOD policies reflects a paradigm shift in how organizations approach mobility, flexibility, and employee empowerment. At the same time, the growing heterogeneity of devices and access points presents considerable challenges in terms of data protection, compliance, and control. In this context, information modeling provides a conceptual and technical foundation for aligning BYOD initiatives with overarching performance and governance objectives (cf. Miller, 2012, pp. 53 ff.; cf. Hunt, 2012, pp. 69 ff.).

Information modeling enables the design and enforcement of BYOD architectures that are transparent, rule-based, and integrated into organizational strategy.

By explicitly defining device roles, access rights, security policies, and compliance requirements, information models help mitigate risks and ensure operational continuity across diverse user environments (cf. Pohlmann and Blumberg, 2006, pp. 45–48; cf. Henderson, 2012, pp. 22–27). Key modeling contributions to BYOD integration include:

- *Access Control Structuring:* Formalized access models specify how individual device types and user roles interact with sensitive data and systems. This includes the categorization of users, mapping of network segments, and dynamic authorization rules to accommodate changing contexts (e.g., remote location, time of access) (cf. Ward and Peppard, 2002, pp. 148–150).
- *Audit Trail Mapping:* Information models serve as templates for recording and reconstructing user activity across devices and systems. They support compliance with internal security protocols as well as external regulatory frameworks, such as ISO/IEC 27001 and the GDPR (cf. Kersten, Reuter, et al. 2011, pp. 98–102; cf. Fischer, 2012, pp. 60 ff.).
- *User Behavior Analytics:* Advanced modeling approaches allow for the integration of behavioral indicators into monitoring processes. These may include frequency of access, usage anomalies, and risk scoring, and can be connected to automated enforcement systems such as MDM and EDR platforms (cf. Henderson, 2012, pp. 22–28).
- *Compliance Alignment:* BYOD modeling frameworks embed legal and policy requirements into workflows and data management procedures. This facilitates demonstrable compliance and promotes accountability among users (cf. Hunt, 2012, pp. 69 ff.; cf. Ginovsky, 2012, pp. 24–27).

Moreover, by consolidating governance, performance, and compliance requirements into a unified modeling environment, organizations are able to treat BYOD not as an exception to existing systems but as an integral component of enterprise architecture. This holistic perspective allows for consistent control, strategic visibility, and responsiveness to changing internal and external conditions. In sum, the contribution of information modeling to BYOD integration lies in its capacity to translate mobile technology challenges into structured, manageable, and performance-oriented architectures, thereby reinforcing both strategic control and operational agility (cf. Ward and Peppard, 2002, pp. 65 ff.).

1.7.5 Implementation Considerations

The implementation of information modeling within strategic performance management requires deliberate planning, methodological rigor, and organizational readiness. As models serve to bridge strategic intent and operational execution, their effectiveness depends not only on their technical sophistication but also on their alignment with existing processes, systems, and stakeholder expectations (cf. Krcmar, 2003, pp. 79–82; cf. Ehrmann, 2007, pp. 45 ff.).

A robust implementation strategy must address issues of scalability, interoperability, usability, and resilience. Poorly designed or isolated models risk becoming obsolete, ignored, or counterproductive. Therefore, implementation must be conceived as a phased, feedback-oriented process that emphasizes continuous improvement, stakeholder engagement, and system integration. Essential dimensions of implementation include:

- *Modular Model Development:* To facilitate maintainability and scalability, information models should follow a modular structure. This allows new business domains, performance indicators, or control logics to be incorporated incrementally without disrupting existing model logic. Such modularity also supports scenario testing and domain-specific refinements (cf. Ehrmann, 2007, pp. 46–49).
- *Cross-System Integration:* In heterogeneous IT environments, the integration of information models across ERP systems, BI tools, governance platforms, and workflow engines is essential. Standardized data interfaces (e.g., eXtensible Markup Language (XML), JavaScript Object Notation (JSON), Representational State Transfer (REST) Application Programming Interface (API)) and middleware services can enhance interoperability, data consistency, and synchronization (cf. Applegate et al., 2002, pp. 158 ff.; cf. Krcmar, 2003, pp. 110–113).
- *Stakeholder-Centric Design:* Information models must be designed with their end users in mind. This includes role-specific views, intuitive visualizations, and clearly defined data flows. Participatory design methods such as workshops and iterative prototyping ensure that the resulting models are both usable and accepted (cf. Ward and Peppard, 2002, pp. 65 ff.; cf. Ginovsky, 2012, pp. 24–27).
- *Resilience Engineering:* Information models must be equipped to handle system disruptions, data inconsistencies, and shifting strategic priorities. Mechanisms such as model versioning, validation routines, and rollback functions contribute to stability and governance continuity (cf. Violino, 2012, pp. 29–31 ff.; cf. Fischer, 2012, pp. 60 ff.).

- *Performance and Compliance Monitoring:* Effective implementation includes establishing routines for monitoring the model's accuracy, relevance, and compliance with regulatory standards (e.g., GDPR, ISO/IEC 27001). Integration with performance dashboards and audit systems enhances transparency and facilitates proactive governance (cf. Kersten, Reuter et al., 2011, pp. 98–102).

Ultimately, the implementation of information models should not be seen as a one-time project, but as a dynamic and continuous capability-building process. Organizations that invest in flexible modeling architectures, cross-functional alignment, and lifecycle governance are more likely to realize sustained strategic value from their performance management systems.

1.7.6 Implementation and Application

The successful application of information models in organizational practice depends on their seamless integration into existing IT infrastructures and business routines. This phase, which bridges model development and operational deployment, entails both technical and organizational demands. In practice, it is not the model alone that determines success, but the ability of the organization to implement it under real-world conditions, manage resistance, and generate value from its use. System integration challenges include ensuring data compatibility, platform interoperability, and the efficient migration of existing databases. Technical complexity is further compounded by the need to maintain performance and scalability during and after rollout. Standardized protocols and modular system architectures are essential to reduce integration friction and preserve the integrity of operational processes (cf. Applegate et al., 2002, pp. 121–125; cf. Elmasri and Navathe, 2015, pp. 158 ff.).

From an organizational perspective, implementation also requires robust change management, clear communication strategies, and a strong commitment of leadership to the transition process (cf. Neely, 2007, pp. 313–317). Resource management becomes critical when allocating financial, technical, and human resources to support implementation while safeguarding ongoing operations (cf. Applegate et al., 2002, pp. 201–204). Additionally, proactive risk management must be embedded to anticipate system or project failures, delays, and compliance issues (cf. Krcmar, 2003, pp. 277–280).

Real-world case studies play a vital role in evaluating the effectiveness of these implementations. They allow organizations to validate theoretical constructs, identify contextual success factors, and adapt best practices to their own environments (cf. Bourgeois et al., 2014, pp. 122–125). The use of qualitative and quantitative

Fig. 1.5 Phases of Implementation and Application of Information Models. (Own illustration, 2025)

evaluation methods, ranging from interviews and process observation to metric-based benchmarking, enables a multi-faceted understanding of the model's value contribution (cf. Darvish et al., 2012, pp. 15 f.).

These empirical findings inform implementation guidelines and strategic recommendations that go beyond technical rollout. Figure 1.5 visualizes the interdependent phases of implementation, from system integration through organizational enablement and case-based validation, culminating in iterative model refinement and long-term value realization. They support refinement of the models, adjustment to organization-specific needs, and long-term value realization. Thus, implementation and application do not represent the end of the modeling process, but rather a critical phase in the iterative lifecycle of continuous performance development.

1.7.7 System Integration

System integration represents a pivotal step in the application of information models, as it determines whether the conceptual and technical design can be embedded in the operative IT landscape of an organization. This phase encompasses a complex interaction of software, data structures, user interfaces, and organizational workflows. A seamless and scalable integration is essential to ensure that the benefits of information modeling, such as improved performance visibility, strategic alignment, and governance, can be realized in day-to-day operations (cf. Applegate et al., 2002, pp. 121–125; cf. Gallaugher, 2023, pp. 122–126).

An analysis of the key integration dimensions reveals two interdependent challenge areas that require simultaneous attention: technical and organizational integration requirements. First, on the technical side, organizations face a series of integration challenges that must be methodically addressed:

- *Compatibility and Interoperability:* One of the central requirements is ensuring compatibility between the newly developed model and the organization's legacy systems, databases, and middleware platforms. The integration must be robust across heterogeneous environments and should ideally be based on standardized protocols and APIs (e.g., REST, Simple Object Access Protocol (SOAP)) to allow modular extensibility (cf. Applegate et al., 2002, pp. 158 ff.).
- *Data Migration and Transformation:* Migration of historical and operational data to new structures entails data mapping, cleansing, and transformation routines that must preserve semantic consistency. Information models must accommodate various data granularities and formats without compromising integrity or traceability (cf. Krcmar, 2003, pp. 222–225).
- *System Performance and Scalability:* The additional computational load resulting from model-driven processes, analytics, and real-time monitoring must be managed without degrading system responsiveness. Performance testing, load balancing, and distributed architecture principles (e.g., microservices) are key strategies to mitigate this (cf. Ward and Peppard, 2002, pp. 148 ff.).

In parallel to the technical dimensions, the organizational layer of system integration must be carefully managed:

- *Change Management:* Integrating a model often requires not only technical deployment but also process redesign. Employees must be supported through structured change programs, user trainings, and clear communication to ensure acceptance and avoid operational resistance (cf. Bernhard, 2000, pp. 32–35).

- *Resource Management:* Successful implementation depends on appropriate allocation of financial, temporal, and personnel resources. Interdisciplinary project teams that bring together business and IT perspectives are a critical success factor (cf. Applegate et al., 2002, pp. 201–204).
- *Risk Management:* Anticipating technical failures, integration delays, or security vulnerabilities is essential. Information modeling projects should include a formal risk management strategy that defines escalation paths, contingency plans, and critical checkpoints (cf. Krcmar, 2003, pp. 277–280).

In sum, system integration is not a purely technical exercise but a multi-dimensional transformation process. Only by addressing both technological interoperability and organizational alignment can the full strategic potential of information models be realized within enterprise infrastructures.

1.7.8 Case Studies and Practical Examples

To complement the theoretical and technical insights surrounding information modeling, the empirical examination of implementation success through case studies and practical examples is essential. These studies serve multiple purposes: they validate conceptual assumptions, identify barriers and success factors in real-world applications, and generate recommendations for both strategic decision-makers and operational stakeholders (cf. Speckbacher et al., 2003, pp. 361 f.; cf. Bernhard, 2000, pp. 30 ff.). An in-depth analysis of case study work is generally structured in three stages. Setting the analytical framework, examining empirical findings, and formulating recommendations:

- *Analytical Framework:* The primary objective of employing case study methodology is to evaluate the effectiveness, scalability, and adaptability of information models across diverse organizational contexts. In addition, case studies provide insight into how specific elements such as governance structures, IT architectures, or organizational culture interact with the model and influence outcomes (cf. Darvish et al., 2012, pp. 18 f.; cf. Bainey, 2016, pp. 158 ff.). A structured combination of qualitative and quantitative methods such as semi-structured interviews, document analyses, structured observations, and performance metric assessments is typically employed to ensure a comprehensive evidence base (cf. Darvish et al., 2012, pp. 15 f.).
- *Empirical Findings:* Case studies highlight both strengths and limitations of the modeled approaches. Key performance indicators include the model's integra-

tion depth, usability, compliance alignment, and contribution to strategic goals (cf. Ginovsky, 2012, pp. 24–27; cf. Bourgeois et al., 2014, pp. 122–125). Findings often reveal that successful implementations are supported by high-level commitment, early stakeholder involvement, and continuous feedback loops. Conversely, resistance to change, poor integration into legacy systems, or lack of user training are frequently cited barriers (cf. Bernhard, 2000, pp. 32–35).
- *Best Practices and Recommendations:* Across cases, certain recurring practices have proven effective, including early alignment of the model with key stakeholders, modular deployment strategies, and the integration of model maintenance responsibilities into existing governance structures (cf. Speckbacher et al., 2003, pp. 365 f.; cf. Ehrmann, 2007, pp. 45 ff.). Based on these insights, organizations are advised to ensure continuous model refinement, secure executive sponsorship throughout the implementation lifecycle, and embed performance feedback mechanisms that support iterative learning and adaptation (cf. Darvish et al., 2012, pp. 19 f.).

Taken together, these case-based insights offer empirically grounded validation and practical guidance that enhance the reliability, contextual fit, and long-term utility of information models. They also illustrate how theoretical principles can be translated into operational excellence across varied organizational settings.

1.8 Scientific Relevance

The study of the interfaces between information management, systems theory and performance management, as carried out by the model for evaluation and performance management using a balanced scorecard, offers a comprehensive analysis of these interdisciplinary areas. This approach is of considerable scientific importance, as it contributes both to the expansion of theoretical knowledge and to the development of practical solutions that are indispensable for the management of information processes in modern organisations (cf. Bernhard, 2000, pp. 10 ff.).

Expansion of theoretical knowledge: The scientific relevance of this topic is evident in several key areas:

- **Information Management**: Information management is concerned with the systematic collection, processing, storage and provision of information to support decision-making processes in organisations. Through the study and development of information models, an understanding of the efficient management and use of information is deepened. This includes the analysis of data flows, the optimisation of information systems and the improvement of data quality. The theoretical insights from this area help to expand the foundations of information management and develop new approaches to addressing the challenges of an increasingly data-driven world (cf. Krcmar, 2003, pp. 23 ff.).

- **Systems Theory**: Systems theory provides a framework for analysing and modelling complex systems and their interactions. In the context of the information model, systems theory enables a deeper understanding of the dynamic relationships between different components of an information system. By applying systems theory principles, models are developed that reflect the complexity of information processes and take into account the interdependencies between data, processes and technologies. This leads to a more comprehensive and in-depth consideration of information systems and their role in organisations (cf. Speckbacher et al., 2003, pp. 365 f.).
- **Performance Management**: Performance Management focuses on measuring and managing organisational performance. The development of information models for performance evaluation contributes to the refinement of the theoretical concepts of performance management. In particular, it examines how performance measurement systems and analytical methods can be used to monitor and improve organisational performance. The insights gained expand our knowledge of how performance management strategies and techniques are applied in different organisational contexts (cf. Bernhard, 2000, pp. 11–14).

Development of practical solutions: In addition to the theoretical expansion, the development of practical solutions plays a central role in the scientific relevance of the topic:

- **Management of information processes**: The practical solutions that arise from the study of the information model are crucial for the management of information processes in modern organisations. This includes the development of methods and tools for the efficient integration and use of data, as well as the implementation of information systems that enable transparent and informed decision-making. By providing practical solutions, organisations are able to make optimal use of their information resources and increase their performance (cf. Applegate et al., 2002, pp. 45 ff.).
- **Strategic Control and Performance Evaluation**: Another practical aspect is the role of information systems in the strategic control and performance evaluation of organisations. Information models provide the necessary data and analyses to

support the strategic goals of the organisation and improve operational efficiency. This includes identifying key indicators, monitoring performance metrics and forecasting future developments. The practical implications of these models help to strengthen the organisation's competitiveness and ensure long-term success (cf. Bernhard, 2000, pp. 14 ff.).

Central questions of organisational research: The topic addresses several central questions of organisational research, including:

- **Efficiency and effectiveness of information systems**: How can information systems be designed and implemented in a way that maximises the efficiency and effectiveness of information processes in organisations (cf. Applegate et al., 2002, pp. 45 ff.)?
- **Integration of data and technologies**: Which methods and techniques are best suited to ensure the integration of different data sources and technologies into a consistent and powerful information system (cf. Ward and Peppard, 2002, pp. 65 ff.)?
- **Strategic decision-making**: How can information models support strategic decision-making in organisations and what impact do they have on long-term planning and control (cf. Speckbacher et al., 2003, pp. 365 f.)?
- **Performance evaluation and control**: Which key figure systems and analytical methods are most effective for evaluating and controlling the performance of organisations (cf. Bernhard, 2000, pp. 11–14)?

The study of the interfaces between information management, systems theory and performance management, especially in the context of evaluating and managing performance using a balanced scorecard, is dedicated to these areas. A significant and current topic in this context is BYOD. The integration of BYOD into the existing information model presents both theoretical and practical challenges and opportunities that need to be analysed comprehensively.

1.9 Expansion of Theoretical Knowledge Through BYOD

BYOD, the concept by which employees use their own devices such as laptops, smartphones and tablets for work purposes, represents a significant development in information management. This concept expands theoretical understanding in several areas:

- **Information Management**: The introduction of BYOD significantly changes the landscape of information management. Traditional information systems are based on defined, centralised devices and networks. BYOD, on the other hand, introduces decentralisation of information sources, which requires new methods for collecting, processing and storing data. It increases the complexity of data management because different devices have different operating systems and security standards. Integrating BYOD into information models therefore requires an adaptation of existing theories and practices of information management (cf. Pohlmann and Blumberg, 2006, pp. 45–49).
- **Systems Theory**: From a systems theory perspective, BYOD represents an extension of the system in which external, non-standardised components are integrated into the organisational network. This significantly increases the number of variables and interactions within the system. Systems theory provides tools for modelling and analysing this increased complexity, including the identification and control of interdependencies and feedback loops. A robust information model must be able to map these dynamic relationships and increased system complexity (cf. Speckbacher et al., 2003, pp. 365 f.).
- **Performance Management**: The impact of BYOD on performance management is complex. On the one hand, BYOD can increase employee productivity and flexibility because they can work with devices they are familiar with. On the other hand, BYOD poses new challenges for performance evaluation, as the use of personal devices blurs the line between work and personal use. This requires the development of new performance measurement systems that take into account both the advantages and potential risks of BYOD (cf. Henderson, 2012, pp. 23–29).

1.9.1 Dveloping Practical Solutions for BYOD

The implementation of BYOD requires targeted solutions to address its unique challenges and unlock its potential. This section outlines both technical and organisational measures necessary for ensuring security, compatibility, and efficient management in the BYOD environment. The integration of BYOD into the information model requires the development of specific practical solutions to overcome the associated challenges and maximise the benefits:

- **Technical solutions**
  - **Security and data protection**: One of the biggest challenges of BYOD is ensuring data security and data protection. Technical solutions such as Mobile Device Management, Virtual Private Networks and encryption technologies are necessary to ensure the security of corporate data on personal devices. An information model must integrate and continuously monitor these security aspects (cf. Pohlmann and Blumberg, 2006, pp. 45–48).
  - **Compatibility and Interoperability**: The variety of devices and operating systems in the BYOD context requires solutions to ensure compatibility and interoperability. Standardised interfaces and protocols are necessary to enable seamless integration of personal devices into the corporate network (cf. Henderson, 2012, pp. 26–29).

- **Organisational measures**
  - **Policies and training**: The introduction of BYOD requires clear policies and training for employees. These policies should regulate the use of personal devices and establish security protocols. Training is necessary to raise employee awareness of security risks and to educate them in the safe use of their devices (cf. Ginovsky, 2012, pp. 24–27).
  - **Resource Management**: BYOD can lead to a redistribution of IT resources, as managing and supporting a variety of devices requires additional resources. Careful planning and allocation of these resources is necessary to ensure the efficiency of the IT department (cf. Hunt, 2012, pp. 69 ff.).

1.9.2 Strategic Control and Performance Evaluation with BYOD

The integration of personal devices into the workplace requires adapting performance management systems to address new challenges and opportunities. Key performance indicators must be expanded to reflect BYOD's impact on productivity, security, and employee satisfaction. Advanced analytics and predictive modelling enable organisations to identify trends, forecast risks, and implement proactive measures, ensuring BYOD aligns with strategic objectives while enhancing organisational efficiency and security. The integration of BYOD into an organisation's performance management and strategic control brings with it new dimensions and requirements:

- **Key performance indicator systems**: Traditional key performance indicator systems must be adapted to measure the impact of BYOD on employee productivity and efficiency. New performance indicators that take into account factors such as the use of personal devices, employee satisfaction and data security must be developed and validated (cf. Hunt, 2012, pp. 71 ff.).
- **Data analysis and predictive modelling**: The application of advanced analytics techniques is critical to identify the patterns and trends in performance data influenced by BYOD. Predictive analytics can be used to forecast the future developments and potential risks of BYOD and to plan proactive measures to optimise the use of personal devices (cf. Violino, 2012, pp. 29 ff.).

1.9.3 Key Issues in Organisational Research with BYOD

The integration of personal devices into organisational processes raises critical questions in research on information systems, strategic management, and performance evaluation. Key issues include balancing efficiency and security, understanding the strategic and operational impacts of BYOD, and developing effective metrics for measuring and evaluating device usage. These challenges highlight the need for interdisciplinary approaches that connect information management, systems theory, and performance management, especially in the context of increasing remote work and evolving workplace dynamics. The integration of BYOD into the information model addresses several key issues in organisational research, including:

- **Information system efficiency and security**: How can information systems be designed and implemented to maximise the efficiency of information processes while ensuring data security in a BYOD environment (cf. Henderson, 2012, pp. 23–27)?
- **Strategic and operational impact of BYOD**: What strategic and operational impact does BYOD have on the organisation and how can these best be managed to maximise the positive effects and minimise the risks (cf. Rodham, 2012, pp. 12 ff.)?
- **Measuring and evaluating BYOD usage**: What methods and metrics are most effective for measuring and evaluating the use of personal devices in the organisation (cf. Hunt, 2012, pp. 70 ff.)?

The study of the interfaces between information management, systems theory and performance management, in particular through the balanced scorecard, deals intensively with these interdisciplinary areas. In the wake of the COVID-19 pandemic, the concept of the home office has taken on unprecedented importance and represents an extension that poses both theoretical and practical challenges and opportunities in these areas.

1.10 Expansion of Theoretical Knowledge Through Home Office

The widespread adoption of home office practices, accelerated by the COVID-19 pandemic, has significantly influenced the theoretical foundations of organisational research. This development has introduced new challenges and opportunities in information management, systems theory, and performance management. Key areas include adapting centralised information systems for distributed work environments, managing the increased complexity of system interactions, and redefining performance metrics to reflect the realities of remote work. These changes highlight the need for theoretical advancements to address the evolving dynamics of the modern workplace. The introduction and increase of home office due to the COVID-19 pandemic is changing the theoretical foundations of information management, systems theory and performance management:

- **Information Management**: The sudden and widespread shift of the work environment to the home office poses new challenges for information management. Traditional, centralised information systems must be adapted to support distributed and decentralised work environments. This requires new approaches for securely capturing, processing and storing data outside the physical office boundaries. The integration of cloud technologies and remote access solutions is becoming a central component of modern information management (cf. Kersten, Reuter et al., 2011, pp. 110 ff.).
- **Systems theory**: From a systems theory perspective, the home office leads to a redistribution of system components and an increased complexity of interactions. Work processes and communication channels must be re-modelled to reflect the dynamic and often non-linear relationships between distributed employees and central enterprise systems. Systems theory approaches help to ensure the stability and resilience of these new working models and to develop adaptation strategies for rapidly changing working conditions (cf. Bundesamt, 2022, pp. 10–13).
- **Performance Management**: Performance evaluation in the home office requires an adaptation of existing key figure systems. Traditional metrics, which are aimed at physical presence and direct monitoring, are no longer applicable. Instead,

new indicators must be developed that take into account aspects such as digital productivity, virtual collaboration and self-management of employees. The theoretical concepts of performance management must be expanded to integrate the specific challenges and opportunities of the home office (cf. Golden and J. F. Veiga, 2005, pp. 302–307).

1.10.1 Developing Practical Solutions for Home Offices

The shift to home office environments necessitates practical solutions to address the technical and organisational challenges of remote work. This includes implementing robust security measures, adapting infrastructure to meet the needs of distributed teams, and establishing clear guidelines and training programs. Effective resource management and support systems are also essential to ensure the seamless functioning of remote work environments and to maximise productivity and security. The integration of the home office into the information model requires the development of specific practical solutions:

- **Technical solutions**
  - **Security measures**: Relocating work to the home office increases the risk of cyber attacks and data loss. Technical solutions such as VPN, two-factor authentication, and encrypted communication channels are necessary to ensure the security of company data. A robust information model must integrate and continuously monitor these security aspects (cf. Kersten, Reuter et al., 2011, pp. 53–56).
  - **Infrastructure**: The technical infrastructure must be adapted to the requirements of the home office. This includes the provision of hardware (such as laptops and mobile devices), software (such as collaboration and communication platforms) and support services that enable the distributed work environments to function smoothly (cf. Bundesamt, 2022, pp. 13 ff.).
- **Organisational measures**
  - **Guidelines and training**: The introduction of home office requires clear guidelines and training for employees. These guidelines should regulate the use of IT resources, security protocols and work performance expectations. Training is necessary to educate employees on the effective use of new

technologies and on best practices for working from home (cf. Bundesamt, 2022, pp. 14 ff.).

- **Resource management**: Managing remote resources requires careful planning and allocation. IT departments must be able to provide fast and effective support for a large number of remote workstations. This may include the introduction of helpdesk systems and remote support tools (cf. Bundesamt, 2022, pp. 15 ff.).

1.10.2 Strategic Control and Performance Evaluation in the Home Office

Adapting strategic control and performance management to home office environments introduces new demands. Performance metrics must evolve to capture factors like virtual collaboration, digital productivity, and employee satisfaction. Leveraging advanced data analysis and forecasting techniques allows organisations to identify trends, address emerging challenges, and enhance the effectiveness of remote work setups. The integration of the home office into an organisation's performance management and strategic control brings with it new dimensions and requirements:

- **Key performance indicators**: Traditional key performance indicator systems must be adapted to enable performance evaluation in the home office. New performance indicators should include aspects of virtual collaboration, the achievement of project goals and employee satisfaction. Measuring digital productivity and the quality of work output are also important indicators to be integrated into the KPI systems (cf. Golden and J. F. Veiga, 2005, pp. 306–309).
- **Data analysis and forecasting**: The application of advanced analytics techniques is crucial to identify patterns and trends in employee performance data while working from home. Predictive analytics can be used to forecast future developments and potential challenges in the home office and to plan proactive measures to optimise remote working environments (cf. Golden and J. F. Veiga, 2005, pp. 311–316).

1.10.3 Key Issues in Organisational Research with Home Offices

The shift to home office environments presents several critical challenges in organisational research. Questions about the efficiency and security of information systems, the strategic and operational impacts of remote work, and effective methods for evaluating employee performance and satisfaction have gained increasing importance. Addressing these issues requires an interdisciplinary approach, combining insights from information management, systems theory, and performance management to develop robust frameworks and models for the evolving workplace. The integration of the home office into the information model addresses several key issues in organisational research, including:

- **Information Systems Efficiency and Security**: How can information systems be designed and implemented to maximise the efficiency of information processes while ensuring data security in a distributed work environment (cf. Kersten, Reuter et al., 2011, pp. 47–51)?
- **Strategic and operational implications of remote work**: What are the strategic and operational implications of remote work for the organisation and how can they best be managed to maximise the positive effects and minimise the risks (cf. Kommission, 2022, pp. 13 ff.)?
- **Measuring and evaluating home office use**: Which methods and metrics are most effective for measuring and evaluating the performance and satisfaction of employees working from home (cf. Golden and J. F. Veiga, 2005, pp. 303–309)?

The intensive study of the interfaces between information management, systems theory and performance management, in particular through the BSC, deals with these interdisciplinary areas. The BSC, a strategic management tool for evaluating performance and controlling organisations, plays a central role in this. It enables a structured and multidimensional view of organisational performance and is therefore essential for the development and application of information models.

1.11 Expansion of Theoretical Knowledge Through the BSC

The BSC significantly enriches theoretical perspectives in information management, systems theory, and performance management. It promotes advanced data integration techniques for comprehensive performance evaluation, provides a framework for analysing multidimensional interactions within organisations, and emphasises a balanced approach to managing financial and non-financial metrics. By linking strategic goals to actionable measures, the BSC fosters a deeper understanding of sustainable and holistic performance management. The BSC extends theoretical understanding in several areas of information management, systems theory and performance management:

- **Information Management**: The BSC requires the systematic collection, processing and analysis of a large amount of data covering various aspects of organisational performance. This includes both financial and non-financial metrics that need to be integrated into an integrated information system. The development of an information model for the BSC therefore requires advanced information management techniques to consistently and reliably process and provide the data (cf. Ehrmann, 2007, pp. 46–49).
- **Systems Theory**: From a systems theory perspective, the BSC provides a framework for modelling the complex interactions between the various dimensions of organisational performance. The BSC is based on the assumption that an organisation's performance is influenced not only by financial results, but also by customer perspectives, internal business processes and learning and development perspectives. These multidimensional relationships can be analysed and optimised using system-theoretical approaches to ensure balanced and sustainable performance management (cf. Speckbacher et al., 2003, pp. 364–368).
- **Performance Management**: The Balanced Scorecard is a central instrument of performance management. It provides a holistic and multidimensional view of an organisation's performance by integrating financial and non-financial metrics. The BSC expands the theoretical concepts of performance management by emphasising the importance of a balanced consideration of the various performance dimensions and by focusing on strategic goals and their implementation (cf. Ehrmann, 2007, pp. 47 ff.).

1.11.1 Development of Practical Solutions for the BSC

Integrating the BSC into organisational frameworks demands practical solutions to address both technical and organisational challenges. Ensuring effective data integration and leveraging automation technologies enables seamless performance monitoring and real-time analysis. Equally important are well-planned implementation strategies and training programs, which foster employee understanding and support for the Balanced Scorecard while promoting a culture of strategic alignment and continuous improvement. The integration of the Balanced Scorecard into the information model requires the development of specific practical solutions:

- **Technical Solutions**
  - **Data Integration**: A central element of the BSC is the integration of different data sources and formats into a consistent and comprehensive information system. This requires advanced data integration strategies that ensure that all relevant performance data is collected, processed, and provided in an accessible format (cf. Ehrmann, 2007, pp. 45–48).
  - **Automation and real-time analysis**: Modern technologies such as Business Intelligence (BI) tools and data analysis platforms can be used to automate the collection and analysis of BSC data. Real-time analysis makes it possible to monitor current performance data and react quickly to deviations (cf. Speckbacher et al., 2003, pp. 377–380).
- **Organisational measures**
  - **Implementation Strategy**: The introduction of BSC in an organisation requires a careful implementation strategy. This includes defining clear objectives, establishing responsibilities and involving all relevant stakeholders. A stepwise implementation can help to increase acceptance and minimise potential resistance (cf. Ehrmann, 2007, pp. 48 ff.).
  - **Training and Change Management**: The effective use of the BSC requires training and change management initiatives to ensure that all employees understand and support the principles and applications of the BSC. This helps to foster a culture of continuous improvement and strategic thinking (cf. Speckbacher et al., 2003, pp. 385–388).

1.11.2 Strategic Control and Performance Evaluation with the BSC

The BSC is a vital tool for effective strategic control and performance evaluation. It facilitates the alignment of organisational activities with strategic objectives by defining measurable performance indicators. Through continuous monitoring and adjustment, the BSC enables proactive management and swift responses to changing conditions. Its integration of financial and non-financial metrics ensures a holistic evaluation of organisational performance, providing a balanced perspective on success and areas for improvement. The BSC plays a crucial role in the strategic control and performance evaluation of an organisation:

- **Strategic alignment**: The BSC helps organisations to define their strategic objectives and translate them into concrete, measurable performance indicators. This ensures that all activities and resources are aligned with the achievement of long-term goals (cf. Ehrmann, 2007, pp. 45 ff.).
- **Continuous monitoring and adjustment**: By regularly monitoring BSC indicators, organisations can continuously assess their performance and make necessary adjustments. This enables proactive management and a rapid response to changes in the business environment (cf. Speckbacher et al., 2003, pp. 365–370).
- **Holistic performance assessment**: The BSC enables a holistic assessment of organisational performance by integrating financial and non-financial metrics. This helps to obtain a balanced picture of performance and ensures that all relevant aspects of the organisation are taken into account (cf. Speckbacher et al., 2003, pp. 369–372).

1.11.3 Key Issues in Organisational Research with the BSC

The BSC raises critical questions in organisational research, particularly regarding the efficiency and effectiveness of information systems, the strategic and operational implications of its implementation, and the evaluation of its use within organisations. Addressing these issues involves exploring the intersections of information management, systems theory, and performance management, offering insights into optimising performance evaluation and control. The integration of complementary frameworks, such as COBIT 2019, further enriches the theoretical and practical understanding of these topics. The integration of the BSC into the information model addresses several key issues in organisational research, including:

- **Efficiency and Effectiveness of Information Systems**: How can information systems be designed and implemented to maximise the efficiency and effectiveness of the Balanced Scorecard and ensure consistent and reliable data collection and analysis (cf. Speckbacher et al., 2003, pp. 373–378)?
- **Strategic and operational implications of the BSC**: What are the strategic and operational implications of using the Balanced Scorecard in the organisation and how can these be best managed to maximise the positive effects and minimise the risks (cf. Ehrmann, 2007, pp. 47–50)?

- **Measuring and evaluating BSC usage**: What methods and metrics are most effective for measuring and evaluating the use of the Balanced Scorecard in the organisation (cf. Speckbacher et al., 2003, pp. 381–388)?

The intensive examination of the interfaces between information management, systems theory and performance management is central to the study of performance evaluation and control of organisations. In this context, COBIT 2019 plays an important role. COBIT 2019 is a comprehensive framework for the governance and management of enterprise information and technology. The integration of COBIT 2019 into existing information models presents both theoretical and practical challenges and opportunities that require comprehensive analysis.

1.12 Expansion of Theoretical Knowledge Through COBIT 2019

Theoretical advancements in information management, systems theory, and performance management are significantly influenced by COBIT 2019. This framework provides a comprehensive approach to IT governance and management, emphasising process standardisation, data security, and alignment with organisational objectives. Its systems theory foundation enables the analysis of complex interactions and interdependencies, while its performance management tools introduce precise metrics and methods for evaluating IT processes. COBIT 2019 thus contributes to the optimisation of organisational structures and the achievement of strategic goals. COBIT 2019 expands theoretical understanding in several areas of information management, systems theory and performance management:

- **Information Management**: COBIT 2019 provides a structured framework for the governance and management of IT resources and processes. It defines detailed control objectives and best practices that ensure IT resources are used effectively to support business objectives. In information management, COBIT 2019 helps standardise processes and ensure consistent, reliable, and secure data management. This includes guidelines for data security, privacy, and compliance, which are integral to a robust information model (cf. Krcmar, 2003, pp. 79–82).
- **Systems Theory**: COBIT 2019 is based on systems theory principles and provides a comprehensive framework for analysing and controlling the interactions between different IT and business processes. The systems theory perspective of COBIT 2019 helps to structure and understand the complexity of IT governance. It provides tools for modelling system interactions and identifying feedback

loops and interdependencies, which are crucial for designing and optimising information systems (cf. Applegate et al., 2002, pp. 120–123).

- **Performance Management**: COBIT 2019 plays an essential role in performance management by defining clear performance metrics and evaluation methods for IT processes. These metrics are aligned with the strategic objectives of the organisation and enable effective monitoring and control of IT performance. Theoretical concepts of performance management are extended by COBIT 2019, as it provides specific guidelines for measuring and improving IT performance (cf. Ward and Peppard, 2002, pp. 65 ff.).

1.12.1 Developing Practical Solutions for COBIT 2019

Practical implementation of COBIT 2019 demands targeted solutions that address both technical and organisational challenges. Effective IT governance structures and security measures are essential for aligning IT resources with organisational goals and mitigating risks. At the same time, organisational strategies, including well-planned implementation frameworks and comprehensive training initiatives, ensure that employees are equipped to support and sustain the governance principles defined by COBIT 2019. The integration of COBIT 2019 into the information model requires the development of specific practical solutions:

- **Technical solutions**

  - **IT governance and management**: COBIT 2019 provides detailed frameworks for IT governance and management to ensure that IT resources are used efficiently and effectively. This includes implementing IT governance structures, roles and responsibilities, and introducing processes and controls that ensure compliance with governance guidelines (cf. Gaulke, 2002, pp. 45–48).
  - **Security and risk management**: COBIT 2019 places a strong emphasis on security and risk management. Technical solutions must be developed to identify, assess and mitigate risks and ensure the security of IT systems. This includes measures for risk assessment, threat analysis and implementation of security controls (cf. Kersten, Reuter et al., 2011, pp. 98–102).

- **Organisational measures**
  - **Implementation Strategy**: The implementation of COBIT 2019 requires a careful strategy that includes aligning organisational structures and processes with the governance guidelines. This involves defining clear governance frameworks, establishing communication and reporting lines, and training employees in COBIT principles (cf. Krcmar, 2003, pp. 125 ff.).
  - **Training and change management**: The successful implementation of COBIT 2019 requires training and change management initiatives to ensure that all employees understand and support the principles and applications of COBIT 2019. Training should focus on the importance of IT governance, the specific requirements of COBIT 2019, and the role of employees within governance structures (cf. Applegate et al., 2002, pp. 150–153).

1.12.2 Strategic Control and Performance Evaluation with COBIT 2019

Integrating COBIT 2019 into strategic control and performance management introduces enhanced capabilities for evaluating IT performance. By defining key performance indicators aligned with organisational objectives, COBIT 2019 facilitates a comprehensive assessment of IT effectiveness, efficiency, security, and compliance. Additionally, advanced data analytics and predictive tools enable organisations to anticipate risks and trends, ensuring proactive measures to optimise IT governance and management. The integration of COBIT 2019 into an organisation's performance management and strategic control brings new dimensions and requirements:

- **Key performance indicators**: COBIT 2019 defines specific key performance indicators that are aligned with the strategic and operational objectives of the organisation. These indicators enable a holistic evaluation of IT performance and support the continuous improvement of IT processes. Performance indicators include metrics on IT effectiveness, efficiency, security, and compliance (cf. Ward and Peppard, 2002, pp. 209–212).
- **Data Analytics and Predictive Analytics**: Applying advanced analytics techniques is crucial to identify patterns and trends in IT performance data. Predictive analytics can be used to forecast future developments and potential risks in the IT area and to plan proactive measures to optimise IT governance and management (cf. Speckbacher et al., 2003, pp. 373–376).

1.12.3 Key Issues in Organisational Research with COBIT 2019

The integration of COBIT 2019 into organisational frameworks highlights several critical research challenges. These include designing information systems that optimise IT efficiency and security while ensuring compliance, understanding the strategic and operational impacts of IT governance, and developing effective methods for measuring and evaluating IT performance. Addressing these issues requires interdisciplinary approaches that connect information management, systems theory, and performance management to enhance organisational effectiveness and resilience. The integration of COBIT 2019 into the information model addresses several key issues in organisational research, including:

- **Efficiency and security of information systems**: How can information systems be designed and implemented to maximise the efficiency and security of IT processes while meeting compliance requirements (cf. Krcmar, 2003, pp. 110–113)?
- **Strategic and operational impact of IT governance**: What strategic and operational impact does the use of COBIT 2019 have on the organisation and how can these best be managed to maximise the positive effects and minimise the risks (cf. Applegate et al., 2002, pp. 135–139)?
- **Measuring and evaluating IT performance**: Which methods and metrics are most effective for measuring and evaluating IT performance and how can these metrics be integrated into strategic control (cf. Ward and Peppard, 2002, pp. 212–215)?

Conclusion and Recommendations from Chapter I

The topic of 'Information model in the system for measuring and the performance of the Balanced Scorecard' provides a comprehensive exploration of the intersections between information management, systems theory, and performance management. The integration of contemporary topics such as BYOD, home office, the Balanced Scorecard, and COBIT 2019 enriches the academic discourse, offering detailed insights into both the theoretical and practical challenges and opportunities presented by these developments.

Organizational control mechanisms play a critical role in ensuring that information systems consistently support strategic objectives, particularly in decentralized work environments shaped by BYOD and remote access. Through structured monitoring, systematic evaluation, and responsive corrective actions, organizations can maintain transparency, enforce compliance, and drive continuous improvement.

Technologies such as MDM, CASB, and EDR enhance these capabilities by providing granular oversight, real-time threat detection, and adaptive response mechanisms. As part of a dynamic feedback loop, these control elements transform abstract governance principles into actionable routines, thereby reinforcing the strategic relevance and resilience of the overall information system architecture.

Modern frameworks and practices such as remote work, flexible device usage, performance evaluation systems, and governance frameworks have fundamentally reshaped organisational approaches. These shifts influence how data is collected, processed, and analysed, the complexity of interactions within and between systems, and the methods used for evaluating organisational performance. To adapt to these changes, organisations must employ innovative strategies that ensure stability, efficiency, and alignment with evolving technological and organisational landscapes.

In the context of information management, the increasing adoption of BYOD and home office necessitates new approaches for securely managing distributed and decentralised data. Cloud technologies and remote access solutions are central to addressing these challenges. The Balanced Scorecard provides a structure for integrating both financial and non-financial metrics into cohesive information systems to support strategic decisions. Complementing this, COBIT 2019 offers detailed control objectives and best practices for effective IT governance and management, ensuring that information processes align with organisational goals.

From a systems theory perspective, the inclusion of BYOD and home office introduces greater complexity to system interactions, requiring a reconfiguration of work processes and communication channels. Systems theory helps organisations manage these dynamics by analysing the relationships and feedback loops within organisational frameworks. The Balanced Scorecard uses systems theory principles to model multidimensional performance relationships, while COBIT 2019 applies these concepts to optimise IT and business process interactions.

Performance management is also significantly enhanced by integrating these frameworks and practices. New metrics, such as digital productivity and virtual collaboration, reflect the realities of BYOD and home office scenarios. The Balanced Scorecard provides a holistic and multidimensional framework for performance evaluation, combining financial and non-financial indicators. COBIT 2019 complements this by offering specific performance metrics for IT processes, ensuring that evaluation methods align with strategic objectives.

Developing practical solutions to integrate these frameworks requires both technical and organisational measures. Technically, organisations must address security concerns through VPNs, two-factor authentication, and encrypted communication channels, as well as implement advanced data integration and automation strategies to streamline performance data analysis. Organisationally, clear guidelines, comprehensive training, and effective change management are essential to foster employee understanding and ensure alignment with governance frameworks like COBIT 2019 and performance tools such as the BSC.

Strategic control and performance evaluation benefit greatly from the Balanced Scorecard and COBIT 2019. These frameworks provide structured methodologies for defining, monitoring, and refining performance metrics. They also address the unique challenges posed by remote work and BYOD, helping organisations develop innovative performance indicators that reflect the demands of modern work environments. By integrating financial insights with IT governance principles, these frameworks enable a comprehensive and adaptable evaluation of strategic progress.

The integration of these topics into organisational information models raises critical questions in organisational research. Issues such as ensuring the efficiency and security of information systems, managing the strategic and operational impacts of workplace transformations, and developing effective metrics for performance evaluation are central to advancing knowledge in this field. Addressing these issues requires interdisciplinary collaboration that bridges information management, systems theory, and performance management to enhance organisational effectiveness and resilience.

In conclusion, the integration of BYOD, home office, Balanced Scorecard, and COBIT 2019 into information models is of significant scientific relevance. These frameworks expand theoretical and practical perspectives on information systems and performance management, addressing key questions in organisational research. By implementing effective information models that reflect these developments, organisations can optimise their processes, improve performance, and secure long-term competitiveness. The COVID-19 pandemic has further underscored the necessity and urgency of these adjustments, driving innovation and transformation in the fields of information systems and organisational management.

Integration of BYOD Into IT-BSC Systems to Optimize it Structures and Strategic Alignment

2

In this chapter, the focus is on presenting the topic-related fundamentals that are essential for a well-founded examination of the research question formulated in the introduction. The emphasis here is on creating a solid foundation for understanding and classifying the subsequent analyses and discussions in the context of the current scientific landscape. It should be noted that the aim of this chapter is not to provide a comprehensive and exhaustive presentation of the respective sub-areas. Rather, the intention is to provide a concise overview of the current state of scientific knowledge, focusing specifically on the aspects relevant to the research question.

2.1 The Bring your Own Device Concept

'Bring Your Own Device' (BYOD) is a business strategy that allows employees to use their personal electronic devices, such as smartphones, laptops and tablets, for work purposes. This practice has become a widespread method of making business processes more efficient and improving employee satisfaction. A thorough understanding of BYOD, its benefits and challenges, is crucial for companies that want to use this strategy effectively. The origin of BYOD lies in technological progress and the increasing prevalence of powerful portable devices. As early as 2009, Intel officially recognised the practice as the 'consumerisation of IT' (cf. Intel, 2009, p. 1). Since then, BYOD has gained popularity worldwide, especially with the rise of remote working and the digital transformation of business processes (cf. K. W. Miller et al., 2012, pp. 10–15).

The advantages of BYOD are manifold. On the one hand, it enables companies to save hardware costs because employees use their own devices. Furthermore, it increases productivity, as employees are often more familiar and comfortable working with their personal devices. It can also improve employee satisfaction and

M. Groß, *Managing IT in the Age of BYOD and Remote Work*,
https://doi.org/10.1007/978-3-658-51216-3_2

engagement by giving them more flexibility and control over how they work (cf. Köffer, 2015, pp. 29–34). At the same time, however, there are also challenges and risks associated with BYOD. These include issues of data security, data protection and IT governance. These issues require specific considerations and strategies to ensure that sensitive corporate information is protected and legal requirements are met (cf. Stanton et al., 2015, pp. 15–19).

It is also important to remember that the implementation of BYOD depends on corporate culture and technological infrastructure. Organisations must be willing and able to adapt their IT strategies and policies to effectively integrate BYOD. This includes developing guidelines for the use of personal devices, implementing appropriate security solutions, and providing support and training for employees. In the following chapters, the relevant aspects of BYOD will be presented to provide a comprehensive understanding of this practice and its impact on modern organisations (cf. Stanton et al., 2015, pp. 33 f.).

2.1.1 Fundamentals Bring Your Own Device

In this chapter, the term BYOD is examined in more detail to provide a clear understanding of its meaning, dimensions and application. BYOD refers to a practice in which employees use their personal electronic devices—including, but not limited to, smartphones, laptops and tablets—to carry out their work. In a broader context, BYOD also encompasses concepts such as Choose Your Own Device (CYOD), Corporate Owned, Personally Enabled (COPE) and Corporate Liable Employee Owned (CLEO), each of which emphasises specific aspects of the use of personal technologies in the work environment(cf. French et al., 2014, pp. 1–5).

It is important to note that BYOD encompasses multiple dimensions. In addition to the purely technical dimension—the devices themselves and the associated technologies—BYOD also includes organisational, behavioural and legal dimensions. The organisational dimension concerns the impact of BYOD on business processes and workflows, including issues of productivity, employee satisfaction and IT governance. The behavioural dimension refers to employees' behaviour and preferences regarding their devices and how this influences their work. Finally, the legal dimension concerns the legal regulations and policies that apply to the use of personal devices in the work environment, particularly with regard to data protection and security (cf. Brodin, 2016, pp. 10–15).

2.1.2 Definition and Concepts

Beyond the conventional BYOD approach, the spectrum is expanding to include alternative concepts such as Choose Your Own Device (CYOD), Corporate Owned, Personally Enabled (COPE) and Corporate Liable Employee Owned (CLEO). This section introduces these concepts and analyses their specifics as well as possible advantages and disadvantages.

CYOD—Choose Your Own Device

While the concept of BYOD is well established, a similar but distinct concept called Choose Your Own Device (CYOD) has also emerged. CYOD allows employees to choose a device from a predefined list of devices that the company provides and manages. In contrast to BYOD, where employees bring their own personal devices, with CYOD, employees choose from the options offered by the company (cf. Elghaly, 2018, pp. 173–182). One major difference between BYOD and CYOD lies in control and security. Since the devices in a CYOD scheme are provided by the company, the company retains more control over the devices and can ensure that they are properly secured and updated. This can help mitigate some of the security and compliance issues often associated with BYOD (cf. Gupta et al., 2013, pp. 12–15).

Another difference lies in the costs. While BYOD helps companies save on hardware costs, CYOD can be more expensive for companies because they have to purchase and maintain the devices. However, these costs can be justified by the advantages in terms of control and security. Finally, employee satisfaction can be another difference between BYOD and CYOD. While BYOD offers employees the greatest possible flexibility by allowing them to use their own devices, CYOD allows employees a certain amount of choice while still maintaining corporate control (cf. Wang, 2020, pp. 102–107).

COPE—Corporate Owned, Personally Enabled

Another concept that is important in the discussion of personal devices in the corporate environment is the 'Corporate Owned, Personally Enabled' (COPE) model. Similar to BYOD and CYOD, COPE has its own specific characteristics and distinctions. The COPE model refers to a strategy in which the company purchases and owns the devices, but employees can use them for personal purposes. In contrast to BYOD, where employees bring their own devices, or CYOD, where employees choose from a list of company-approved devices, companies purchase the devices under COPE and then allow employees to use them for both work and personal purposes (cf. Brodin, 2016, pp. 11–15).

A key advantage of the COPE model is that it ensures control and security of corporate data, as the company has full control over the devices. Furthermore, companies can ensure that all devices have the necessary security features and updates (cf. Elghaly, 2018, pp. 11 ff.). Another advantage is that the COPE model offers employees greater flexibility than the traditional corporate device model, as they can also use the devices for personal purposes. This can help to increase employee satisfaction and productivity, as they no longer have to switch between personal and work devices (cf. Brodin, 2016, pp. 10–15).

Nevertheless, there are challenges, particularly in terms of separating personal and professional data on the same devices and ensuring employee privacy. Therefore, the successful implementation of COPE requires careful planning and policy design. Overall, the COPE model can be an effective solution for companies that want to experience the benefits of personal device use while ensuring control and security of corporate data (cf. Brodin, 2016, pp. 18 ff.).

CLEO—Corporate Liable, Employees Owned

In the variety of models that relate to the use of personal devices in a professional context, the 'Corporate Liable Employee Owned' (CLEO) model stands out. This model offers a unique approach that bridges the boundaries between the previously discussed models. In the CLEO model, employees own their devices, but companies assume responsibility (liability) for them. This means that the company is responsible for the maintenance, security, and compliance of the devices, even though the devices are owned by the employees (cf. Gupta et al., 2013, pp. 13 f.). A key advantage of the CLEO model is that it combines the advantages of BYOD (e.g., employee satisfaction and productivity) with the control and security of COPE. By taking responsibility for the devices, the company can ensure that they are properly secured and maintained, while employees have the freedom to use their own devices (cf. Elghaly, 2018, pp. 12 ff.).

The challenges of the CLEO model are similar to those of BYOD and COPE. On the one hand, the company must ensure that it has control over the devices to minimise security risks. On the other hand, it must respect employee privacy since the devices are owned by employees. These challenges require careful policies and management practices (cf. Wang, 2020, p. 13).

2.1.3 BYOD Development in the Timeline

The BYOD concept has undergone a remarkable evolution over the years. This chapter traces the development of the term BYOD along a timeline. The origins of BYOD lie in the late 2000s, when the proliferation of smartphones and other portable devices increased. Employees began using their personal devices for work to increase productivity and achieve a better work-life balance. In 2009, Intel officially recognised the phenomenon as the 'consumerisation of IT' (cf. K. W. Miller et al., 2012, pp. 1 f.).

The early 2010s marked the 'Golden Age' of BYOD. Many companies introduced BYOD policies to take advantage of the benefits in terms of productivity, employee satisfaction and cost efficiency. It was also during this time that the first challenges in terms of security and compliance became apparent (cf. Köffer, 2015, pp. 1–3). By the mid-2010s, organisations began to develop and implement alternative models to BYOD, including CYOD, COPE, and CLEO. These models were introduced to address the control, security, and compliance challenges of BYOD (cf. Gupta et al., 2013, pp. 13–16). In the late 2010s and early 2020s, the importance of BYOD and similar models continued to grow due to the increasing prevalence of remote work and digital transformation. The COVID-19 pandemic has further intensified these trends, as many companies have switched to remote work and employees are increasingly reliant on their personal devices (cf. Wang, 2020, pp. 2 ff.).

2.1.4 Opportunities of BYOD Usage

One of the main arguments in favour of implementing BYOD in companies is the potential for cost savings. This chapter examines the financial opportunities and considerations associated with BYOD. The cost savings of BYOD can be realised in several areas. Firstly, companies can save significant hardware costs because employees provide their own devices. This can mean significant savings, especially in larger organisations with many employees [cf. Secondly, software and licence costs can also be reduced, especially if employees use their own applications and software subscriptions. Furthermore, maintenance and support costs can be reduced, as employees are often able to maintain and repair their own devices (cf. Willis and Madsen, 2013, p. 12).

However, it is important to remember that BYOD can also incur additional costs. These include, for example, the costs of implementing and managing security solutions, providing training and support for employees, and adapting IT systems and applications to a wide range of devices and operating systems. In addition, organisations must also consider the legal and financial implications of issues such as liability, data protection and compliance. This may include, for example, the cost of legal advice and the development of BYOD policies (cf. French et al., 2014, p. 14).

In addition to the potential cost savings, BYOD also offers other opportunities, particularly in terms of employee mobility, efficiency and satisfaction. Employee mobility is an important aspect of BYOD. By allowing employees to use their personal devices for work, they have the option of working from anywhere as long as they have access to the internet. This can improve flexibility and work-life balance, and enable employees to work more efficiently (cf. Köffer, 2015, p. 16). Furthermore, BYOD can also increase employee efficiency. Since employees are often more familiar with their personal devices and may be able to operate them better and faster than company devices, this can lead to increased productivity. It can also improve communication and collaboration because employees can more easily access their devices and applications and use them for work (cf. Andriole, 2012, pp. 18 ff.).

Finally, BYOD can also increase employee satisfaction. Employees often appreciate the flexibility and control that BYOD offers, and they can be happier and more engaged when they can use their own devices for work. However, it is important to note that these benefits do not come without challenges. Organisations need to ensure that they provide appropriate policies and support to ensure security and compliance and to support employees in their use of their devices. Overall, BYOD strategies offer significant opportunities to improve employee mobility, efficiency and satisfaction. However, companies need to plan and manage carefully to maximise these benefits and minimise potential risks (cf. Wang, 2020, pp. 20 f.).

2.1.5 Business Management Consideration

A comprehensive business assessment of BYOD requires an examination of the costs that companies would incur if they decided against implementing BYOD. This chapter sheds light on these aspects. Without a BYOD strategy, companies usually have to bear the costs of providing devices for their employees (cf. Versteegen, 2003, pp. 99–102). These hardware costs can be significant, especially in larger organisations. These costs include not only the purchase costs of the devices themselves, but also the costs of maintaining and updating them (cf. Willis and Madsen, 2013, p. 12). Another significant cost factor is the software and licences. Companies often need to purchase licences for a range of applications and services that run on the devices provided. These costs can add up significantly over time, especially when upgrades or additional licences are needed (cf. French et al., 2014, p. 14). In addition, the costs of managing and supporting the devices can be significant. This includes the cost of IT support and training, device and system maintenance, and managing security and compliance requirements (cf. J. Harris et al., 2012, p. 16).

Finally, there are also indirect costs to consider, including potential productivity losses when employees cannot use their preferred devices or applications, as well as the impact on employee satisfaction and engagement. Overall, it is important that companies include all these cost factors in their business assessment of BYOD. While BYOD has its own costs and challenges, it can also help companies avoid or reduce many of the expenses mentioned above. Implementing a BYOD strategy does come at a cost. It is a project that can incur both human and material costs. Human and material costs can arise when a company plans, implements and manages a BYOD strategy. These include expenses for project management, IT infrastructure, security, training and support (cf. Willis and Madsen, 2013, pp. 18 ff.).

First of all, planning and implementing a BYOD project can require significant human resources. This can include both internal employees (e.g. IT staff, project managers, compliance and security experts) and external consultants. These costs can be significant, especially if specialised expertise or additional resources are needed (cf. French et al., 2014, pp. 13–16). In addition, BYOD requires an appropriate IT infrastructure. This may include both hardware (e.g. servers, network equipment) and software (e.g. Mobile Device Management (MDM) systems, security solutions). While some of these expenses can be offset by using employees' own devices, other costs, particularly those related to security and administration, may increase (cf. J. Harris et al., 2012, pp. 16 f.).

Training and support costs are another important factor. Employees need to be trained on how to use their devices securely and effectively for work, and they may need assistance with setting up and using their devices. In addition, training and support may be required for IT staff responsible for managing the BYOD strategy. These costs can include both direct costs (e.g. personnel, infrastructure) and indirect costs (e.g. productivity losses due to downtime) (cf. Willis and Madsen, 2013, p. 18). In terms of direct costs, companies may need to hire or train additional helpdesk staff to support the variety of devices and systems that employees bring with them. In addition, the costs for support infrastructure, such as helpdesk software or support tools, may increase. It may also be necessary to hire specialised external service providers, especially if specific expertise or resources are needed (cf. French et al., 2014, pp. 18 ff.). In terms of indirect costs, employee downtime caused by personal device issues can impact employee productivity. Furthermore, the expenses for managing security problems or data loss associated with personal devices can be significant. Although expenses and financial savings play an important role in the business case for BYOD, there are also numerous non-monetary aspects that should be considered (cf. J. Harris et al., 2012, pp. 16 ff.):

1. **Employee Satisfaction and Productivity**: A BYOD strategy can improve employee satisfaction and productivity by giving employees the freedom and flexibility to use their own devices. These devices are usually the ones that employees are most familiar with and can use most efficiently, which can lead to productivity increases (cf. Köffer, 2015, pp. 11 f.).
2. **Recruiting and retaining talent**: BYOD can also be a valuable tool for attracting and retaining professionals. Many employees, especially younger generations, value the opportunity to use their own devices for work and may be attracted to companies that offer BYOD (cf. Andriole, 2012, p. 16).
3. **Security and Compliance**: While BYOD can pose security and compliance challenges, it also provides an opportunity to adopt more robust and flexible security practices. For example, the use of Mobile Device Management (MDM) or Mobile Application Management (MAM) solutions can help to protect and control corporate data on personal devices (cf. French et al., 2014, pp. 18 f.).
4. **Innovation and adaptability**: Finally, BYOD can help to foster a culture of innovation and adaptability in a company. Employees using their own devices and applications can find new and innovative ways of doing their jobs, which in turn can contribute to the company's overall innovative strength (cf. J. Harris et al., 2012, pp. 20 f.).

2.1.6 General and Specific Risks

While BYOD offers significant advantages and opportunities, it also involves a number of risks. This chapter provides an overview of the general and specific risks that can arise when using BYOD:

1. **Risks for employee satisfaction**
   The BYOD strategy not only offers opportunities but also risks for employee satisfaction. Although the approach potentially increases employee flexibility and autonomy, it also raises concerns about privacy and work-life balance (cf. Köffer, 2015, pp. 17 f.). One of the main concerns is employee privacy. When personal devices are used for work purposes, there may be a concern that the company could have access to personal information or activities (cf. J. Harris et al., 2012, pp. 21 f.). This can negatively affect satisfaction and trust in the company's management (cf. Andriole, 2012, p. 32).

Another critical element is the blurring of the boundaries between work and private life. The constant accessibility and the possible pressure to be available outside of regular working hours can lead to stress and exhaustion (cf. French et al., 2014, pp. 34–37). These effects can have a negative impact on both employee productivity and satisfaction in the long term (cf. Köffer, 2015, p. 36).

2. **Security and Compliance Challenges**
   The implementation of BYOD presents companies with several challenges, particularly in terms of data security and compliance. One of the most significant risks is the potential data loss that can arise from various scenarios. For example, employees could accidentally or intentionally lose sensitive information, for example through the loss of the device itself or through the use of insecure cloud services and networks (cf. Gartner, 2023, pp. 1 f.; cf. ISC(2), 2023, pp. 5–8).
   Another significant risk is the vulnerability to cyber attacks. Personal devices are often less well protected against such attacks, especially if they are not regularly updated or if no appropriate security mechanisms are implemented. Cyber attacks can not only result in the loss or compromise of sensitive company data, but can also endanger the integrity of the entire corporate network (cf. Gartner, 2023, p. 3; cf. Center, 2023, pp. 6 ff.).
   Furthermore, there are specific challenges in the area of compliance. The heterogeneous device landscape in a BYOD environment makes it difficult to ensure that all devices comply with the applicable legal and internal regulations. This is particularly important with regard to data security and data protection regulations (cf. Gartner, 2023, pp. 5 f.).
3. **Lost or stolen devices**
   Another specific risk associated with BYOD is the risk of lost or stolen devices. Using personal devices for work increases the likelihood of sensitive corporate information being lost or stolen, especially when employees are on the road or working outside the office. If a device is lost or stolen, all company information stored on or accessible through it may be compromised (cf. French et al., 2014, pp. 18–21).
   Furthermore, there is a risk that unauthorised individuals may access the device and retrieve or misuse sensitive company information. This can lead to data breaches, reputational damage and potential legal consequences (cf. Andriole, 2012, p. 16). There are a number of measures that companies can take to mitigate this risk. These include implementing security measures such as passwords, encryption, and remote wipe capabilities, providing training to employees on how to use and store their devices securely, and implementing policies and

procedures in the event a device is lost or stolen (cf. J. Harris et al., 2012, pp. 20 f.).

4. **Management and Support Risks in BYOD Environments**
   The integration of BYOD into a company's IT infrastructure brings with it a number of risks and challenges for administration and support. In a BYOD environment, IT departments must be able to manage a heterogeneous landscape of devices, operating systems and applications. HARRIS ET AL. point out that this diversity can lead to increased costs and a more complex IT landscape (cf. J. Harris et al., 2012, pp. 20 f.). The challenge begins with the inventory of the devices and continues with configuration and security. Different operating systems require specialised knowledge and tools for administration, which increases the need for IT teams to invest in additional training and software (cf. Andriole, 2012, pp. 22 f.). Furthermore, incompatible systems and applications can cause problems when integrating them into the existing IT infrastructure, which makes support more difficult (cf. Köffer, 2015, p. 24).
   An additional layer of complexity is added by the need for continuous compliance monitoring. Organisations must ensure that all devices comply with security policies and regulations, which in turn requires ongoing monitoring and occasional audits (cf. French et al., 2014, p. 26). To minimise these risks, appropriate management strategies and tools are required. One approach would be to implement a Unified Endpoint Management (UEM) system that allows all devices and operating systems to be managed from a central interface (cf. J. Harris et al., 2012, pp. 26–29).
5. **Insecure connections**
   One of the specific risk categories associated with the implementation of BYOD relates to the use of insecure connections. When employees use their personal devices for work, they usually have the freedom to access corporate resources from virtually any location. This can often mean that they have to rely on public or insecure Wi-Fi networks to connect. Such networks pose a significant security risk as they can easily be compromised by cybercriminals targeting sensitive company information (cf. French et al., 2014, pp. 18 f.).
   Furthermore, there is a risk that employees may install or use insecure apps or services on their devices that can either intentionally or accidentally open security vulnerabilities. These apps can also be used to transfer or store sensitive company information, increasing the risk of a data loss or a data protection violation (cf. Andriole, 2012, p. 16). To mitigate these risks, companies can take a number of measures. These may include providing secure connectivity options, such as VPNs, training employees on how to use networks and apps

securely, and implementing technology to monitor and control device usage (cf. J. Harris et al., 2012, pp. 20 ff.).

6. **Data exchange risks**
   Data exchange poses a specific and significant risk in a BYOD environment. In a BYOD environment, employees often have the ability to exchange data between their personal devices and corporate networks. While this can improve employee flexibility and productivity, it also introduces significant risks. These include the possibility of accidental or intentional sharing of sensitive company data, the possibility of data being stored on insecure or unauthorised devices or services, and the possibility of data being compromised during transmission (cf. French et al., 2014, pp. 80 f.).
   These risks can have significant impacts, including the loss or disclosure of sensitive company data, reputational damage, and potential legal ramifications. In some cases, they can also affect the company's ability to meet compliance requirements (cf. Andriole, 2012, pp. 17 f.). To mitigate these risks, organisations can take a number of measures. These include implementing data control and management tools, training employees on secure data sharing practices, implementing policies and procedures for data sharing, and using security technologies such as data encryption and secure connection options (cf. J. Harris et al., 2012, p. 21).

2.2 Home Office Evolution in Context of the COVID 19 Pandemic

The COVID-19 pandemic has fundamentally changed the concept of workplace design worldwide and made remote working a mainstay of the global economy. Previously, remote working was seen as an alternative and flexible working method favoured only by a minority. However, it has now become the main working model for a wide range of professions and companies. The unexpected and abrupt shift to remote working due to lockdown measures has brought both advantages and challenges. This chapter examines the development of remote working during the pandemic and the associated legal perspectives.

In the context of the pandemic, companies have recognised the value of flexibility and adaptability, and technology has proven to be an essential tool for business continuity. The rapid shift to remote working has shown that productivity and efficiency are not necessarily tied to a physical location. At the same time, the shift to remote working has raised new legal issues and challenges, ranging from labour law to data protection and occupational health and safety.

Employees now have the right to work from home under certain conditions, but they must also comply with company policies and standards that apply to the home office. For their part, companies must ensure that they respect these rights while also ensuring compliance with legal requirements. The legal complexity arising from the home office affects not only employers and employees, but also governments, which must create appropriate legal frameworks.

The following sections will discuss the development of the home office during the COVID-19 pandemic, analyse the legal issues and perspectives associated with it, and examine how these changes could affect the future of work. It will also discuss the implications of the legal aspects of the home office for employees and employers and the solutions available to overcome the legal challenges that have arisen.

2.2.1 Home Office Development

Early concepts of home office are not new and date back to the 1970s, when technological progress offered the first opportunities for remote work (cf. Nilles, 1975, p. 15). The invention of personal computers and the advent of the Internet later in the 1990s expanded these opportunities (cf. Duvall, 2005, pp. 25 f.). However, at the beginning of the 21st century, home office was seen as a niche practice that was more common in certain industries or functions, such as IT or customer care (cf. Bloom et al., 2015, p. 10).

It is important to understand the early approaches to home office, as they provide the framework for the current shift to home office during the COVID-19 pandemic. While in the early phases of home office, the technological infrastructure and legal frameworks were often inadequate or non-existent, these elements have developed and improved over the years. One of the main challenges in introducing home office in the past was ensuring productivity and the quality of work in a remote working environment (cf. Bloom et al., 2015, pp. 186 f.).

In terms of legal aspects, the early approaches to home office were largely characterised by the lack of a specific legal framework (cf. Gollmann et al., 2006, pp. 15–19). The rights and obligations of employees and employers with regard to home office were often regulated by individual employment contracts, which were not always sufficient to protect the interests of both parties (cf. Eurofound and the International Labour Office, 2017, p. 19). As time passed and the practice of remote working grew, legal regulations were developed to fill this gap, but these have often still not kept pace with the rapid development of technology and changing work practices (cf. Mann and Holdsworth, 2003, pp. 225–228).

While the COVID-19 pandemic has accelerated the implementation of remote working, historical context shows that this is an evolution built on decades of experience and adaptation. It is important to consider this historical perspective to understand the current challenges and opportunities of remote working.

2.2.2 Technological Advances and their Implications

Technological advances have been crucial in enabling and encouraging remote work. The first remote work experiments began in the 1970s and 1980s, thanks to developments in telecommunications technology and the personal computer revolution (cf. Nilles, 1975, p. 15; cf. Duvall, 2005, p. 9). In the 1990s, the advent of the internet and e-mail provided greater access to remote work (cf. Duvall, 2005, pp. 10 f.). However, recent advances in technology have exponentially increased the potential for remote work. Cloud computing, videoconferencing technologies, instant messaging, and mobile technologies have transformed the way people communicate and collaborate, blurring the lines between the physical office and where work is actually done (cf. Hjorth and Peters, 2019, p. 10).

In the context of the COVID-19 pandemic, these technologies have facilitated the transition to remote working. According to a study by Defilippis et al. (cf. 2020, p. 10), employees quickly adapted to new technologies during the lockdown while maintaining the same or even higher levels of productivity. However, in the context of legal aspects, technological advances have also created new challenges. Increasing digitalisation has raised questions regarding data protection and security that were previously less present in traditional office environments (cf. Sullivan and Staas, 2014, pp. 225 f.). Governments and organisations must continue to work to develop and update legal frameworks that both take into account technological developments and ensure the rights and safety of workers (cf. Bentley et al., 2020, p. 530).

2.2.3 Changes in Work Culture and Structures

The rapid shift to remote working has caused a significant change in the work culture and structure in many organisations. A study by Felstead and Henseke (2017) emphasises that remote working requires a different view of work, focusing on the outcome of work rather than the traditional control of when and where work is done. Increased use of remote working has also helped to break down traditional hierarchies, as employees at all levels of an organisation work in similar working environments (cf. Kelliher and D. Anderson, 2010, p. 76). It has the potential to foster a more inclusive work culture by offering more flexibility and autonomy, which can be particularly beneficial for workers with caring responsibilities, those with disabilities or those living in remote areas (cf. Eurofound, & the International Labour Office, 2020, pp. 19 f.).

However, there are also concerns about the impact of remote working on workplace culture. For example, the lack of in-person interactions and social ties in the workplace can lead to isolation and feelings of alienation (cf. Gajendran and Harrison, 2007, pp. 743 f.). In addition, the blurring of work and personal life that remote work often entails can lead to overwork and stress (cf. Boswell and Olson-Buchanan, 2007, p. 1182). In terms of legal aspects, these changes in work culture and structure require labour laws and regulations to be reviewed and updated. For example, companies must ensure that they can guarantee the health and safety of their employees despite the physical distance (cf. Biron and van Veldhoven, 2016, p. 10). Furthermore, new rules and agreements are needed to address data protection and security issues in the home office environment (cf. Sullivan and Staas, 2014, pp. 225 f.).

2.2.4 The Covid 19 Pandemic and the Rise of the Home Office

The COVID-19 pandemic has permanently changed the world of work and made home office an essential form of work. Before the pandemic, home office was the exception in many companies and industries, while in times of the pandemic it became the rule (cf. Bick et al., 2020, p. 10). According to a study by Brynjolfsson et al. (2020), 50% of employees in the US switched to working from home within a few weeks (cf. Brynjolfsson et al., 2020, pp. 2–5). The rapid shift to remote working has had both positive and negative effects. On the plus side, many employees and companies have come to appreciate the flexibility of working from home. Studies have shown that, under the right conditions, productivity can be maintained or even improved when working from home (cf. Defilippis et al., 2020, p. 10). Furthermore, the option to work from home could help to reduce commuting and thus the environmental impact of transport (cf. S.-H. Chen and Kuo, 2021, pp. 5 f.).

On the negative side, however, there are also challenges. The blurring of work and personal life can lead to stress and burnout (cf. Boswell and Olson-Buchanan, 2007, pp. 1182 f.). The lack of social interaction and isolation can affect the well-being of employees (cf. Gajendran and Harrison, 2007, p. 743). From a legal perspective, the pandemic has also produced a number of challenges. Questions of data protection and security are of particular concern as many employees access sensitive company information from their homes (cf. Sullivan and Staas, 2014, p. 225). Furthermore, if the workplace is the employee's home, how can employers fulfil their duties regarding occupational health and safety?

The pandemic has emphasised remote working as an essential part of the response to the crisis. The need to maintain physical distance and limit the spread of the virus has led many companies to send their employees to work from home (cf. Brynjolfsson et al., 2020, pp. 2 f.). This abrupt transition to remote working has created its own challenges. Organisations had to quickly switch to digital work tools and train their employees in the use of new technologies (cf. Defilippis et al., 2020, p. 10). New processes and communication protocols were also required to ensure collaboration and productivity in a remote setting (cf. Choudhury et al., 2021, pp. 10 f.). Despite these challenges, remote working has enabled organisations to maintain their operations and retain some sense of normalcy during a time of unprecedented disruption. It has also provided an opportunity to challenge traditional working models and explore innovative approaches to work (cf. Kniffin et al., 2021, p. 10).

In terms of legal aspects, the shift to the home office has highlighted the need for clearer regulations and guidelines. Companies must ensure that they respect the labour rights of their employees while also ensuring health and safety in the workplace, even if that workplace is the employee's home (cf. Eurofound, & the International Labour Office, 2020, pp. 19). Data protection and security issues are also of key importance as more and more employees access sensitive company information from home (cf. Sullivan and Staas, 2014, pp. 225). The global pandemic has not only highlighted remote working as a response to the current crisis, but also as a possible way forward for the future of work post-pandemic. In the US, a study by Brynjolfsson et al., 2020 showed that about half of the workers transitioned to remote work within a few weeks. In Europe, research by Eurofound, & the International Labour Office (2020) showed that about 37% of workers started working from home during the pandemic, compared to about 10% before the pandemic.

While some of these changes are likely to be temporary, there are signs that remote working could play a greater role post-pandemic. A survey by PWC (2021) found that 83% of employers believe that the transition to remote working during the pandemic has been successful. More than half of the employers plan to enable home office even after the pandemic, and 68% of employees would like to have a hybrid way of working that combines home office and on-site work (cf. Sullivan and Staas, 2014, p. 225; cf. Biron and van Veldhoven, 2016, pp. 10 f.).

2.2.5 Legal Perspective on Mobile Working

The legal aspects of working from home are diverse and complex. They affect a range of issues, including working hours, labour law, health and safety at work, data protection and data security. In the area of labour law, it is important that the rights and obligations of employers and employees are clearly defined. This includes issues such as remuneration, working hours, holiday entitlements and protection against dismissal (cf. Klußmann, 1997, pp. 15–18). In many jurisdictions, the principle applies that employees working from home should enjoy the same rights and protections as employees working in a physical workplace (cf. Eurofound and the International Labour Office, 2017, p. 19).

The question of working hours is particularly relevant in the context of working from home. Traditional working time models are often based on the employee's presence at the workplace. However, in a home office, the boundaries between work and leisure time can become blurred, which can lead to overtime and overwork (cf. Eurofound, & the International Labour Office, 2020, pp. 18 f.). Therefore, complying with working time laws and ensuring adequate rest periods can be challenging in a home office (cf. T. A. Bentley et al., 2016, pp. 9 ff.). Health and safety is another important consideration. Employers have a duty in many jurisdictions to ensure the safety and health of their employees in the workplace. However, in the context of remote working, this can be challenging as the employer has no direct access or control over the employee's workplace (cf. Biron and van Veldhoven, 2016, pp. 10 f.). The COVID-19 pandemic has highlighted the need to address these and other legal issues related to remote working. It is crucial that the legal framework keeps pace with the evolving practice of remote working to protect the rights and interests of employees and employers (cf. Calder, 2013, pp. 25–29).

Data protection and data security are central legal aspects in the context of the home office. With the increasing digitalisation of work and the shift of workplaces to the home office, these questions have become more important (cf. Sullivan and Staas, 2014, p. 19). In the European Union, data protection is regulated by the General Data Protection Regulation (GDPR), which sets strict rules for the processing of personal data. Employers who send their employees to work from home must ensure that they comply with these rules. This includes taking appropriate technical and organisational measures to ensure the security of the data being processed (cf. European Parliament and Council, 2016, n.pag.).

In terms of data security, there is a risk that home office environments may be more vulnerable to security breaches than traditional office environments. Employees working from home may be at increased risk of cyberattacks due to unsecured networks, the use of personal devices (BYOD), or the improper handling of information (cf. S.-H. Chen and Kuo, 2021, pp. 5 f.). Therefore, it is important for employers to implement appropriate security policies and to educate their employees regarding data security (cp. Wright et al., 2020, pp. 10 f.). Overall, ensuring data protection and data security is an important challenge in the context of working from home. It is crucial that companies rise to this challenge and that the legal framework is updated and adapted to take into account the new realities of work. The design of agreements and contracts for mobile working, especially working from home, is a central legal aspect of this form of work. These agreements set out the conditions for the home office and regulate issues such as working hours, remuneration, workplace equipment and data handling (cf. Eurofound and the International Labour Office, 2017, pp. 20 f.). An important point is working hours. When working from home, the boundaries between work and leisure time can become blurred, and it can be more difficult to monitor compliance with working time laws (cf. Eurofound, & the International Labour Office, 2020, pp. 18 ff.). Mobile working agreements should therefore include clear rules on working hours and rest periods to prevent overwork and burnout (cf. T. A. Bentley et al., 2016, p. 10).

Another important point is data protection and security. Remote working arrangements should include provisions that govern the handling of sensitive data and ensure that employees take the necessary measures to protect it (cf. Sullivan and Staas, 2014, pp. 19 f.). They should also include guidelines for the use of devices and software used to carry out the work (cf. S.-H. Chen and Kuo, 2021, p. 5). Employers should also ensure that their remote working arrangements take into account health and safety in the workplace. This may include providing appropriate work equipment, conducting risk assessments or providing guidance on how to set up an ergonomic workplace (cf. Eurofound and the International Labour Office, 2017, pp. 18 f.). Designing agreements and contracts for mobile work is a complex task that requires careful consideration and knowledge of the relevant legal provisions. It is crucial that these agreements meet the needs and rights of employees and employers and provide a fair and secure framework for mobile working (cf. Andriole, 2012, pp. 14–17).

2.2.6 Home Office Advantages and Disadvantages

Working from home offers a number of advantages for both employees and employers. For employees, working from home can provide greater flexibility by facilitating work–life balance and eliminating the need for commuting time (cf. Hill et al., 1998, p. 220). This can be especially beneficial for employees who have family commitments or live in rural areas far from the workplace (cf. Felstead and Henseke, 2017, p. 78). In addition, remote working can give employees more autonomy in how they organise their work and their environment (cf. Kelliher and D. Anderson, 2010, pp. 219 f.).

For employers, the benefits of remote working can include increased productivity and efficiency, reduced operating costs, and greater ability to attract and retain talent (cf. Diana E. Bailey and Kurland, 2002, p. 240). Research has shown that, under the right conditions, home offices can improve productivity by reducing workplace disruptions and allowing workers to organise their work around their individual preferences and rhythms (cf. Bloom et al., 2015, p. 180). Furthermore, companies can save significant costs by reducing their need for office space (cf. S.-H. Chen and Kuo, 2021, pp. 5 f.).

However, it is important to note that the benefits of remote working depend heavily on the specific circumstances and proper implementation. Organisations need to provide appropriate support and resources and develop clear policies and agreements for remote working to maximise these benefits and minimise potential drawbacks. Although remote working offers numerous advantages, it also presents challenges and potential risks. Challenges for employees include isolation, a lack of separation between work and personal life, potential overtime, and difficulties in maintaining motivation and productivity (cf. Golden, J. Veiga, et al., 2006, pp. 1023 f.; cf. Gajendran and Harrison, 2007, p. 146).

Isolation can lead to reduced job satisfaction, lower company loyalty and increased stress levels (cf. Golden, J. Veiga, et al., 2006, pp. 1027 ff.). Blurring the lines between work and leisure can also lead to stress and overwork and can disrupt employees' work-life balance (cf. Boswell and Olson-Buchanan, 2007, p. 340). For employers, data protection and security pose a significant challenge (cf. Sullivan and Staas, 2014, p. 225). As more and more employees access sensitive company information from home, it is crucial to implement appropriate security measures and ensure compliance with data protection regulations. Furthermore, monitoring employee performance and ensuring compliance with working time laws and health and safety regulations can be difficult when working from home (cf. Eurofound and the International Labour Office, 2017, pp. 19 f.).

2.2.7 Effects of Home Office on Employees

The impact of remote working on job satisfaction and work-life balance for employees is mixed and depends heavily on individual circumstances and the design of the remote work arrangement. On the positive side, remote work can improve work-life balance by offering employees more flexibility in how they organise their working hours and environment (cf. Kossek et al., 2006, pp. 1070 f.). This can be especially beneficial for employees who have family commitments or live in rural areas far from the workplace (cf. Hill et al., 1998, p. 332). Some studies have shown that employees who work from home report higher job satisfaction levels than their on-site colleagues (cf. Gajendran and Harrison, 2007, p. 1309).

On the other hand, however, working from home can also lead to a blurring of work and leisure time, which can result in stress and overwork (cf. Boswell and Olson-Buchanan, 2007, pp. 598). In addition, the isolation that can come with working from home can lead to reduced job satisfaction and a lower sense of belonging to the company (cf. Golden J. F. Veiga, and Dino, 2008, pp. 364 f.). Overall, these findings suggest that working from home can have both positive and negative effects on job satisfaction and work-life balance. It is therefore important that companies carefully design and support the home office to maximise these potential benefits and minimise the drawbacks (cf. Fischer, 2012, pp. 112–116).

Social isolation and communication are important aspects to consider when working from home. Employees who work from home may have fewer personal interactions with colleagues and supervisors, which can lead to feelings of isolation and alienation (cf. Golden, J. Veiga, et al., 2006, p. 1066). This isolation can in turn have a negative impact on job satisfaction, commitment, and loyalty to the company (cf. Golden, J. Veiga, et al., 2006, p. 1071). Communication poses a particular challenge when working from home. While digital technologies make it possible to communicate and work from almost any location, they cannot fully replace face-to-face interactions and non-verbal communication (cf. Kurland and D. E. Bailey, 1999, pp. 598 f.). This can affect the quality of collaboration and the ability to build and maintain relationships (cf. Hinds and D. E. Bailey, 2003, pp. 322 f.). However, companies can take measures to reduce social isolation and improve communication. These include regular virtual meetings, the use of collaboration tools, and the promotion of informal interactions and social activities (cf. Fonner and Roloff, 2010, pp. 240–244). It is crucial that companies recognise the potential negative effects of social isolation and communication challenges in the home office and take measures to mitigate them (cf. Mirza et al., 2012, pp. 14–19).

The impact of the home office on employee productivity and performance is an important topic in research and practice. Some studies have shown that, under the right conditions, remote work can increase productivity (cf. Bloom et al., 2015, p. 172). These studies argue that remote workers experience fewer distractions and interruptions and that they can better customise their work and environment to their individual preferences and rhythms. However, it is also important to emphasise that these productivity gains depend on a range of factors, including the type of work, technological support and the skills and preferences of the workers (cf. Felstead and Henseke, 2017, pp. 410–414). In addition, it may be more difficult to monitor and evaluate work performance when working from home, which can pose challenges for management and performance reviews (cf. Kurland and D. E. Bailey, 1999, p. 30). Another important aspect is autonomy in the home office. While increased autonomy can boost productivity, it can also lead to stress and overwork if employees have difficulty organising their work and controlling their working hours (cf. Kossek et al., 2006, p. 1075).

2.3 The Balanced Scorecard as an IT Controlling Instrument

The BSC is a powerful management tool that helps companies translate their strategies into operational goals and measure their performance in several key areas. This chapter introduces the concept of the scorecard and explains how it can be used as a management tool.

The Balanced Scorecard was developed by ROBERT S. KAPLAN and DAVID P. NORTON in the 1990s and provides a structured framework for measuring and managing business performance from four perspectives: financial, customer, internal processes, and learning & growth (cf. Kaplan and Norton, 1992, pp. 71–79).

1. **Financial perspective**: This perspective considers traditional financial metrics such as sales and Return on Invested Capital (ROIC). The main objective is to measure and manage the company's financial performance to maximise shareholder value.
2. **Customer perspective**: Here, the focus is on customer satisfaction, loyalty and performance. Metrics may include customer satisfaction, market share or customer retention.
3. **Internal process perspective**: This perspective focuses on the efficiency and effectiveness of a company's internal processes, including production processes, supply chain management and innovation processes.

4. **Learning and Growth**: This perspective is about the organisation's ability to adapt, learn and grow. It includes the development of employee skills, cultural development and infrastructure for growth and learning.

The BSC enables organisations to clearly define and communicate their strategies, translate them into operational objectives, and measure their progress towards those objectives. By combining performance measures from these four perspectives, the scorecard provides a 'balanced' view of organisational performance that goes beyond traditional financial metrics. The BSC was originally developed to provide a more balanced view of organisational performance that goes beyond financial metrics. It integrates financial and non-financial measures to provide a more holistic view of organisational performance. Furthermore, it emphasises the role of internal processes and learning and growth in creating value and improving performance (cf. Grembergen and Haes, 2009, pp. 282 ff.).

In terms of IT control, the BSC also provides a framework for measuring and managing IT performance. It can help to understand the contributions of IT to business goals and to assess the effectiveness of IT processes. It can also help identify the areas in which IT investments and initiatives can have the greatest impact (cf. Grembergen and Haes, 2009, p. 167). The BSC has its roots in the theory of corporate strategy and strategic management and is often used in conjunction with other management concepts and techniques such as strategic planning, performance management, and process management. Overall, the BSC provides a comprehensive framework for performance measurement and management that takes into account both the strategic and operational aspects of organisational performance (cf. Kaplan and Norton, 1996b, pp. 25 f.).

2.3.1 Criticism of Traditional Control Systems

Traditional management control systems, which are often geared exclusively towards financial metrics, have been the subject of some criticism, which led to the development of the BSC in the 1990s. These criticisms are, in essence:

- **Short-term orientation**: Traditional management control systems often focus on short-term financial metrics, which can lead to decisions that compromise long-term goals and strategies (cf. Kaplan and Norton, 1992, pp. 71–77).
- **Lack of strategic focus**: Many traditional management systems provide little orientation regarding the strategic direction of the company. They focus on

operational efficiency without taking into account the company's strategy and long-term goals (cf. Kaplan and Norton, 1996a, pp. 75–80).

- **Neglect of intangible assets**: Traditional control systems place little value on intangible assets such as customer relationships, employee expertise and organisational culture. However, these factors play a crucial role in the long-term success of the company (cf. Kaplan and Norton, 2004, pp. 13–17).
- **Lack of balance**: Traditional management systems tend to emphasise certain areas of the company, particularly financial aspects, while neglecting others, such as internal processes, customer satisfaction and learning ability. This can lead to an unbalanced view of company performance (cf. Kaplan and Norton, 2001, pp. 11–15).

The BSC was developed in response to these criticisms. It offers a balanced view of corporate performance by taking into account other important aspects alongside financial indicators. It also promotes a long-term strategic focus and takes into account both tangible and intangible values. The scorecard is characterised by its balance, which manifests itself in four main features:

1. **Balance between financial and non-financial metrics**: The BSC combines financial metrics, which reflect the company's past performance, with non-financial metrics, which predict the company's future performance. This enables management to monitor both the company's short- and long-term performance (cf. Kaplan and Norton, 1992, pp. 71–77).
2. **Balance between internal and external performance measures**: The BSC takes into account both internal performance measures (e.g. process efficiency, employee competence) and external performance measures (e.g. customer satisfaction, market position). This allows a holistic understanding of the company's performance (cf. Kaplan and Norton, 1996a, pp. 80–83).
3. **Balance between performance drivers and result indicators**: While traditional control systems often focus on result indicators, the BSC also integrates performance drivers into its measurement system. This helps to understand and manage the influence of activities and processes on business performance (cf. Kaplan and Norton, 2004, pp. 13 f.).
4. **Balance between short- and long-term goals**: The BSC promotes a balance between short-term operational goals and long-term strategic goals. It enables management to translate long-term strategy into short-term operational goals and to monitor their achievement (cf. Kaplan and Norton, 2001, pp. 11 f.).

2.3.2 The Perspective Concept of the BSC

The BSC is based on four essential perspectives that serve as a basis for evaluating and managing corporate performance (figure 2.1):

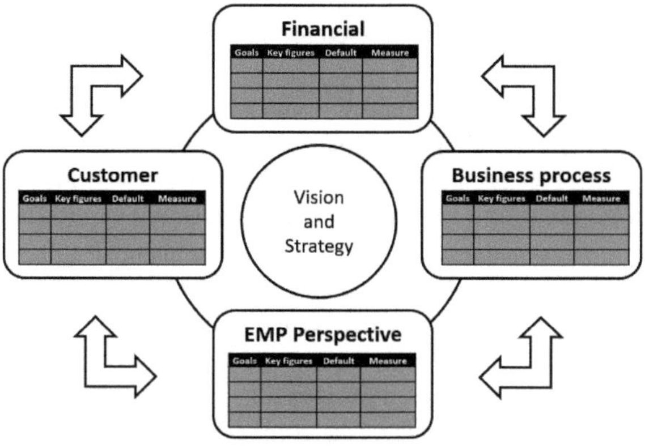

Fig. 2.1 4 BSC Perspectives. (Own illustration. 2023, adapted from Kaplan and Norton, 1996a)

1. **The financial perspective**
   The financial perspective is one of the four key perspectives of the BSC. It focuses on the financial performance of the company and is often closely linked to the interests of stakeholders, particularly shareholders.
   The indicators in the financial perspective are intended to reflect the financial health and profitability of the company. Typical metrics in this perspective include sales, profit, costs, Return on Investment (ROI), Economic Value Added (EVA) and cash flow. These metrics help management and stakeholders assess and manage the financial success of the company (cf. Kaplan and Norton, 1992, pp. 76 f.).
   It is important to note that the financial perspective is closely linked to the other three perspectives of the BSC. The improvements in the areas of customer perspective, internal processes and learning & growth should ultimately lead to improved financial performance (cf. Kaplan and Norton, 1996a, p. 79 f.).
   Although the financial perspective plays a crucial role in the BSC, Kaplan and Norton point out that focusing exclusively on financial metrics can lead to short-term thinking and decision-making. Therefore, it is important that the financial

perspective is considered in balance with the other perspectives of the BSC to ensure a long-term and sustainable improvement in business performance (cf. Kaplan and Norton, 1992, pp. 76 f.).

2. **The customer perspective**

   The customer perspective of the BSC emphasises the importance of customer orientation and satisfaction for a company's success. It focuses on defining goals and metrics that reflect the value added for the company's customers (cf. Kaplan and Norton, 1992, pp. 77 f.).

   Key figures in the customer perspective can relate to various aspects of the customer relationship, including customer satisfaction, customer loyalty, customer acquisition, customer profitability, and market share. These key figures help the company understand how well it meets the needs and expectations of its customers and how it can improve its customer relationships.

   Kaplan and Norton argue that the customer perspective is closely linked to the other perspectives of the BSC. Improvements in internal processes and in the learning and growth perspective, for example, can lead to improved customer satisfaction and loyalty. These improvements can then ultimately contribute to improved financial performance of the company (cf. Kaplan and Norton, 2004, pp. 15 f.).

   Despite its importance, the customer perspective is often neglected in traditional performance measurement systems. The BSC corrects this neglect by placing the customer perspective at the centre of its strategic management method. This promotes a stronger customer orientation and helps the company to understand and improve its value creation from the customer's point of view (cf. Kaplan and Norton, 2001, pp. 13 f.).

3. **The internal process perspective**

   The internal process perspective of the BSC focuses on the internal operational processes and activities that contribute to the company's value creation. It helps the company to optimise its internal processes in order to effectively achieve the objectives in the other three perspectives—finance, customers and learning & growth—(cf. Kaplan and Norton, 1992, pp. 78 f.).

   The internal process perspective can refer to a wide range of processes, including production processes, logistics and supply chain processes, customer service processes and innovation processes. Indicators in this perspective could include process quality, process efficiency, cycle time, and process cost. These metrics help management understand how well the internal processes are working and where improvements are possible and necessary (cf. Kaplan and Norton, 1996a, pp. 81 f.).

Furthermore, Kaplan and Norton emphasise that the internal process perspective is closely linked to the other perspectives of the BSC. Efficient and effective internal processes can, for example, lead to higher customer satisfaction and improved financial performance (cf. Kaplan and Norton, 2004, pp. 16 f.).
In contrast to traditional performance measurement systems, which often focus on external outcome indicators, the BSC emphasises the importance of internal processes. This helps the company to focus on the activities that form the basis for its success (cf. Kaplan and Norton, 2001, pp. 14 f.).

4. **The learning and development perspective**
The learning and development perspective of the BSC emphasises the importance of continuous improvement and innovation through learning and development of the employees and the organisation as a whole. It highlights that people, their skills and their motivation have a critical influence on the success of an organisation (cf. Kaplan and Norton, 1992, pp. 79 f.).
The learning and development perspective can include a variety of indicators, including employee satisfaction, employee retention, training and development, innovation rate, and cultural development. These indicators help management understand how well the company develops and promotes its employees and how well it fosters a culture of learning and innovation (cf. Kaplan and Norton, 1996a, pp. 82 f.).
Furthermore, Kaplan and Norton emphasise that the learning and development perspective is closely linked to the other perspectives of the BSC. For example, improving employee skills and motivation can lead to improved internal processes and customer satisfaction, which ultimately leads to improved financial performance (cf. Kaplan and Norton, 2004, pp. 17 f.).
In contrast to traditional performance measurement systems, which often focus on short-term, quantifiable results, the BSC emphasises the importance of learning and development for the long-term success of the organisation. This fosters a culture of continuous improvement and innovation and helps the organisation to adapt to changing market conditions and thrive (cf. Kaplan and Norton, 2001, pp. 15 f.).

2.3.3 Cause-effect Relationships between Parameters

The BSC is not just a collection of key figures, but also a model for cause-and-effect relationships that reflect the company's strategy. The BSC concept postulates that improvements in certain areas (causes) lead to improvements in other areas (effects) (cf. Kaplan and Norton, 1996a, pp. 78 f.). In the BSC, these cause-and-effect relationships are represented by the four perspectives (financial, customers, internal processes, learning & development) and the associated key figures. The underlying assumption is that investments in learning and development (e.g. training and further education of employees, development of a culture of innovation) lead to improvements in internal processes (e.g. higher process efficiency, better product quality). These improvements lead to higher customer satisfaction and loyalty, which ultimately leads to improved financial performance (cf. Kaplan and Norton, 2004, pp. 13–18).

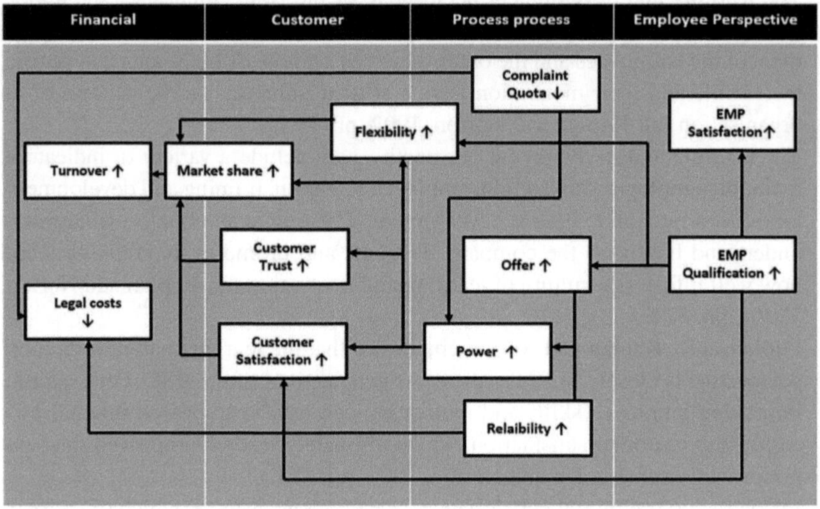

Fig. 2.2 Cause-and-effect relationships in the BSC. (Own illustration, 2023, adopted from Kaplan and Norton, 2001)

The cause-and-effect relationships in the BSC offer several advantages. They enable management to understand the impact of decisions and actions in one area on other areas. They also support communication and understanding of the corporate strategy by showing the connections between different activities and objectives (figure 2.2). Finally, they help to identify and focus on the performance drivers that have the greatest impact on the organisation's strategic objectives (cf. Kaplan and Norton, 2001, pp. 11–16). Despite their advantages, Kaplan and Norton point out that developing and implementing cause-and-effect relationships in the BSC can be challenging. It requires a deep understanding of the corporate strategy and the factors influencing corporate success. Furthermore, it may be necessary to review and adjust the cause-effect relationships over time to reflect changes in corporate strategy or the business environment (cf. Kaplan and Norton, 2004, pp. 19 f.).

2.3.4 Application Possibilities and Limitations of the BSC as a Controlling Instrument

The BSC has established itself as an effective tool for implementing strategy. It provides a structured approach to translating the organisation's strategy into measurable objectives and metrics and to monitoring progress towards those objectives (cf. Kaplan and Norton, 1996a, pp. 78–81). By providing a clear and coherent framework for strategy implementation, the BSC can help foster understanding and acceptance of the strategy throughout the organisation. It can also help to communicate the strategy at all levels of the organisation and to promote alignment between employees' individual goals and activities and the organisation's strategy (cf. Kaplan and Norton, 2001, pp. 11–16).

Furthermore, the BSC can serve as a tool for monitoring and adjusting the strategy. By regularly reviewing the BSC, management can assess whether the strategy is being successfully implemented and whether adjustments are needed due to changes in the internal or external environment (cf. Kaplan and Norton, 2004, pp. 13–18). Despite its strengths, the BSC also has some limitations as a strategy implementation tool. Developing and implementing a BSC can be complex and time-consuming. It requires a deep understanding of corporate strategy and the ability to translate that strategy into measurable objectives and metrics. Furthermore, the effectiveness of the BSC can depend on the quality of the underlying data and the willingness and ability of employees to use the BSC (cf. Kaplan and Norton, 2001, pp. 17 f.).

The BSC can be used effectively to promote shareholder value. Shareholder value is a central target value for many companies and often forms the core of the financial perspective in the BSC (cf. Rappaport, 1986, p. 17). By focusing on financial key figures such as profitability, sales growth and cost reduction, the BSC helps the company to improve its financial performance and increase shareholder value. At the same time, the BSC emphasises that improving financial performance often depends on improvements in other areas, such as the customer perspective, the internal process perspective and the learning and development perspective. In this way, the BSC supports balanced management that takes into account both short-term financial goals and long-term strategic goals (cf. Kaplan and Norton, 1992, pp. 76 f.).

However, the BSC also has some limitations in terms of promoting shareholder value. While the financial perspective of the BSC helps to measure and manage shareholder value, it cannot capture all the factors that influence shareholder value. For example, macroeconomic factors, competitive conditions and regulatory changes can have a significant impact on shareholder value, but are not directly considered in the BSC. Furthermore, the BSC can only be as good as the strategy it supports. If the company's strategy is not geared towards increasing shareholder value, the BSC alone cannot increase this value(cf. Kaplan and Norton, 2004, pp. 14 f.).

The BSC can serve as a strategic early warning system. It provides a framework for continuously monitoring the organisation's performance in relation to its strategic objectives and can help identify potential problems or opportunities early on (cf. Kaplan and Norton, 1996a, pp. 78–81). A BSC captures a wide range of performance indicators from four perspectives—financial, customer, internal processes, and learning & development. By regularly monitoring these indicators, management can identify trends and patterns that indicate emerging issues or opportunities. For example, falling customer satisfaction scores could indicate issues with product quality or customer service that need to be addressed. Similarly, an increase in employee turnover could indicate problems with job satisfaction or corporate culture that need to be addressed (cf. Kaplan and Norton, 2001, pp. 11–16).

However, the BSC can only serve as an effective early-warning system if it is properly implemented and utilised. This requires careful selection of performance indicators, reliable data collection and analysis, and a strong management commitment to use the BSC. Furthermore, the BSC should be regularly reviewed and adjusted to ensure that it remains relevant and useful (cf. Kaplan and Norton, 2004, pp 17f). Despite its strengths, the BSC also has some limitations as an early warning system. It can only monitor internal performance indicators and may therefore overlook external factors that could affect the company, such as changes in the competitive landscape or economic environment. Furthermore, the BSC can only point to known risks and opportunities and may therefore be caught off guard by unknown or unexpected events (cf. Kaplan and Norton, 2001, pp. 16 f.). The BSC can serve as an effective communication tool within a company. It provides a structured model for presenting the corporate strategy and its implementation, which can be communicated to all employees at all levels of the company (cf. Kaplan and Norton, 1996a, pp. 81 f.).

By clearly presenting the strategic objectives and the associated performance indicators in the four perspectives, the BSC can help to ensure that all employees have a common understanding of the corporate strategy and their role in its implementation. It can also serve to clarify the link between individual tasks and performance and the strategic objectives of the company. This can increase employee motivation and commitment to achieving strategic goals (cf. Kaplan and Norton, 2001, pp 15f). However, the BSC can only serve as an effective communication tool if it is regularly used and updated, and if communication in both directions—from management to employees and from employees to management—is encouraged. Furthermore, the effective use of BSC as a communication tool requires an open and transparent corporate culture in which questions, concerns and ideas can be freely expressed and discussed (cf. Kaplan and Norton, 2004, pp 13–18). Despite its strengths, the BSC also has some limitations as a communication tool. It can only communicate aspects of corporate strategy and performance that are represented in its four perspectives and the associated performance indicators. It can therefore overlook other important aspects of corporate strategy or culture. Furthermore, the BSC can support communication, but it cannot change the underlying skills, attitudes and behaviours of employees that are needed for effective communication (cf. Kaplan and Norton, 2001, pp. 17 f.).

2.3.5 Background and Significance of the IT Balanced Scorecard

The IT Balanced Scorecard is an application of the BSC concept specifically for IT management. It is used to measure and control the performance of IT organisations and to establish a clear link between IT objectives and the strategic goals of the company as a whole (cf. Grembergen and Haes, 2009, pp. 18 ff.). The IT-BSC takes into account the specific requirements of IT and adapts the perspectives of the traditional BSC accordingly. Often, the four classic perspectives of the BSC (financial, customers, internal processes, learning and growth) are adapted to IT contexts (cf. Grembergen, 2000, pp. 15–19). The main purpose of the IT BSC is to support the management of IT performance and to establish a clear link between IT initiatives and business results. It enables managers to look at IT performance from different perspectives and understand the contribution of IT to the achievement of business objectives. Furthermore, it supports communication and understanding between IT and business units and promotes the alignment of IT strategy with business strategy (cf. Grembergen and Haes, 2009, pp. 19 ff.).

Although the basic concept of the BSC is retained in the IT-BSC, there are some important differences that are geared to the specific needs and requirements of IT. Firstly, the four classic perspectives of the BSC are often modified or redefined in the IT-BSC to better reflect the IT context. For example, the financial perspective could be renamed 'IT value contribution' to emphasise the focus on creating business value through IT investments. The customer view could focus on internal customers and be referred to as 'user satisfaction' (cf. Grembergen, 2000, pp. 22 f.).

Secondly, the IT-BSC emphasises the strategic role of IT and the contribution of IT to achieving business goals. It is specifically designed to clarify the link between IT initiatives and business outcomes and to align IT strategy with business strategy (cf. Grembergen and Haes, 2009, pp. 15–17). Thirdly, the IT BSC deals more with technical and operational aspects of IT performance. It can include specific IT metrics and indicators that are not present in a general BSC, such as system availability, help desk performance, project delivery or software quality (cf. Grembergen, 2000, pp. 22).

The IT BSC plays a crucial role in IT governance and performance. As a strategic management and measurement system, it enables companies to assess and manage the performance of their IT organisations and to establish a clear link between IT objectives and the strategic objectives of the company as a whole (cf. Grembergen, 2000, pp. 12–15). In terms of IT governance, the IT-BSC provides a framework for defining and communicating IT strategy and objectives and measuring performance against those objectives. It promotes the alignment of IT strategy with business strategy and supports communication and understanding between IT and business units (cf. Grembergen and Haes, 2009, pp. 18 f.). The IT BSC also helps to improve IT performance. It enables managers to look at IT performance from multiple perspectives, including financial performance, customer satisfaction, internal process performance, and learning and growth capabilities. This can help to increase the effectiveness and efficiency of IT processes and maximise the value that IT contributes to business success (cf. Grembergen, 2000, pp. 25–28).

2.3.6 The Perspectives of the IT Balanced Scorecard

In the context of the IT BSC, a specific adaptation of the general BSC approach for corporate management, the defined perspectives differ in structure and orientation from the traditional perspectives of the general corporate BSC:

1. **IT User Satisfaction:** In the IT BSC, the financial perspective is often referred to as 'IT value contribution' and refers to the ability of IT to create economic value for the company. This includes both the direct financial results of IT, such as cost control and efficiency, and its contribution to increasing the company's revenues and profitability (cf. Grembergen and Haes, 2009, pp. 18 ff.).

The financial perspective can be measured by a variety of metrics, including IT costs, Return on Investment (ROI) of IT projects, cost avoidance through IT innovations, and the contribution of IT to achieving the financial goals of the organisation (cf. Grembergen, 2000, pp. 22 f.).
A key aspect of this perspective is the need to quantify and communicate the value proposition of IT. This can be challenging as the value of IT cannot always be measured directly in financial terms. However, it can be crucial to promoting understanding and recognition of the value of IT across the organisation (cf. Kaplan and Norton, 1992, pp. 77 ff.).

2. **The IT customer perspective:**
The IT-BSC customer perspective focuses on the satisfaction of internal and external customers with IT services. In this context, 'customers' can be both internal users within the company and external customers who use the company's IT-based products or services (cf. Grembergen and Haes, 2009, p. 20).
This perspective can include a wide range of metrics, including user satisfaction with IT support and services, the reliability and availability of IT systems, the quality of IT projects and products, and IT's ability to respond to customer needs and requirements (cf. Grembergen, 2000, pp. 21 f.).
A key challenge in this perspective is to understand and meet customer expectations and requirements while efficiently managing IT costs and resources. This requires close collaboration and communication between IT and customers to ensure a shared understanding of requirements and priorities (cf. Kaplan and Norton, 1996a, p. 78).
3. **The IT Internal Process Perspective:**
The IT-BSC internal process perspective focuses on the effectiveness and efficiency of IT internal processes. It aims to measure and improve the quality, performance, and costs of these processes to optimise IT service delivery and maximise IT value contribution (cf. Grembergen and Haes, 2009, pp. 18 ff.).
The metrics that can be used in this perspective include, for example, process performance, system availability, IT support response time, compliance with Service Level Agreements (SLA), and the quality and timeliness of IT project delivery (cf. Grembergen, 2000, pp. 19–22).
This perspective also emphasises the need for continuous improvement of IT processes. By identifying and eliminating process weaknesses and inefficiencies, organisations can increase productivity, reduce costs and improve customer satisfaction (cf. Kaplan and Norton, 1992, pp. 76–79).
4. **The IT learning and development perspective:**
The IT learning and development perspective in the IT-BSC focuses on the IT organisation's ability to improve, adapt and prepare for future challenges. It

includes aspects such as the development of skills and competencies, employee satisfaction, innovation capability and willingness to change (cf. Grembergen and Haes, 2009, pp. 18 ff.).
The metrics in this perspective can measure the training and development of IT staff, the implementation of new technologies and processes, the satisfaction and motivation of IT staff, and the IT organisation's ability to adapt to change (cf. Grembergen, 2000, pp. 19–22).
This perspective emphasises the role of learning and development as essential factors for the long-term performance and success of IT. Through continuous learning and improvement, the IT organisation can improve its performance, expand its capabilities, and be more responsive to changing needs and challenges (cf. Kaplan and Norton, 1992, pp. 78 ff.).

2.3.7 Key Figures and Metrics in the IT Balanced Scorecard

Selecting and defining relevant IT key performance indicators is an essential aspect of implementing the IT BSC. These metrics should measure the performance of the IT organisation from different perspectives and show a clear link between IT objectives and the strategic objectives of the company (cf. Grembergen and Haes, 2009, pp. 18 ff.). The specific metrics may vary depending on the company and industry, but should cover the four perspectives of the BSC.

When selecting IT metrics, it is important that they are clearly defined, measurable, relevant and time-bound. They should have a clear link to the organisation's strategic objectives and should be regularly reviewed and adjusted to ensure their relevance and effectiveness (cf. Kaplan and Norton, 1992, pp. 71 ff.). A central element of the IT-BSC is the relationship between the key performance indicators and the four perspectives: IT value contribution, user satisfaction, internal processes, and learning and growth. Each of these perspectives contains a number of key performance indicators that serve to measure and control performance in that area (cf. Grembergen and Haes, 2009, pp. 16 f.).

1. The financial perspective includes metrics that measure the economic value of IT, such as IT costs, return on investment (ROI) of IT projects and cost avoidance through IT innovations.
2. The customer perspective focuses on customers' satisfaction with IT services, measured by metrics such as user satisfaction, system availability and adherence to service level agreements (SLAs).

3. The internal process perspective measures the effectiveness and efficiency of IT processes through metrics such as process performance, project delivery time and quality, and the efficiency of IT support.
4. The learning and development perspective refers to the IT organisation's ability to improve and adapt, measured by metrics such as employee satisfaction, training and development of IT staff, and implementation of new technologies and processes. (cf. Grembergen, 2000, pp. 17 ff.).

An important aspect of the IT BSC is the connection between these perspectives and key performance indicators. Each indicator should have a clear link to the organisation's strategic objectives in one of the four perspectives. Furthermore, the indicators should be linked to each other to provide a holistic view of IT performance and to show the impact of improvements in one area on other areas (cf. Kaplan and Norton, 1992, pp. 77 ff.).

Measuring and monitoring IT performance is a key element of the IT BSC. By using metrics in the four perspectives, the IT BSC enables a comprehensive assessment of IT performance and a clear link between IT objectives and the organisation's strategic goals (cf. Grembergen and Haes, 2009, pp. 11 f.). A variety of methods and tools can be used to measure and monitor IT performance. These may include dashboards, reports and analyses that are regularly generated and reviewed to assess performance in the various areas and identify opportunities for improvement. Furthermore, it is important that IT performance measurement is not seen as a one-off activity, but as an ongoing process. IT performance should be monitored regularly and the metrics should be adjusted and updated to ensure their relevance and accuracy and to reflect changes in the business environment or IT strategies (cf. Kaplan and Norton, 1992, p. 79).

2.3.8 Implementation of the IT Balanced Scorecard

The introduction of an IT BSC requires careful planning and implementation. The basic steps for introducing an IT BSC are listed below:

- **Strategic alignment**: This is the first and most important step in implementing the IT-BSC. It involves understanding the business strategy and deriving the IT strategy that is aligned with it.
- **Definition of perspectives and key performance indicators**: This step involves defining the four perspectives and selecting the key performance indicators to be

measured in each perspective. These indicators should measure IT performance from different perspectives and have a clear link to IT and business objectives.

- **Data collection and analysis**: This step involves collecting and analysing data for the selected metrics. This can be done by using IT systems, dashboards and reporting tools.
- **Review and adjustment**: After implementing the IT-BSC, performance should be regularly monitored and the IT-BSC adjusted as needed. This may involve changes in metrics, target values or improvement initiatives.
- **Communication and training**: This step involves communicating the IT BSC and training employees in how to use it. This can help to promote understanding and acceptance of the IT BSC throughout the company. (cf. Grembergen and Haes, 2009, pp. 16–20).

Implementing an IT BSC can be an effective way to improve IT performance and promote the alignment of IT with business strategy. However, it requires careful planning, implementation and continuous review and adjustment.

The integration of the IT BSC into the corporate BSC is an essential aspect of implementing the IT BSC. It allows IT performance to be seen in the context of overall business performance and to understand how IT contributes to the organisation's strategic objectives (cf. Grembergen and Haes, 2009, pp. 18 ff.). This integration can be done by linking IT metrics to metrics in the business BSC. For example, IT performance measures that measure customer satisfaction or internal process performance could be linked to the corresponding measures in the corporate BSC. This way, it can be shown how IT performance influences the overall performance of the company (cf. Grembergen, 2000, pp. 17–21). Furthermore, the IT BSC should be integrated into the regular review and update of the corporate BSC. This can help to ensure that the IT BSC remains up-to-date and relevant and that the IT goals and initiatives are aligned with changing business strategies and goals. The integration of the IT BSC into the corporate BSC can help to clarify the strategic role of IT in the company and to promote the alignment of IT with the business strategy (cf. Kaplan and Norton, 1996a, pp. 108–111).

The implementation of an IT-BSC can pose various challenges. One of the main challenges is the alignment of IT objectives and strategies with business strategies. It can be difficult to identify and measure the right IT metrics that are directly related to business objectives (cf. Grembergen and Haes, 2009, pp. 19 ff.). Another challenge is to gain acceptance and commitment from IT staff and management (Figure 2.3). Implementing the IT-BSC often requires changes to existing processes and structures and may meet resistance. Therefore, it is important to ensure clear communication and training and to clarify the advantages of the IT-BSC (cf. Kaplan

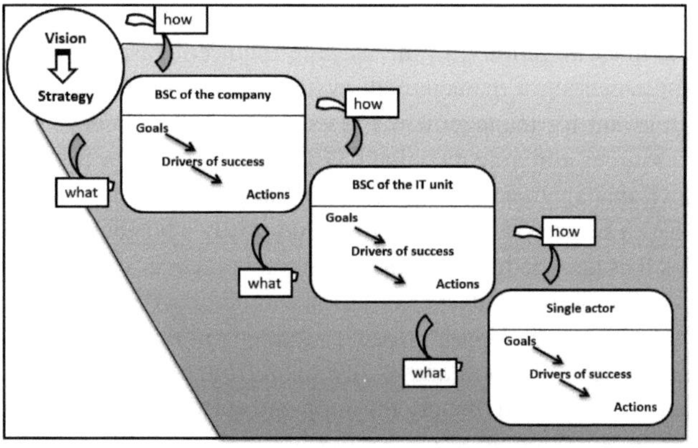

Fig. 2.3 Integration IT-BSC into the company BSC. (Own illustration, 2023)

and Norton, 1996a, pp. 111–114). The success factors for implementing the IT-BSC include strong leadership and support from management, clear communication and understanding of the IT-BSC and its benefits, careful planning and implementation, including selecting the right IT metrics, and continuously reviewing and adjusting the IT-BSC to ensure its relevance and effectiveness (cf. Grembergen, 2000, pp. 22 f.).

2.4 Implementation of a Management System with COBIT

Control Objectives for Information and Related Technology (COBIT) is a framework developed by ISACA, an international professional association of IT governance, risk, and cyber security professionals. Since its first publication in 1996, COBIT has been continuously developed and is now available in the COBIT 2019 version (cf. ISACA, 2019a, p. 2). COBIT 2019 is a comprehensive framework for managing and governing IT. It provides principles, practices, analytical tools, and models that help improve an organisation's IT governance and management capabilities, thus enabling IT to make a greater contribution to business success (cf. Haes and Grembergen, 2019, pp. 8–11). Implementing a management system in the context of COBIT 2019 can help to establish a systematic, structured and holistic approach to GEIT. It can help to improve the effectiveness of IT systems and processes, minimise risks, ensure compliance and promote IT alignment with business strategy. However, implementing such a system requires careful planning and execution and must be tailored to the specific requirements and objectives of the company. Implementing a management system in the context of COBIT 2019 is particularly relevant for management and executives. They benefit from the comprehensive resources and guidance that COBIT 2019 offers for improving IT governance and IT management (cf. ISACA, 2019a, pp. 6–10). Implementing such a system requires a basic understanding of the company's business processes and IT systems, as well as knowledge of the principles and practices of IT management and IT governance. Furthermore, the organisation should be willing and able to provide the necessary resources and commitment to implement it. Successful implementation also requires active support and involvement from top management, as it often requires extensive changes to the organisation and culture of the company (cf. Haes and Grembergen, 2019, pp. 9–12).

2.4.1 The Fundamentals of COBIT

COBIT is a framework that provides guidelines for the management and governance of enterprise IT. Originally introduced by ISACA in 1996, COBIT has since been continuously developed to meet the changing needs and trends in IT governance and management (cf. ISACA, 2019a, pp. 8 ff.). The original version of COBIT focused on the IT auditor function by providing control objectives for IT processes. However, with the publication of COBIT 3.0 in 2000, more emphasis was placed on IT management and governance. Four domains were introduced: planning and organisation, acquisition and implementation, delivery and support, and monitoring and evaluation. In the COBIT 4.1 version, published in 2007, a maturity model was introduced that enabled organisations to assess the maturity of their IT processes and identify opportunities for improvement. COBIT 5, published in 2012, integrated a number of other ISACA frameworks, including Val IT and Risk IT, and introduced a series of enablers to facilitate the implementation of IT governance. The latest version, COBIT 2019, further expands the framework and provides more flexibility and customisability to tailor it to the specific needs and objectives of each organisation (cf. Haes and Grembergen, 2019, pp. 1 f.). COBIT 2019 is based on a set of principles that form the foundation for IT management and IT governance. The following principles are at the core of COBIT 2019 :

1. **Stakeholder Value**: COBIT emphasises that IT and information should create value by contributing to the achievement of stakeholders' objectives.
2. **Holistic Approach**: COBIT recognises that IT governance and IT management cannot take place in isolation, but must be embedded in the context of the entire organisation.
3. **Governance System**: COBIT recognises that effective IT management and governance requires a governance system supported by a clear allocation of roles, responsibilities, structures and processes.
4. **Management System**: COBIT recognises the importance of a management system that provides a structured, coherent and holistic approach to IT governance (cf. ISACA, 2019a, pp. 4 f.) .

These principles are supported by a set of concepts and tools, including the COBIT domains, processes, objectives and KPIs, the enablers and the maturity model. Together, they provide a comprehensive and structured approach to IT management and IT governance (cf. Haes and Grembergen, 2019, pp. 4 f.).

2.4.2 Introduction to COBIT 2019 Framework Architecture

The architecture of the COBIT 2019 framework provides a structured and coherent method for designing and implementing an effective IT management and governance system. It is based on a set of components that interact and work together to support the achievement of IT and business objectives (cf. ISACA, 2019a, pp. 5 ff.). At the heart of the COBIT architecture is the principle of 'Governing System and Components'. This principle represents the implementation of governance and management through a series of interconnected components. These components include the objectives of the organisation, the stakeholder requirements, the governance and management system, the processes, the practices and the activities used to achieve these objectives (cp. ISACA, 2019a, p. 10). The components are organised in a way that allows a systematic and holistic view of the IT management and governance system to be obtained. They enable a clear view of IT objectives and the relationship between IT objectives and business objectives. They also support the identification and management of IT risks, the control of IT resources, and the measurement and improvement of IT performance (cf. Haes and Grembergen, 2019, pp. 6 f.). The COBIT architecture provides the basis for implementing and managing an effective IT management and governance system (Figure 2.4). It provides a structured model that enables a systematic and holistic view of IT management and governance, helping to promote IT alignment with business objectives and maximise the value of IT to business success (cf. ISACA, 2019c, p. 13).

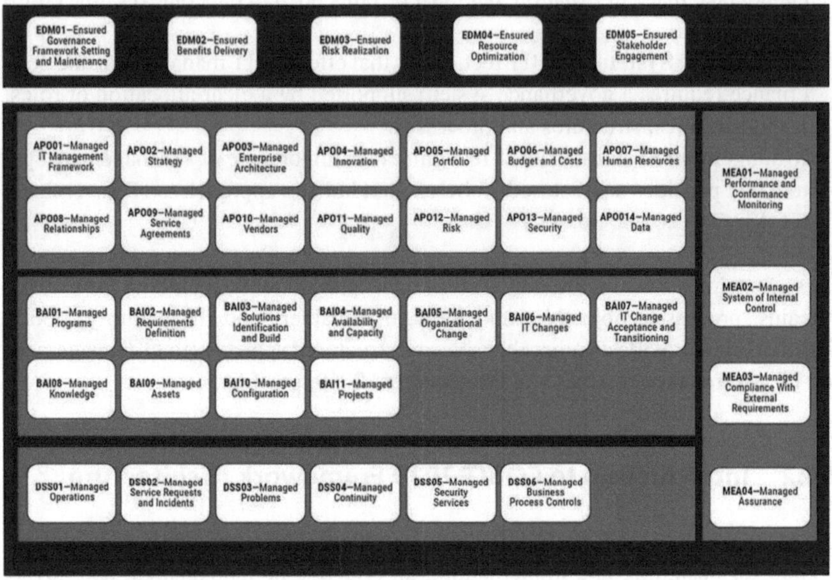

Fig. 2.4 COBIT 2019 Governance process Model (ISACA, 2019c)

The COBIT 2019 framework is structured into five domains (Figure 2.4), which cover the most important areas of IT governance and management: Evaluate, Direct and Monitor (EDM); Align, Plan and Organize (APO); Build, Acquire and Implement (BAI); Deliver, Service and Support (DSS); and Monitor, Evaluate and Assess (MEA). In other words, these areas support the governance and management of enterprise IT (GEIT), from strategy and planning, to design and implementation, to deployment and support, and finally to monitoring and evaluation of all relevant governance instruments. Each of these domains plays a critical role in IT governance and management and contributes to the creation of business value through IT (cf. ISACA, 2019a, p. 8):

1. **Governance of Enterprise IT (GEIT)**
   COBIT 2019 identifies five domains that cover the various areas of IT governance and IT management. These domains form the framework of the COBIT 2019 framework and serve to organise and structure the various aspects of IT management and IT governance. The fifth domain, GEIT, is particularly important as it addresses the overarching aspects of IT governance (cf. ISACA, 2019a, pp. 12 f.).
   The GEIT domain encompasses the decisions made at the highest management level to ensure IT alignment with business objectives, manage IT risks, optimise IT resources and measure and improve IT performance. It includes processes and activities that serve to define and assign responsibility for IT governance, develop and implement IT strategy, evaluate and manage IT risks, and monitor and evaluate IT performance (cf. ISACA, 2019a, p. 13). The GEIT domain is closely linked to the other four COBIT domains (APO, BAI, DSS and MEA). Together, these domains provide a comprehensive and structured approach to IT management and governance, helping to promote IT alignment with business objectives and maximise the value that IT contributes to business success (cf. Haes and Grembergen, 2019, pp. 12 f.).
2. **Strategic alignment**
   One of the five domains of the COBIT 2019 framework is strategic alignment, which is implemented in the Align, Plan and Organize (APO) domain. This domain encompasses the processes required to define, plan, and align the IT strategy with the business strategy (cf. ISACA, 2019a, pp. 14 f.).
   Strategic alignment is a central aspect of IT governance and IT management. It ensures that the IT strategy and IT objectives are aligned with business strategies and objectives, and that IT contributes to achieving these objectives. This requires close co-operation between IT management and business management and continuous alignment of the IT strategy with changing business conditions and requirements.
   The APO domain includes a set of processes designed to define the IT strategy, execute IT planning, develop the IT architecture, manage IT investments, manage IT projects, manage IT services, and manage IT risks. These processes support the strategic direction and help to maximise IT performance and the value that IT contributes to business success (cf. Haes and Grembergen, 2019, p. 15).
3. **Service provision**
   Service provision is another important domain in the COBIT 2019 framework and is represented in the domain Deliver, Service and Support (DSS). This domain deals with the processes and activities required to provide and support

IT services in order to meet business requirements (cf. ISACA, 2019a, pp. 16 f.).
IT service delivery refers to the ability of IT to provide services that meet business needs and create value. This includes not only the technical provision of IT services, but also the management of IT services to ensure that they are provided effectively and efficiently, that they meet user expectations, and that they help achieve business objectives.
The DSS domain includes a number of processes that serve to define and manage IT services, manage IT operations, handle service requests and incidents, ensure service continuity, manage security services and IT resources. These processes support the provision of services and help to improve the quality, effectiveness and efficiency of IT services, and to maximise the value that IT contributes to business success (cf. Haes and Grembergen, 2019, pp. 16 f.).

4. **Risk Management**
   In the COBIT 2019 framework, risk management is an integral component that is primarily anchored in the APO domain. In particular, the APO12 'Manage Risk' process is dedicated to the identification, assessment and management of IT-related risks (cf. ISACA, 2019a, pp. 18 f.). Effective IT risk management requires a systematic and proactive approach to identifying, assessing, and treating risks that could impair IT's ability to support business objectives and create value. This includes risks that may arise from technical failures, security breaches, data loss, IT project failures, and other IT-related events.
   The COBIT 2019 framework provides a comprehensive approach to IT risk management based on the principles of risk assessment, treatment, communication and monitoring. It defines a set of processes and activities that serve to identify, assess, treat, communicate and monitor IT risks, and provides metrics and target values that serve to measure and improve the effectiveness of IT risk management (cf. Haes and Grembergen, 2019, 18f).
5. **Resource Management**
   Resource management plays an important role in the COBIT 2019 framework, particularly in the APO and DSS domains. Processes such as APO07 'Manage IT Human Resources', APO08 'Manage Relationships', APO10 'Manage Suppliers', and DSS01 'Manage Operations', all focus on various aspects of IT resource management (cf. ISACA, 2019a, pp. 20 f.).
   Resource management refers to the effective and efficient management of IT resources, including human resources, hardware, software, networks, data and services. Effective management of IT resources is essential to ensure the availability, reliability, performance and security of IT services, and to support business objectives and create value.

COBIT 2019 provides a structured and systematic approach to resource management. It defines a set of processes and activities that serve to plan, acquire, manage, monitor, and optimise IT resources. It also provides metrics and target values that can be used to measure and improve the effectiveness and efficiency of resource management (cf. Haes and Grembergen, 2019, pp. 21) Fig. 2.5.

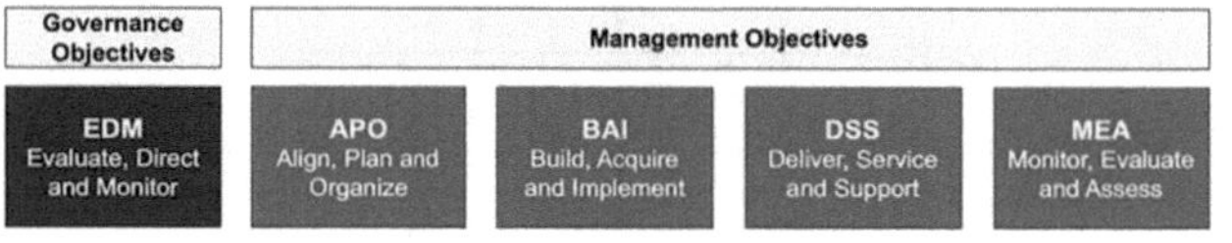

Fig. 2.5 COBIT 2019 Objectives (ISACA, 2019c)

2.4.3 Process Model and KPIs of COBIT

The COBIT 2019 framework defines a total of 40 processes, which are organised into five domains (APO, EDM, BAI, DSS and MEA). Each of these domains represents a specific aspect of IT management and governance, and the processes within them provide a structured and systematic approach to implementing and improving IT management and governance practices (cf. Haes and Grembergen, 2019, p. 25).

The structured and consistent design of such a process is depicted in Figure 2.6 and includes a variety of elements that ensure all relevant aspects of a process are considered. This structure is essential to ensure a consistent and standardised approach to IT governance that supports the integration of BYOD into the management system of an IT BSC.

1. **Process description**:
   Clarifies the purpose and objectives of the process. In terms of integrating BYOD, the process description could cover the effective use of personal devices for business purposes and ensuring data security and compliance (cf. Gaulke, 2020, pp. 102 f.).
2. **Process objectives**:
   Define the results that the process should achieve. Here, the objective could be to increase end-user satisfaction by allowing them to use their preferred devices through the integration of BYOD (cf. Gaulke, 2020, pp. 115 f.).
3. **Management Practices**:
   Core activities within the process, often further subdivided into activities and

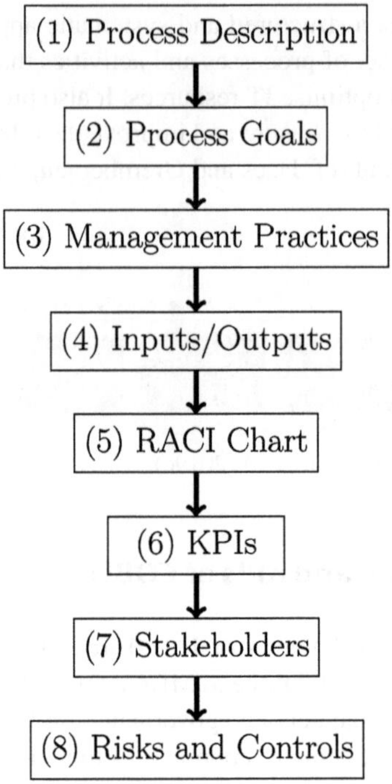

Fig. 2.6 Generic Structure of a COBIT 2019 Process. (Own illustration, 2023)

tasks. For example, a practice could be to regularly review and update the BYOD policies to ensure they are aligned with current best practices and legal requirements (cf. Gaulke, 2020, pp. 128 f.).

4. **Inputs and Outputs**:
   Define what the process requires as input and what it produces as output. An input could be a risk assessment, while an output could be a revised BYOD policy (cf. Gaulke, 2020, pp. 140 ff.).
5. **RACI chart**:
   Identifies roles and responsibilities. This could be used to determine that the IT department is responsible (R) for implementing and maintaining the BYOD strategy, while individual employees are responsible (A) for complying with the guidelines (cf. Gaulke, 2020, p. 152).
6. **Target and key performance indicators (KPIs)**:
   Specific metrics for performance measurement and evaluation. A possible KPI

could be the number of security incidents caused by BYOD, with the goal of reducing this number (cf. Gaulke, 2020, pp. 165 f.).

7. **Stakeholders involved**:
   People or groups that are involved in or affected by the process. Stakeholders could be the IT department, management, and the end users themselves (cf. Gaulke, 2020, pp. 178 ff.).
8. **Risks and controls**:
   Identifies risks and defines control mechanisms. The focus here could be on identifying data protection risks and developing strategies to minimise these risks, such as regular security training for employees (cf. Gaulke, 2020, pp. 190 f.).

The processes and their components can be adapted to the specific requirements and complexity of the respective organisation and the specific BYOD implementation. Implementing COBIT is an iterative process that requires regular reviews and adjustments (cf. ISACA, 2019c, p. 17).

2.4.4 COBIT Implementation Process

Implementing COBIT in an organisation requires careful planning and execution. The COBIT 2019 framework provides a comprehensive implementation guide to help organisations improve their IT governance and management processes and maximise the benefits of implementing COBIT (cf. ISACA, 2019a, pp. 32 f.). The COBIT implementation process is a multi-stage process that begins with recognising the need for change and defining the objectives and scope of the implementation. This is followed by a planning and mobilisation phase, in which the specific measures for implementing COBIT are defined and the necessary resources and skills identified. Then comes the execution phase, in which the planned measures are carried out and the results monitored and evaluated. Finally, there is the sustainable application phase, in which the implemented measures are reviewed and adjusted to improve their effectiveness and maximise their benefits (cf. Grembergen and Haes, 2018, p. 11–14.)

Throughout the implementation process, as illustrated in Figure 2.7, there are a number of critical success factors to consider. These include leadership commitment and support, the involvement of all stakeholders, the development of competencies and skills, effective communication and change management, tailoring COBIT to the specific needs and conditions of the organisation, and the use of metrics and indicators to monitor and improve implementation (cf. Haes and Grembergen, 2019,

p. 33). Implementing COBIT in an organisation is a structured process consisting of several steps. Each of these steps is crucial to the successful implementation of COBIT and requires careful planning, execution and monitoring. These steps are explained in detail below (cf. ISACA, 2019a, pp. 22–25):

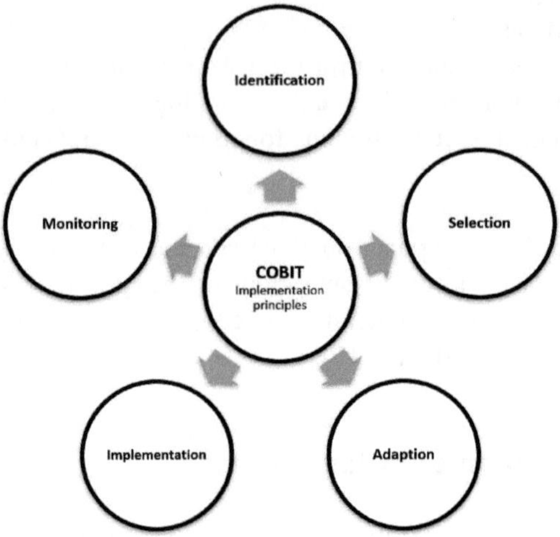

Fig. 2.7 COBIT Implementation 5 Phase Guide. (Own illustration, 2023)

1. **Identification of business objectives and context**
   The first step in implementing COBIT 2019 is to identify the business objectives and context. This is a crucial phase to ensure that the implementation of COBIT is aligned with the specific needs and objectives of the organisation (cf. ISACA, 2019a, pp. 22 f.).
   Identifying the business objectives requires a close analysis of the organisation's strategic goals and priorities. This may include the business model, strategic plans, performance targets, and the organisation's current challenges and opportunities. These objectives should then be aligned with the IT organisation's objectives to ensure that IT is effectively supporting the business goals (cf. Grembergen and Haes, 2018, pp. 11 f.).
   The business context refers to the specific conditions and circumstances in which the organisation operates. This includes the size and structure of the organisation, the industry and market in which it operates, the regulatory requirements and standards to which it is subject, the IT landscape and capabilities, and the

culture and behaviour of the organisation. A thorough knowledge of the business context is critical to identifying and selecting the most appropriate and effective COBIT practices and processes for the organisation (cf. Haes and Grembergen, 2019, pp. 28 f.).

2. **Selection of relevant COBIT components**
   After identifying the business objectives and context, the selection of relevant COBIT components follows. This step involves choosing the specific COBIT processes, practices, objectives, and metrics to implement in order to achieve the identified business objectives and address the specific needs and challenges of the business context (cf. ISACA, 2019a, pp. 24 f.).
   The selection of relevant COBIT components should be based on a careful analysis of the business needs and objectives, the IT landscape and capabilities, the current IT governance and management practices, and the specific risks and challenges of the organisation. It should also consider the involvement and feedback of relevant stakeholders, including leadership, IT staff, users, and other interested parties (cf. Grembergen and Haes, 2018, pp. 13 f.).
   Furthermore, the selection of COBIT components should be flexible and iterative, where implementation can start on a smaller scale and be gradually expanded based on the results achieved and the knowledge gained. There should also be constant review and adjustment of the selected COBIT components to improve their effectiveness and ensure their relevance and adaptability to the changing conditions and needs of the organisation (cf. Haes and Grembergen, 2019, pp. 30 f.).
3. **Adaptation of the COBIT framework to the corporate environment**
   Adapting the COBIT framework to the specific needs and requirements of the organisation is an essential step in implementing COBIT. The COBIT framework was designed to be flexible and adaptable to different organisational contexts, objectives, risks, and resources (cf. ISACA, 2019a, pp. 24 f.).
   This tailoring process may include adapting the COBIT processes, practices, objectives and metrics to the organisation's specific business processes, IT landscape, organisational structure and culture. It may also involve selecting and adapting specific COBIT tools and techniques to meet the organisation's specific needs and conditions. The tailoring should be done on the basis of a thorough analysis of the organisation's objectives, context and relevant COBIT components. It should also include close collaboration and alignment with relevant stakeholders to take into account their needs and expectations and ensure that the adapted implementation of COBIT effectively supports business objectives and creates value (cf. Grembergen and Haes, 2018, pp. 13 f.).

Ultimately, customising COBIT should be a dynamic and continuous process that allows for constant review and adjustment of the implemented COBIT components to improve their effectiveness and ensure their relevance and adaptability to the changing needs and conditions of the organisation (cf. Haes and Grembergen, 2019, pp. 30 f.).

4. **Implementation of COBIT in the organisation**
   The introduction of COBIT into the organisation is a crucial step in the implementation of COBIT. This step involves the actual implementation of the selected and adapted COBIT components in the organisation and the monitoring of their effectiveness and performance (cf. ISACA, 2019a, pp. 26 f.).
   The introduction of COBIT should be done in several phases, starting with educating and raising awareness among employees and managers about COBIT and its benefits, followed by implementing the selected COBIT processes and practices and aligning organisational structures and systems with COBIT requirements (cf. Grembergen and Haes, 2018, pp. 15 f.).
   During the implementation, there should be continuous monitoring and evaluation of the implemented COBIT components to assess their performance and their contribution to achieving the organisation's objectives. This should be done by using metrics and indicators and by regular audits and reviews. Based on these assessments, adjustments and improvements should be made to enhance the effectiveness and efficiency of COBIT (cf. Haes and Grembergen, 2019, pp. 32 f.).
5. **Continuous monitoring and improvement**
   Continuous monitoring and improvement are crucial aspects of implementing COBIT. They ensure that the implemented framework remains effective and is constantly adapted to changing business conditions and requirements (cf. ISACA, 2019a, pp. 30 f.).
   Continuously monitoring the COBIT implementation involves regularly assessing the performance of the implemented processes and practices. This includes regularly reviewing metrics and performance indicators, conducting audits and assessments, and gathering feedback from users and stakeholders (cf. Grembergen and Haes, 2018, pp. 17 f.).
   Continuous improvement of COBIT implementation involves the systematic identification and implementation of improvements based on the results of monitoring. Improvements may include changes to processes and practices, training and development of staff, adaptation of tools and technology, and enhancement of governance and management structures (cf. Haes and Grembergen, 2019, p. 24 f.).

2.4.5 The Usage of COBIT

COBIT 2019 can be applied in different scenarios to achieve various objectives, depending on the specific needs and challenges of the organisation. This section describes some of the typical application scenarios of COBIT 2019 (cf. ISACA, 2019a, pp. 30 f.).

1. **IT governance and management**:
   COBIT can be used to improve IT governance and management by providing a structured and standardised approach to controlling and managing IT resources and processes. This can help improve IT efficiency and performance, better align IT with business objectives, improve risk management practices, and comply with regulatory requirements (cf. Grembergen and Haes, 2018, pp. 17 f.).
2. **IT strategy and planning**: COBIT can be used to support IT strategy and planning by providing a structured approach to identifying and prioritising IT objectives, defining IT strategies and plans, identifying and assessing IT risks and opportunities, and planning and budgeting IT resources and investments (cf. Haes and Grembergen, 2019, pp. 24 f.).
3. **IT performance management**:
   COBIT can be used to measure and improve IT performance by providing a set of standardised IT performance metrics and indicators, as well as a structured approach to measuring, monitoring and improving IT performance (cf. ISACA, 2019a, p. 31).
4. **IT risk management**:
   COBIT can be used to improve IT risk management by providing a structured and holistic approach to identifying, assessing, managing and monitoring IT risks based on the principles of governance, risk management and control (cf. Grembergen and Haes, 2018, pp. 17 f.).

The application of COBIT brings a number of benefits to an organisation, but it also presents challenges. Knowledge and understanding of these aspects is crucial for effective implementation and use of COBIT (cf. ISACA, 2019a, pp. 4 f.).

Benefits:

1. **Alignment of IT and business**:
   COBIT enables better alignment of IT objectives and activities with business objectives and strategies, which can lead to a higher business value proposition for IT (cf. Grembergen and Haes, 2018, p. 20).

2. **Improved IT governance and management**: By introducing standardised and best-practice-based processes, practices and controls, COBIT can help to improve IT governance and management (cf. Haes and Grembergen, 2019, p. 26).
3. **Risk management**:
   COBIT provides a structured and holistic approach to IT risk management that can help minimise IT risks and strengthen IT resilience (cf. ISACA, 2019a, p. 5).
4. **Compliance**:
   With COBIT, organisations can better ensure compliance with legal, regulatory and contractual requirements, which reduces the risk of compliance violations and associated penalties (cf. Haes and Grembergen, 2019, p. 36).

Challenges:

1. **Implementation effort**:
   Implementing COBIT can require significant resources and efforts, including time, money, and human resources (cf. Grembergen and Haes, 2018, p. 21).
2. **Resistance to change**:
   As with any organisational change, there may be resistance to the introduction of COBIT, especially if it requires significant changes to existing processes, practices and cultures (cf. Haes and Grembergen, 2019, p. 37).
3. **Complexity**:
   COBIT is a large and complex framework that requires a high level of expertise and understanding to be effectively implemented and used (cf. ISACA, 2019a, p. 5).

Success Factors:

The successful implementation and use of COBIT depends on a variety of factors. Some of the most important success factors are listed below (cf. ISACA, 2019a, pp. 10f):

1. **Leadership and commitment of management**:
   The commitment and support of management is crucial for the successful implementation of COBIT. Management should recognise the importance and bene-

fits of COBIT and actively promote the implementation and use of COBIT (cf. Grembergen and Haes, 2018, p. 22).

2. **Clearly defined goals and strategies**:
   The goals and strategies for implementing and using COBIT should be clearly defined and aligned with business goals and strategies. This helps to ensure that COBIT is aligned with business needs and to maximise its business value (cf. Haes and Grembergen, 2019, p. 38).
3. **Skills and abilities**:
   The successful implementation and use of COBIT requires specific skills and abilities, including an understanding of the COBIT framework and how to apply it, as well as the ability to manage and lead change. Developing these skills and abilities should be a priority(cf. ISACA, 2019a, p. 11).
4. **Organisational culture**:
   Organisational culture plays an important role in the successful implementation and use of COBIT. A culture that promotes change, innovation and continuous improvement can enhance the acceptance and effectiveness of COBIT (cf. Grembergen and Haes, 2018, p. 23).
5. **Continuous monitoring and improvement**: Continuously monitoring and improving the implemented COBIT components is crucial to maintaining their effectiveness and relevance. This requires regularly measuring and evaluating the performance and benefits of COBIT, as well as continuously identifying and implementing improvements (cf. Haes and Grembergen, 2019, p. 39).

Conclusion and Recommendations from Chapter II

The integration of information models for performance evaluation and control of organisations is crucial for the collection, processing and analysis of data necessary for informed management decisions. Theoretically, the topic is based on information management and systems theory, whereby the development of information models is structured and optimised by these theoretical frameworks. Information models are used to identify and measure key performance indicators (KPIs), which are essential for managing business processes. In practical terms, information models are relevant for implementation and integration into existing IT systems and business processes, enabling improved data quality and decision-making. Effective information management involves the collection, processing, storage and provision of information to support decision-making processes. Systems theory helps to structure and model complex information flows and decision-making processes, which is important for developing robust information models. Their practical relevance is demonstrated by the improvement in performance evaluation, as information models enable the systematic collection of performance data, thereby supporting informed management decision-making. However, implementing information models requires technical expertise and an in-depth understanding of organisational structures and processes.

In today's digitalised business world, the combination of 'Bring Your Own Device' (BYOD) guidelines, home office strategies, Balanced Scorecard (BSC), IT Balanced Scorecard (IT-BSC) and the COBIT framework forms a complex, multifactorial ecosystem. This ecosystem presents both attractive advantages and serious challenges for companies. BYOD strategies have the potential to offer a range of benefits, including reduced IT costs and increased employee satisfaction. By allowing employees to use personal devices for work tasks, companies can achieve maximum convenience and efficiency, ultimately leading to greater adaptability to market changes. However, this also results in risk factors such as insecure network connections and complicated authorisation management, which can make the company vulnerable to security breaches.

In addition, the COVID-19 pandemic has greatly accelerated the adoption of home office working models. These models offer advantages such as an improved work-life balance and the opportunity to realise productivity gains. However, they also present companies with challenges such as the social isolation of employees and new legal implications, for example with regard to data protection and labour law. Integrating these factors into a company's existing performance management system, as represented by BSC and IT-BSC, requires careful planning and execution. The COBIT framework serves as a guide to integrate these complex elements into a coherent strategy. COBIT enables a structured evaluation and control of IT resources and processes, which in turn enables optimised performance measurement and management. Thus, the successful implementation and management of this multifactorial ecosystem is a task of considerable complexity that requires comprehensive strategic planning and continuous adjustments. However, it also offers the opportunity to sustainably improve the efficiency, effectiveness and strategic alignment of IT organisations.

The BSC and its IT-specific variant, the IT BSC, have established themselves as effective tools in performance management. They enable a multi-layered view of corporate performance by integrating various perspectives such as finances, customers, internal processes and learning and growth capabilities. In the IT landscape, the IT-BSC supports the harmonisation of business and IT strategies by defining measurable KPIs and objectives that are aligned with overarching business objectives. However, the effectiveness of these management tools depends on a variety of factors. On the one hand, the quality of the underlying strategy plays a crucial role. A poorly conceived or unclearly defined strategy can lead to suboptimal results despite the use of BSC or IT-BSC. On the other hand, the willingness of staff to actively use these tools and get involved in the process is an important factor for success.

In this complex scenario, the COBIT framework serves as a sound architecture for implementing and managing IT governance. COBIT provides structured guidelines and practices that facilitate the integration of business and IT strategies. However, the complexity of implementing COBIT should not be underestimated. It not only requires well-thought-out planning and strategy, but also a high level of commitment from management. The introduction of the framework requires continuous monitoring and adjustment to ensure that the IT organisation remains in line with changing business requirements and regulatory frameworks. Thus, while BSC and IT-BSC are powerful tools, their full potential can only be realised in a well-thought-out and dynamically adapted framework. The COBIT framework provides this framework, but it requires that both executives and IT staff in the organisation are actively engaged and willing to make the necessary efforts for continuous adaptation and improvement.

When all these components—BYOD, home office, BSC/IT-BSC and COBIT—are considered together, it becomes clear that their effectiveness and benefits lie not only in their individual application, but especially in their synergetic interaction. This is a complex ecosystem whose elements are in a dynamic relationship with each other and thus requires a holistic view. Careful planning is a fundamental building block in this context. It is important to define both short-term and long-term goals and metrics that are aligned with the corporate strategy. Only in this way can BYOD strategies or home office models be effectively integrated into the performance measurement and management system of an IT balanced scorecard.

Another critical factor is the implementation of appropriate control mechanisms. These should cover both technical and organisational aspects. For example, when using BYOD, specific security protocols and authorisation structures are necessary to ensure the integrity of corporate data. At the same time, management must ensure that the relevant stakeholders, from IT departments to end users, are involved in the development and implementation of the processes. Continuous monitoring and adjustment form the backbone of this multifactorial system. With the help of the COBIT framework, a robust governance structure can be established that provides both constant performance measurement and the necessary flexibility for change. This monitoring should not only include KPIs and other performance metrics, but also qualitative indicators such as employee satisfaction or customer loyalty.

In summary, companies that manage these various elements in a coordinated and integrated way can maximise the benefits of this ecosystem and minimise the associated risks. This holistic approach ultimately creates sustainable added value that increases both the efficiency and effectiveness of the IT organisation and has a positive influence on the overall performance of the company.

Research Methodology For Integrating BYOD Into IT-BSC Systems

3

The research design defines the framework for the procedure in which the hypotheses put forward by the author are tested. This arrangement is primarily aimed at examining the relevant topics in isolation and distinguishing them from possible disruptive factors.

3.1 Statement of Research Hypothesis

In the context of the COVID-19 pandemic, the global business world has undergone profound changes. These changes have had a significant impact on organisational structures and working methods. Particularly noteworthy is the transition to the home office model, which has made the concept of BYOD a central component of business activities. The introduction of BYOD strategies increases the flexibility and autonomy of employees, but at the same time highlights the importance of appropriate IT management systems. In this context, tools such as IT-BSC and the COBIT framework are becoming increasingly important as they help to measure and control IT performance (Fig. 3.1).

Taking into account the detailed analyses and findings, which were presented in detail in CHAP. 2, the author raises the decisive **research hypothesis MH** on this basis. This hypothesis postulates that the integration of BYOD into the management system of an IT BSC enables a substantial increase in the efficiency, effectiveness and strategic coherence of IT structures within the established COBIT framework. This research claim, which is based on a thorough analysis of relevant information and research results, forms the foundation for further research and debate in the context of the discussed topic.

M. Groß, *Managing IT in the Age of BYOD and Remote Work*,
https://doi.org/10.1007/978-3-658-51216-3_3

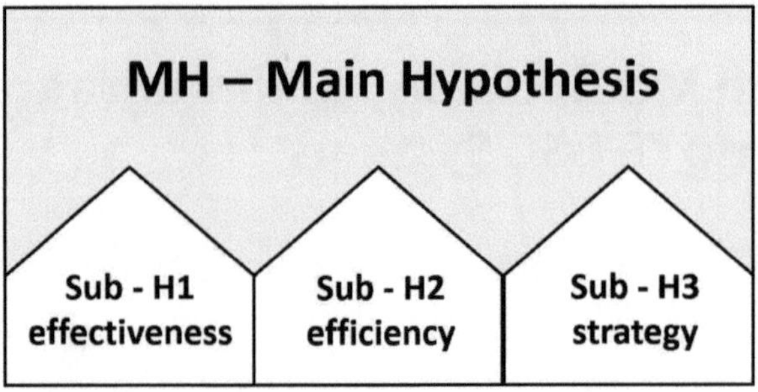

Fig. 3.1 Hypothesis Research Model. (Own illustration, 2023)

(MH) "The systematic integration of BYOD into the IT-BSC management system significantly improves the efficiency, effectiveness and strategic coherence of IT structures within the COBIT framework in the context of the organisation and management of information processes."

Based on the comprehensive literature analyses, it can be seen that an integrative incorporation of BYOD into the structures of the IT management system has significantly positive effects on the utilisation of resources in the area of information technology. The available literature studies shed light on the fact that this integration tends to result in a more efficient utilisation of IT resources. This result is based on the finding that by incorporating BYOD practices into the management system of an IT BSC, a reduction in IT costs and an optimised use of existing resources can be realised.

Based on these research observations, the first **sub-hypothesis (H1)** arises, which states that the integration of BYOD into the management system significantly leads to a more efficient use of resources in the IT area. This hypothesis reflects the understanding that the synergetic linking of BYOD initiatives and the IT-BSC contributes to a significant improvement in operational efficiency and thus increases the potential for cost savings and resource-optimised processes within the IT ecosystem.

(H1) "The integration of BYOD strategies into IT management systems promotes optimised resource utilisation and contributes to a significant reduction in operating costs within the COBIT framework."

Beyond the discussed efficiency gains, the integration of BYOD into the IT management system represents a significant opportunity to substantially increase the value of the IT services provided. This finding is supported by extensive scientific research that indicates that the merging of BYOD practices with an IT-BSC system leads to improved management and governance of IT services. This, in turn, aims to optimise the value of the IT services provided and ensure an enhanced fulfilment of end-user requirements in line with COBIT best practices.

In view of these scientific findings, the **sub-hypothesis H2** arises, which postulates that the integration of BYOD into the IT-BSC system causes a noticeable increase in the value of IT services. This hypothesis reflects the view that the strategic integration of BYOD practices is not only aimed at efficiency, but also at creating added value for the IT services offered, thus maximising the quality and relevance of IT offerings in the context of business objectives.

(H2) "The implementation of BYOD methods in the IT-BSC system leads to more effective control of IT services and processes, whereby the requirements of the end users are met more efficiently and in accordance with the COBIT guidelines."

In the midst of the increasing relevance of information technology for companies, especially in the context of the integration of BYOD, hypothesis H3 was developed in response to the emerging synergy between IT and business objectives. The increasing penetration of IT infrastructures with BYOD practices underscores the need for a closer strategic alignment of corporate goals and IT strategies. Against this backdrop, hypothesis H3 was formulated, stating that the integration of BYOD creates the basis for an optimised strategic alignment between corporate and IT goals.

(H3) "The integration of BYOD helps to achieve a better strategic alignment between business and IT objectives and strengthens the IT department's ability to adapt to external changes."

This hypothesis is based on the insight that combining BYOD initiatives with the principles of IT-BSC promotes greater flexibility and adaptability of the IT organisation to a changing business environment. It helps to increase the agility of IT structures and thus enables the IT organisation to improve its positioning within the COBIT framework. **Sub-hypothesis H3** accordingly emphasises the strategic importance of BYOD integration as a catalyst for improved business-IT alignment and the ability to better adapt to the changing requirements of the business environment.

3.2 Conceptual Model

A far-reaching, conceptual model is needed to meet the complex requirements of integrating BYOD and aligning IT-BSC within the COBIT framework. This model also takes into account the aspects of compliance, which become particularly relevant when these three areas are combined.

1. **Classification of companies**
   In the first step, the companies examined must be classified in terms of their specific implementation of compliance guidelines, their previous use of BYOD and the integration of the IT-BSC in the context of COBIT. This classification enables a differentiated analysis of different operational environments and their individual approaches to the challenges presented

   (a) **Organisation Profile**: Here, organisations are categorised based on their size, industry and business scope.
   (b) **BYOD Implementation Status**: This looks at the extent to which BYOD has already been implemented, from beginners to advanced stages.
   (c) **IT-BSC Integration**: This point refers to how intensively the IT-BSC is applied within the company in the COBIT context.

2. **Influencing factors and control necessities**:
   As a first and fundamental step, the compliance and classification basis of the company is analysed to determine the specific requirements and challenges that arise with BYOD and IT-BSC integration in the company. The focus here is on the strategic importance and dependencies of IT services, particularly with regard to the COBIT guidelines.

   (a) **Strategic Importance**: The importance of IT services in the context of BYOD and IT-BSC is emphasised. The goal is to determine how these services contribute to the overall success of the company.
   (b) **Management Challenges**: This section identifies the specific challenges that arise when managing IT services in a BYOD environment.

(c) **Dependency analysis**: This point deals with the dependencies between IT services, the integration of BYOD and the principles of the COBIT framework.

3. **Compliance and alignment of IT-BSC in COBIT with BYOD**:
Building on the classification, it is crucial to consider compliance in the context of BYOD and IT-BSC. It is important to clarify the extent to which the COBIT framework provides guidelines and best practices for aligning the IT-BSC with BYOD in terms of legal and internal company compliance requirements. This phase identifies potential risks, security requirements and other regulatory factors that arise from the integration of BYOD and the alignment of the IT-BSC, and offers strategies for managing them:

(a) **Risk Analysis**: First, it is necessary to identify potential risks arising from the integration of BYOD and the alignment of IT-BSC under COBIT. This includes security risks, data protection issues and other compliance challenges. Guidelines and best practices: After identifying the risks, the guidelines and best practices of the COBIT framework are analysed to understand how they can help to manage these risks.
(b) **Strategic Alignment**: This section highlights the central role of compliance in the overall context of business strategies, IT strategies and BYOD. This sub-topic emphasises how alignment with business objectives can be achieved while taking compliance requirements into account.

4. **Degree of implementation of the integration of BYOD and alignment with IT-BSC and COBIT**: The status quo of implementation and alignment in the companies examined is examined here. With the help of a maturity model, the degree of integration of BYOD and the alignment of IT-BSC in accordance with the COBIT 2019 framework is determined.

(a) **Maturity model**: This model is used to assess the current state of development of the companies in terms of integration and alignment. It evaluates how far companies have progressed in their BYOD strategy and how well their IT BSC is aligned with the COBIT framework. Within the framework of COBIT, different levels of capability, also known as capability levels, are assigned to the individual process activities. This categorisation is a central element of the capability maturity model, which is based on *Capability Maturity Model Integration (CMMI) V2.0*. The process capability scheme includes a total of six levels, which are listed below:

i. *Incomplete*: At this level, the processes are not yet fully defined and implementation is patchy.
ii. *Initial*: The processes are in an initial state and show an initial degree of organisation.
iii. *Managed*: At this level, the processes are managed and there is a certain degree of control over process activities.
iv. *Defined*: Here the processes are well defined, documented and implemented consistently throughout the organisation.
v. *Quantitative*: The processes are quantitatively understood and can be controlled by measurable targets.
vi. *Optimising*: At the highest level, the processes are optimised and continuously improved to optimise performance.

For a process to achieve a certain level of proficiency between 1 and 5, it is necessary that all activities assigned to it are successfully carried out at the respective level.

(b) **Best Practices**: Companies that are particularly successful in certain areas are identified and analysed to identify 'best practices'.

5. **Evaluation of results**:
In the final step, the effectiveness and success of the measures and strategies taken in the context of BYOD, IT-BSC and COBIT are analysed. This includes an evaluation of satisfaction, the effects achieved and the future fields of action identified.

(a) **Success measurement**: This point refers to quantifiable metrics and KPIs that measure the success or failure of the integration and alignment.
(b) **Feedback collection**: This is where feedback from relevant stakeholders is collected and analysed to gain insights into practical implementation and the challenges faced.
(c) **Future planning**: Finally, the study looks at what measures companies plan to take to further optimise their integration and alignment in the future.

3.3 Alignment of BYOD into the IT-BSC with COBIT

The ongoing digitalisation and increasing complexity of the IT landscape in companies are leading to an increased need to standardise and control IT strategies and processes. Two concepts that are particularly important in this context are the BSC and COBIT. In addition, the concept of BYOD has become widespread in response to the flexibility and mobility required by the modern working world.

IT BSC is a framework for measuring and controlling the performance of IT processes and systems using predefined performance indicators, known as KPI. It is part of a company's strategic management and helps align IT strategy with business objectives (cf. Kaplan and Norton, 1996a, pp. 71–74).

COBIT is used to ensure effective, efficient and controlled use of IT resources to achieve business objectives (cf. ISACA, 2019a, pp. 1–5). The BYOD concept allows employees to use their own devices, such as smartphones, tablets or laptops, for work tasks. However, this requires special security measures and guidelines to ensure data integrity and security, as well as integration into existing IT systems and processes (cf. K. W. Miller et al., 2012, pp. 1–3). The integration of BYOD into the management system of an IT-BSC in the context of COBIT requires careful planning and implementation in order to reap the benefits of BYOD while minimising risks. Especially with regard to compliance requirements, it is crucial that both the COBIT framework and the IT-BSC can adequately respond to the challenges of BYOD (cf. Tarantino, 2012, pp. 2 ff.).

3.3.1 Importance of Integrating BYOD into the Management System

The integration of BYOD into the management system of an IT BSC has significant effects on the alignment of the IT strategy and the effectiveness of IT governance. Firstly, BYOD offers companies a range of potential benefits. Employees can work with devices that they are familiar with, which can increase productivity and employee satisfaction. Furthermore, companies can save costs by no longer having to pay for hardware and instead using their employees' devices (cf. J. Harris et al., 2012, pp. 3 f.).

However, the integration of BYOD into IT-BSC also means that companies need to develop and monitor new metrics to evaluate the performance and security of the BYOD policy. These might include metrics that capture the number of devices, the types of applications used, the time and frequency of use, and the number and type of security incidents (cf. L.-D. Chen et al., 2013, pp. 1231–1234). Secondly, the introduction of BYOD increases the risk of security breaches, as personal devices are often less well protected than corporate devices and more easily lost or stolen. Therefore, the IT BSC must also include KPIs for monitoring and controlling IT security in this context. This can be supported by using COBIT, as this framework provides specific guidelines for managing information security and risk (cf. ISACA, 2019a, pp. 11 ff.).

Thirdly, the introduction of BYOD may result in the need to introduce new processes to ensure the management and support of these devices. This may require the revision of the existing IT BSC and also the introduction of new KPIs. Ultimately, the integration of BYOD into the management system of an IT BSC can lead to a better alignment of IT strategy with business objectives by enabling a more agile and efficient IT environment. At the same time, it can help to strengthen IT governance by ensuring that the risks of BYOD are effectively managed and monitored (cf. Tarantino, 2012, p. 8).

3.3.2 COBIT Compliance Understanding

In the context of information technology, compliance encompasses the observance of rules, laws and guidelines that are defined both internally by corporate policies and externally by legislation and standards (cf. Siponen, Mahmood, et al., 2014, pp. 765 f.). The importance of compliance in the IT landscape has increased significantly in recent times. This is particularly relevant in the context of growing data leaks and security incidents. A well-designed IT compliance management system minimises the risk of such incidents and strengthens the trust of customers and stakeholders in the company's data handling (cf. Soomro et al., 2016, pp. 545 f.).

In the COBIT methodology, compliance is a core area of IT governance. This includes not only adherence to external rules and regulations, but also compliance with internal company guidelines. The idea behind this is to ensure the efficiency and effectiveness of IT processes and to promote corporate goals (cf. ISACA, 2019a, pp. 24–27). The updated COBIT 2019 framework places particular emphasis on the role of compliance in the context of 'systemic governance and management'. According to this, corporate governance should be designed in such a way that all processes and activities function integrally and efficiently. In this context, compliance ensures the necessary transparency and control (cf. ISACA, 2019a, pp. 28 ff.).

COBIT recognises the growing importance of compliance in the digital world and offers specific guidance and tools for effective IT compliance management. Implementing these tools and guidelines helps companies to minimise compliance risks (cf. ISACA, 2019a, pp. 32–35). COBIT offers a comprehensive collection of best practices, principles and tools aimed at establishing an effective IT governance and management system. In particular, COBIT 2019 focuses on ensuring IT compliance. To do this, it takes into account various components such as organisational structures, information flows and services, all of which should be in line with compliance requirements (cf. ISACA, 2019a, pp. 24 f.).

To ensure compliance, COBIT proposes specific guidelines and tools. These include, for example, cascading compliance objectives that support the alignment of compliance and business objectives. These cascades enable the setting and tracking of compliance objectives at different organisational levels (cf. ISACA, 2019a, pp. 26 f.).

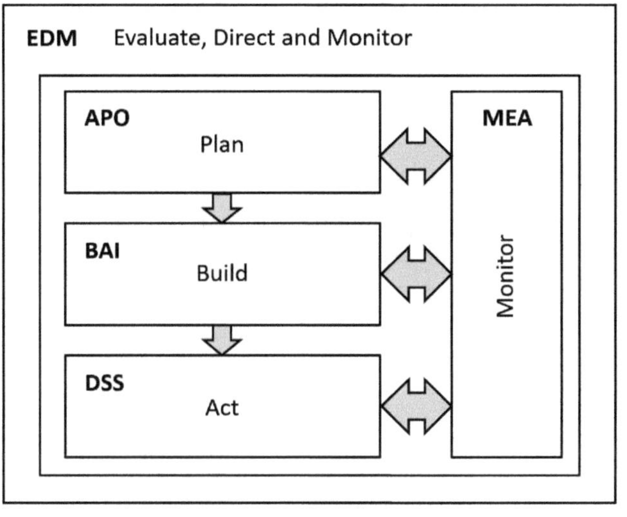

Fig. 3.2 COBIT compliance understanding using EDM. (Own illustration, 2024)

In addition, COBIT provides a comprehensive process for assessing and managing compliance, known as 'Evaluate, Direct, and Monitor' (EDM). This includes identifying risks, creating compliance strategies, implementing control mechanisms, and continuously monitoring compliance performance (cf. ISACA, 2019a, pp. 29–32). Finally, COBIT 2019 recognises that compliance is a dynamic and continuous process (Fig. 3.2). The framework therefore provides guidance and tools for the continuous improvement of compliance, including compliance metrics and scorecards, audits and reviews, and the introduction of compliance management systems (cf. ISACA, 2019a, pp. 34 f.).

3.3.3 IT Compliance as Part of the COBIT Goal Cascade

In the COBIT framework, the consideration of compliance requirements is represented by the goal cascade model, which illustrates the relationship between business and IT goals (cf. ISACA, 2019a, pp. 24 f.). As illustrated in Fig. 3.3, the strategic business goals play a key role as a starting point for further decisions and activities in IT governance and IT management. These goals directly influence the business and IT strategy and the associated priorities (cf. ISACA, 2019a, pp. 26 f.).

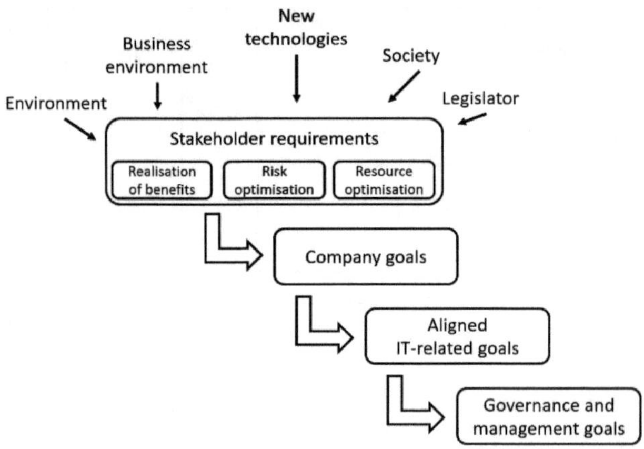

Fig. 3.3 COBIT 2019 Goal Casacade. (Own illustration, 2023 based on (cf. Gaulke, 2020, p. 19)

In the context of the target cascade, IT compliance plays a superordinate role. It is seen as a strategic business objective that serves as a framework for all IT activities (cf. Weill and Ross, 2004, pp. 11–14). COBIT's IT objectives are aligned with these business objectives and are transformed into measurable process and control objectives that guide IT governance and IT management (cf. ISACA, 2019a, pp. 33 f.). Therefore, the fulfilment of compliance objectives is a critical factor for the success of IT governance and IT management in the BYOD context (cf. Haes and Grembergen, 2015, pp. 21–24). These high-level objectives are further broken down into more specific IT governance and IT management objectives in COBIT, which are supported by the COBIT 2019 framework (cf. ISACA, 2019a, pp. 2 ff.).

In COBIT, the IT governance objectives focus on the strategic alignment and value generation through IT (cf. Weill and Ross, 2004, pp. 11–14). Two specific business objectives in COBIT explicitly address the area of compliance:

- **Business Objective 3**: Compliance with external laws and regulations.
- **Business Objective 11**: Compliance with internal guidelines.

The structure of the 13 IT objectives set out in the COBIT framework specifically focuses on IT compliance. Within these objectives, two stand out in particular, which deal directly and primarily with the implementation and maintenance of compliance in IT processes and structures, underlining their central importance within the COBIT framework.

- **IT objective 1**: IT compliance and support in complying with external laws and regulations.
- **IT objective 11**: IT compliance with internal guidelines (cf. Klotz, 2019, p. 16).

These IT objectives are closely linked to the business objectives and are reflected in the perspectives of the BSC. While IT objective 1, which deals with external compliance, is assigned to the financial perspective of the BSC, IT objective 11, which deals with internal compliance, is assigned to the internal perspective of the BSC (cf. ISACA, 2019b, pp. 29 f.).

The special attention paid to the formulation of IT goal 1 enables a differentiated view of IT compliance and compliance supported by IT. This differentiation emphasises the significant role of IT compliance in pursuing the organisation's compliance goals. As shown in Table 3.1, there are two categories of support quality: primary and secondary support, each with its own meaning (cf. Klotz, 2019, p. 17). IT governance places a strong emphasis on compliance. Organisations are required to design IT processes and activities to be compliant with relevant laws, standards, and internal policies. To achieve this, a holistic compliance management approach is necessary (cf. ISACA, 2019a, pp. 5–9).

The COBIT IT management objectives focus on the operational area and include factors such as the efficient use of IT, the provision of services, and ensuring security and compliance (cf. Haes and Grembergen, 2015, pp. 22–25). To ensure IT compliance, measures are embedded in daily IT operations. This includes, among other

Table 3.1 Support of the compliance-related corporate goals through IT goals. (Own representation based on (cf. Klotz, 2019, p. 17))

IT Goal	Business Goal	03 Compliance with external laws and regulations	11 Compliance with internal policies
01 IT compliance and support in adhering to external laws and regulations		Primary	Secondary
11 IT compliance with internal policies		Primary	Primary

things, setting up compliance controls and regular audits to monitor (cf. ISACA, 2019a, p. 10). The COBIT target hierarchy sees compliance as a strategic factor that significantly influences both IT and business strategy. An orderly and methodical approach is therefore essential (cf. ISACA, 2019a, p. 7). The starting point for IT compliance in the COBIT framework is clearly defined compliance objectives at the organisational level (cf. ISACA, 2019a, pp. 9 f.).

The COBIT hierarchy of objectives particularly emphasises the importance of compliance as a governance objective. Two of the 13 corporate objectives are directly related to compliance (cf. ISACA, 2019a, p. 32). The alignment objectives continue to reflect the corporate objectives and are an integral part of a BSC. In particular, IT objective 1 and IT objective 11 emphasise the importance of IT compliance in the context of corporate strategy (cf. ISACA, 2019a, p. 36). The objective hierarchy provides a structured framework for developing IT governance and IT management objectives in the context of IT compliance. The governance objectives include aspects such as strategic alignment and compliance management, while the management objectives focus on operational implementation (cf. Weill and Ross, 2004, pp. 13–16; cf. Haes, 2005, pp. 23–25). Embedding IT compliance in the COBIT target hierarchy promotes a compliance culture that strengthens IT performance in the compliance area. This makes compliance an integral part of the corporate strategy (cf. ISACA, 2019a, p. 9 f.).

3.3.4 IT Compliance in the Components of the IT Governance System

In a rapidly changing world of technology, it is becoming increasingly important that IT organisations follow certain rules and standards. This is an important part of the IT management system and helps to ensure that everything is in line with applicable laws and best practices. The COBIT framework is a key resource in this regard, dividing IT processes into four main areas: planning, building, delivering, and monitoring (cf. ISACA, 2019a, p. 14). The area of monitoring is specifically responsible for controlling compliance with rules and standards (cf. ISACA, 2019a, pp. 16 f.). It is important that such control mechanisms not only exist, but are also regularly reviewed (cf. Siponen, Willison, et al., 2012, pp. 36–40).

Furthermore, it is crucial to embed a culture of compliance in IT processes (cf. ISACA, 2019a, pp. 21–25). The company management has the task of ensuring that compliance is adhered to (cf. I. G. Institute, 2011, pp. 52–55; cf. ISACA, 2019a, pp. 26–28). The clear assignment of roles is of great importance for the effective implementation of compliance (cf. Siponen, Willison, et al., 2012, pp. 61 f.).

In COBIT, IT governance and IT management objectives are closely linked to the general IT objectives of an organisation, in particular to objectives 1 and 11. Of the 40 possible objectives in this area, ten are specifically focused on ensuring that the organisation adheres to laws and regulations, i.e. is compliant. Among these ten specialised goals, two are particularly important for compliance, while the other eight play a supporting role (cf. Klotz, 2019, p. 19). This relationship is shown in Table 3.2.

In the contextualisation of IT compliance within the framework of internal guidelines, ten IT governance and IT management goals can also be identified, which are shown in Table 3.3. Within the framework considered, the goals can be divided into two main categories based on their functional significance and role:

- **Three** of the goals are designed to fulfil a primary support function. This means that they are at the forefront, providing fundamental and direct support and assistance in the core areas. These goals are crucial to effectively addressing the main requirements and activities.
- The other **seven** objectives are defined as secondary support elements. They serve more as complementary or supportive factors that, while not in the foreground, nevertheless contribute significantly to overall performance and efficiency. These secondary objectives help to strengthen and complement the primary objectives by providing additional resources, guidelines or processes.

Table 3.2 IT Goal Nr. 1: Support for IT Governance with BYOD. (Own representation, 2023, based on Klotz, 2019, p. 19)

IT Goal No. 1:		IT Compliance and Support for Compliance with External Laws and Regulations
Primarily supported by...		
1.	**EDM01:**	Ensured governance framework setting and maintenance
2.	**MEA03:**	Managed compliance with external requirements
Secondarily supported by...		
1.	**EDM03:**	Ensured risk optimization
2.	**APO01:**	Managed I&T management framework
3.	**APO13:**	Managed security
4.	**APO14:**	Managed data
5.	**DSS05:**	Managed security services
6.	**MEA01:**	Managed performance and conformance monitoring
7.	**MEA02:**	Managed system of internal control
8.	**MEA04:**	Managed assurance

It is noteworthy that these objectives are largely consistent with those that favour IT objective 1. The differences mainly manifest themselves in the way in which the support is qualified as primary or secondary. The only exceptions in this regard are the objectives APO13 and APO14, which are not considered. Instead, EDM05, which focuses on stakeholders, and DSS06, which focuses on business processes, are added (cf. Klotz, 2019, pp. 20).

A robust Compliance-Management-System (CMS) is essential for the proper management of data and information. To achieve this, roles such as data owner, data controller and data protection officer must be clearly defined (ISACA, 2019a, p. 30). The clear assignment of roles supports effective data management (I. G. Institute, 2011, pp. 56 f.). To ensure data integrity, special security measures such as encryption and data loss prevention strategies are necessary (Siponen, Willison, et al., 2012, pp. 71–74).

Table 3.3 IT Goal No. 11: IT Compliance with Internal Policies. (Own representation, 2023, based on Klotz, 2019, p. 20)

IT Goal No. 11:		IT Compliance with Internal Policies
Primarily supported by...		
1.	**APO01:**	Managed I&T management framework
2.	**MEA02:**	Managed system of internal control
3.	**MEA04:**	Managed assurance
Secondarily supported by...		
1.	**EDM01:**	Ensured governance framework setting and maintenance
2.	**EDM03:**	Ensured risk optimization
3.	**EDM05:**	Ensured stakeholder engagement
4.	**DSS05:**	Managed security services
5.	**DSS06:**	Managed business process controls
6.	**MEA01:**	Managed performance and conformance monitoring
7.	**MEA03:**	Managed compliance with external requirements

3.3.5 Complementary COBIT Processes for BYOD Integration

While compliance is a key factor for the efficiency, effectiveness and strategic direction of IT organisations, it is not the only aspect to consider when implementing BYOD. Apart from compliance, other factors such as employee satisfaction and retention are equally relevant. Particularly in times of the COVID-19 pandemic, where remote working and home offices have become increasingly important, convenience and time savings are becoming more important for employees. BYOD solutions offer the flexibility to work with familiar devices in a short implementation time, which in turn increases job satisfaction and productivity.

In addition, BYOD strategies also offer significant cost-saving potential for organisations, as the acquisition and maintenance costs for devices can be reduced or even eliminated. It is therefore necessary to take a holistic view of BYOD implementation, which not only takes compliance guidelines into account, but also aspects such as employee satisfaction, convenience, time and cost savings. The selection of the appropriate COBIT processes should therefore be based on a comprehensive analysis of the various advantages and disadvantages, risks and opportunities of introducing BYOD. For all of these, suitable controlling instruments must be selected from the COBIT framework, which are explained in detail below.

The APO processes provide the foundation for achieving the goals set out in your research hypothesis (Table 3.4). For example, the APO01 process supports the identification of opportunities to increase IT efficiency through BYOD. APO03 helps to create clear BYOD guidelines that promote both IT governance and strategic alignment. This is reflected in the APO04 and APO10 processes, which help to define BYOD standards and improve the relationship between IT and the business unit. In addition, the APO processes contribute to an optimised management structure. The APO11 process, for example, shows how IT organisations can better exploit the advantages of BYOD integration. APO08 strengthens communication with stakeholders about BYOD initiatives and their influence on the IT Balanced Scorecard.

In terms of risk management, the APO processes, in particular APO09 and APO12, help companies to identify and assess BYOD-related risks. This contributes to improved control and increased IT security. Finally, the APO05 and APO13 processes are essential for effective resource management. They support not only the management of IT resources, but also human resource management, which is crucial for successful BYOD integration.

The BAI processes in the COBIT framework play a key role in integrating BYOD strategies into the IT-BSC system (Table 3.5). The BAI01 process helps to create a structured business case. By analysing business requirements, it creates a clear roadmap for BYOD integration, which supports the strategic direction of the IT organisation. The BAI03 process is particularly relevant for optimising IT services and processes, which links it directly to the H2 sub-hypothesis. By applying BYOD practices in this process, better alignment with end-user needs is achieved, which in turn increases the effectiveness of IT services.

With regard to the H1 sub-hypothesis, the BAI04 process is crucial. It focuses on solution integration and contributes to the development of standards for BYOD integration. This enables more efficient use of IT resources. Finally, the BAI07 process aims at the effective release of new or changed services and solutions. This well-managed release of changes promotes the IT organisation's adaptability to business changes, which supports the H3 sub-hypothesis.

The COBIT processes DSS01 to DSS06 are fundamental for measuring performance and managing IT organisations, especially with regard to BYOD integration (Table 3.6). The DSS01 process specialises in increasing IT efficiency through improved management of IT services, which directly supports the H1 sub-hypothesis. The DSS02 process focuses on increasing the effectiveness of IT service

Table 3.4 Relevance of COBIT 2019 APO Processes for the Research Question

Suporting APO COBIT Process	Relevance for Research Question
APO01	Supports the identification and evaluation of options for improving IT efficiency through BYOD integration.
APO02	Aids in the management of budgets and costs, supporting the investigation of efficiency improvements through BYOD integration.
APO03	Encourages the development of a clear BYOD policy to improve IT governance and strategic alignment.
APO04	Supports the definition and maintenance of BYOD standards to enhance the effectiveness of IT services.
APO05	Allows for more effective management of IT resources through BYOD integration.
APO06	Can assist in examining the potential of BYOD to improve strategic alignment between business and IT goals.
APO08	Encourages the relationship between stakeholders and supports communication regarding BYOD initiatives and their influence on the IT balanced scorecard.
APO09	Assists in identifying and evaluating risks associated with BYOD integration to ensure IT security.
APO10	Supports the relationship between IT and business, thereby promoting strategic alignment through BYOD.
APO11	Enables an improved management structure to better leverage the benefits of BYOD integration.
APO12	Assists in managing risks associated with BYOD integration to ensure effective controls.
APO13	Supports the management of human resources to effectively manage and control BYOD integration.

delivery through better management of service requests, which supports the H2 sub-hypothesis.

The DSS03 process focuses on improving IT service effectiveness, which can be achieved through a well-managed BYOD strategy. This strengthens the effectiveness aspects of the main research hypothesis. In terms of strategic alignment, the DSS05 process promotes better alignment with business objectives through optimised management of services and projects, which corresponds to the H3 sub-hypothesis. Finally, the DSS06 process emphasises IT security, which supports the main research hypothesis by effectively managing security services in a BYOD

Table 3.5 Relevance of COBIT BAI processes for the research question

Supporting BAI COBIT Process	Relevance for Research Question
BAI01	Assists in crafting a structured foundation to assess the impacts of BYOD integration on the efficiency and effectiveness of IT organizations.
BAI03	Focuses on identifying and selecting solutions, thereby fostering the effectiveness of IT services by aligning with end-user requirements.
BAI04	Plays a pivotal role in developing and implementing standards for BYOD integration, enhancing the efficiency of IT resources.
BAI07	Supports strategic alignment by managing the release and implementation of new or changed services and solutions, enabling swift adaptation to business changes.

Table 3.6 Relevance of COBIT DSS processes for the research question

Supporting DSS COBIT Process	Relevance for Research Question
DSS01	Supports the H1 sub-hypothesis by promoting efficient management of IT services that could be enhanced through BYOD integration.
DSS02	Contributes to improving the effectiveness of IT service delivery through better management of service requests and agreements within the scope of BYOD.
DSS03	Aids the H2 sub-hypothesis by fostering a more effective IT service delivery achieved through a well-managed BYOD strategy.
DSS05	Backs the H3 sub-hypothesis by encouraging better strategic alignment through optimal management of organizational services and projects.
DSS06	Assists in ensuring IT security and supporting the main hypothesis through effective management of security services in a BYOD integration environment.

environment. These versatile processes show the complex nature of IT-BSC in the COBIT framework and emphasise the importance of efficiency, effectiveness and strategic alignment for improving IT-organisation performance.

In this context, the EDM processes play a key role (Table 3.7). EDM01 lays the foundation for clear guidelines and specifications for BYOD integration, which strengthens the strategic orientation of IT organisations, as addressed in the H3

Table 3.7 Relevance of COBIT EDM processes for the research question

Supporting EDM COBIT Process	Relevance for Research Question
EDM01	Supports the establishment of clear policies and frameworks for BYOD integration, thereby facilitating a better strategic alignment between business and IT goals, aiding in the substantiation of the main research hypothesis.
EDM03	Addresses the management of risks associated with BYOD integration, encouraging effective and secure BYOD integration, consequently promoting the efficiency of IT services and processes.
EDM05	Enhances the optimization of IT value contribution through performance monitoring, ensuring that IT initiatives and processes effectively contribute to achieving business objectives, supportive in examining the main research hypothesis.

sub-hypothesis. This improves the coordination of business and IT objectives and increases flexibility in the event of business changes. The EDM03 process focuses on risk management in the context of BYOD integration. Effective risk mitigation not only promotes the effectiveness of IT services, as described in sub-hypothesis H2, but also creates a secure framework for the use of personal devices in the workplace. EDM05 acts as a catalyst for increasing IT value contribution. By monitoring the performance and ensuring the effectiveness of IT initiatives in relation to business objectives, the main hypothesis is supported. In particular, the added value of BYOD integration in the context of IT-BSC is emphasised here. In summary, these processes emphasise the importance of well-considered planning and constant monitoring of BYOD integration. They provide an in-depth perspective for examining the effects of this integration on efficiency, effectiveness and strategic alignment within the COBIT framework.

The COBIT processes listed in Table 3.8 provide sustainable support for the BSC. MEA01 focuses on performance monitoring and shows that clear BYOD guidelines can improve the quality of IT services. This is achieved by constantly monitoring and analysing IT strategies. MEA02, which focuses on reporting methods, increases transparency and accountability by regularly reporting on the performance and impact of BYOD integration. This not only promotes efficiency and effectiveness, but also supports a strategic alignment in line with the COBIT framework. MEA03 addresses compliance with external requirements. By implementing BYOD efficiently, IT organisations can ensure compliance while increasing user satisfaction and improving adaptability to market changes.

Table 3.8 Relevance of COBIT MEA processes for the research question

Supporting MEA COBIT Process	Relevance for Research Question
MEA01	Supports the BYOD integration by emphasizing the IT structures' performance-monitoring activities, which enable ongoing monitoring and assessment of IT strategies.
MEA02	Promotes transparency and accountability by enhancing the reporting practices of IT services, which is pivotal in enhancing the efficiency and effectiveness of IT organizations.
MEA03	Focuses on adhering to external requirements and standards to maintain the necessary compliance while elevating user satisfaction through BYOD integration.
MEA04	Offers a roadmap for establishing a management audit process that facilitates continuous monitoring and improvement of BYOD integration.

Finally, MEA04 provides guidance on introducing a monitoring process that continuously reviews organisational structures and processes. This is crucial to the continuous improvement of BYOD integration and supports the achievement of strategic goals, as well as increasing efficiency and effectiveness in IT organisations. Overall, these processes enable continuous improvement and strategic alignment of BYOD integration, while also promoting efficiency and effectiveness in IT organisations.

In summary, the selected COBIT processes contribute significantly to supporting the research hypothesis by providing a framework that promotes the integration of BYOD practices within the BSC, while improving the efficiency, effectiveness and strategic alignment of IT organisations within the COBIT framework.

3.3.6 COBIT Design Approach for the Integration of BYOD

The COBIT 2019 Design Guide presents a process-oriented approach to IT governance and creates an integrated framework for implementing and controlling IT processes in organisations. It emphasises the importance of IT strategy and the consideration of IT objectives in the corporate strategy. It also takes into account compliance requirements (cf. ISACA, 2019a, pp. 26–28).

The integration of BYOD into the IT BSC in the context of COBIT requires a well-thought-out and strategically planned approach. This is where the COBIT

Design Guide comes into play, enabling a clear understanding of the objectives and requirements and providing a systematic and structured approach.

The COBIT design approach focuses on clear objectives and specific design processes that build on them. It takes into account both the company's goals and IT-specific goals, such as greater flexibility for employees or cost savings (cf. J. Harris et al., 2012, pp. 47–50). The process begins with a thorough review of the current IT landscape and an analysis of the requirements and challenges that BYOD brings with it. An important part of this analysis is considering compliance requirements and the associated risks. Based on these findings, appropriate IT processes and solutions are designed and implemented. These should achieve the defined goals while ensuring compliance with compliance standards (cf. ISACA, 2019a, pp. 29 f.). This approach enables a targeted integration of BYOD by prioritising both business and IT objectives while taking into account the necessary security and compliance aspects.

IT BSC measures IT performance from various perspectives, including finance, customers, internal operations and innovation. When integrating BYOD, it is important to consider the many implications for these areas. For example, BYOD can achieve financial savings, but it can also pose challenges such as data protection (cp. Naranjo-Gil, 2012, pp. 12–17). The implementation of BYOD is complex and should be managed through a structured approach as recommended in the COBIT Design Guide. This approach focuses on clearly defined business objectives that provide a guiding principle for IT decisions (cf. ISACA, 2019a, pp. 27–30). Such goals could be improving employee satisfaction or saving costs and should be considered specifically in the context of BYOD (cf. J. Harris et al., 2012, pp. 51 f.; cf. Naranjo-Gil, 2012, pp. 76–79) (Fig. 3.4).

Risks, such as data protection and data security, are crucial factors in the implementation of BYOD. COBIT 2019 offers specific processes such as APO12 for risk management, which can be useful here (cf. Gupta et al., 2013, pp. 21–29; cf. ISACA, 2019a, pp. 51–55). In addition, there are IT-specific challenges, such as data security and device management, for which COBIT 2019 provides processes such as DSS02 and APO11 (cf. Köffer, 2015, pp. 26 ff.; cf. ISACA, 2019a, pp. 51 f.). Last but not least, compliance with compliance standards plays an important role. COBIT 2019 offers special processes for this, such as APO13 for information security management (cf. Andriole, 2012, pp. 29 f.; cf. ISACA, 2019a, pp. 51–54). In summary, the integration of BYOD into an IT-BSC requires a comprehensive understanding and consideration of various factors such as corporate goals, risks, IT-specific challenges and compliance (cf. Muller et al., 2019, pp. 41 f.; cf. Schooley and Marien, 2020, pp. 29 f.).

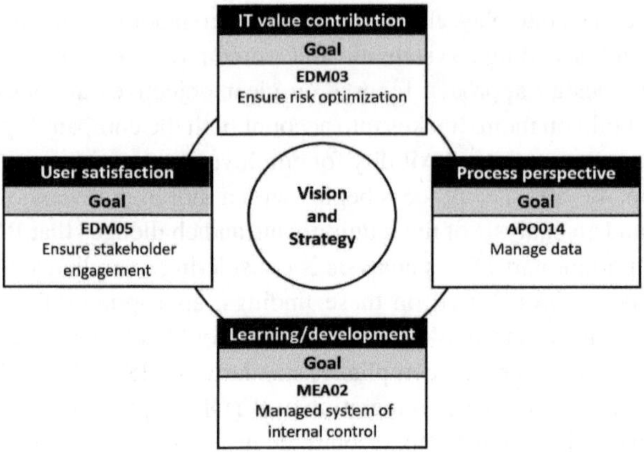

Fig. 3.4 IT-BSC BYOD COBIT Alignment. (Own illustration, 2023, based on (cf. Gaulke, 2020, p. 174))

3.3.7 Implementation of IT Compliance Measures for BYOD According to COBIT

In today's digitalised business world, the implementation of compliance measures for BYOD plays a crucial role. In this context, the COBIT 2019 Implementation Guide provides valuable guidelines for implementing IT compliance with regard to BYOD. The COBIT Implementation Guide is a framework specifically designed to help organisations implement Governance and Management of Enterprise IT (GEIT) based on the COBIT 2019 framework. The guide emphasises a phased implementation approach to ensure the acceptance and long-term success of the GEIT system (cf. ISACA, 2019a, pp. 27–30). The implementation guide places a strong emphasis on understanding the requirements and objectives of the stakeholders before implementing appropriate IT compliance measures. In the context of BYOD, for example, the stakeholders' objectives could include:

- Ensuring the security of corporate data on employees' personal devices.
- Complying with legal and regulatory requirements regarding data protection and security.
- Improving employee productivity and efficiency by allowing them to use their own devices (cf. P. Institute, 2020, pp. 42–45).

Implementing IT compliance measures for BYOD could therefore include actions to enhance IT security, conduct risk assessments, develop BYOD policies and procedures, and train employees. It is also important to note that implementing IT compliance measures for BYOD is an ongoing process that requires regular reviews and adjustments to keep pace with changing business needs and technological developments (cf. M. A. Harris et al., 2018, pp. 28 f.).

Implementing IT compliance measures for BYOD in accordance with the COBIT 2019 Implementation Guide requires a thorough understanding of the needs and objectives of the stakeholders, as well as continuous review and adjustment of the measures. In this context, the Implementation Guide provides valuable orientation for organisations. Effectively assessing and controlling the implementation of compliance measures is a crucial aspect of IT governance. In the context of BYOD, this is particularly relevant as compliance with regulations and policies is often complicated by the challenges associated with using personal devices for business purposes.

Assessing compliance implementation in the case of BYOD should be based on a systematic review and evaluation of the compliance measures introduced. This can be achieved through internal or external audits, self-assessments and reviews, the application of compliance checklists and frameworks, and the monitoring of specific compliance indicators (cf. Herath and Rao, 2009, pp. 21–25). Specific areas to be considered in the evaluation of compliance implementation in BYOD include, but are not limited to:

- employee compliance with BYOD policies and procedures.
- security and integrity of corporate data on personal devices.
- compliance with legal and regulatory requirements related to data protection and security.
- control of compliance implementation with BYOD (cf. Stavrou et al., 2018, pp. 46 ff.).

Monitoring compliance implementation for BYOD involves constant monitoring and adjustment of compliance measures to ensure that they are effective and meet changing business and technology requirements. The COBIT framework recommends a number of practices for controlling compliance implementation, including implementing regular compliance reviews, establishing compliance control mechanisms such as compliance dashboards and reports, and conducting risk and compliance assessments (cf. ISACA, 2019a, pp. 66 f.). It is important to emphasise that controlling compliance implementation in the case of BYOD is not only a technical task, but also an organisational challenge that requires effective communication, training and a culture of compliance (cf. Weiss and E. Anderson, 2020, p. 30).

Assessing and controlling the implementation of compliance in a BYOD environment is a critical aspect of IT governance. The COBIT framework provides valuable orientation and best practices in this context. Monitoring and reporting on IT compliance measures in relation to BYOD is crucial to ensure ongoing compliance and to be able to react to potential violations or problems in a timely manner. Monitoring IT compliance with BYOD involves constant control and analysis of compliance with relevant policies, regulations, and standards. This can be achieved by setting up automated compliance monitoring tools and systems, as well as regular audits and reviews (cf. Weiss and E. Anderson, 2020, pp. 28 ff.). It is important that the monitoring of compliance measures for BYOD not only takes into account technical aspects, but also organisational and human factors, such as employee compliance with BYOD policies and procedures (cf. Bulgurcu et al., 2010, pp. 46 f.). The purpose of IT compliance reporting in a BYOD environment is to provide stakeholders inside and outside the company with regular and transparent information about the status and effectiveness of the implemented compliance measures. Within the COBIT 2019 framework, IT compliance reporting can take the form of compliance reports, dashboards and scorecards that present key compliance indicators and metrics (cf. ISACA, 2019a, pp. 68 ff.). Reporting should include both quantifiable metrics (e.g. number of compliance violations, level of compliance) and qualitative information to provide a comprehensive picture of compliance performance (cf. Herath and Rao, 2009, p. 79).

Conclusion and Recommendations from Chapter III

The integration of Bring Your Own Device (BYOD) into the management system of an IT Balanced Scorecard (IT-BSC) within the COBIT 2019 framework is indeed a challenging undertaking. It requires a multidisciplinary approach that takes into account technical, organisational and strategic aspects. Within this complex structure, compliance requirements play a central role. Adherence to compliance guidelines is not just a formality, but serves as a catalyst for a number of advantages. On the one hand, it enables systematic control of the IT infrastructure and the associated processes, which manifests itself in effective risk minimisation. This is particularly relevant when integrating BYOD, as such strategies naturally go hand in hand with increased exposure to security risks. A well-founded compliance strategy not only identifies such risks, but also mitigates them appropriately. On the other hand, compliance is an integral part of the IT governance objectives as formulated in the COBIT 2019 framework. Aligning BYOD and IT-BSC strategies with the compliance requirements of COBIT not only improves risk management, but also strengthens the company's overall IT governance structure. This helps to achieve greater efficiency and effectiveness in the IT organisation and also supports the strategic alignment of IT with business objectives.

In this context, the COBIT framework serves as an overarching structure for evaluating and managing IT performance. The MEA (Monitoring, Evaluation and Assessment) domain plays a key role in the area of compliance. This includes monitoring and assessing compliance with guidelines, regulations and internal procedures that enable robust IT governance. The importance of the MEA domain is emphasised by the fact that it forms the basis for consistent and reliable performance measurement and evaluation, which in turn is essential for the integrity and credibility of the IT organisation. Nevertheless, the other COBIT domains should not be neglected, as they each cover specific aspects of IT management that directly or indirectly affect different areas of the business. For example, the APO (Align, Plan and Organize) domain is of central importance for planning and optimising IT strategies. Through effective IT strategy planning and resource allocation, the APO domain can have a significant impact on employee satisfaction by ensuring better alignment of IT and business objectives.

The Deliver, Service and Support (DSS) domain is responsible for providing and supporting IT services and, in this context, also influences the retention of stakeholders. Efficient and responsive IT service management can increase the satisfaction of internal and external stakeholders, thereby strengthening the relationship with them. EDM (Evaluate, Direct and Monitor) is the domain that controls IT governance and management at a meta level. It is crucial for cost and risk management and provides guidelines for effective control of IT resources. By optimising decision-making processes and improving control of the IT infrastructure, the EDM domain can contribute to cost efficiency and minimisation of operational risks. Finally, the Build, Acquire and Implement (BAI) domain is responsible for the design and implementation of IT solutions. By effectively building systems and applications, it significantly influences the efficiency and adaptability of the IT organisation, which is particularly advantageous in dynamic business environments.

While integrating BYOD into the IT BSC presents a complex challenge, it offers significant advantages for IT strategy and corporate competitiveness. By incorporating BYOD metrics into the IT BSC, IT managers can achieve a closer alignment between operational activities and overarching business objectives. This results in improved efficiency, for example through optimised use of IT resources and a possible reduction in operating costs. Furthermore, the inclusion of BYOD can strengthen the company's competitiveness by enabling greater agility and flexibility in the IT strategy. It is important to underscore that implementing BYOD and maintaining IT compliance should not be viewed as one-time activities, but rather as continuous processes. In a rapidly changing technological and regulatory environment, it is imperative that companies have the agility and adaptability to regularly evaluate and, if necessary, adjust their strategies and approaches. This includes the continuous monitoring of key performance indicators, periodic reviews of compliance guidelines and adaptation to new regulatory requirements. The dynamic nature of this approach requires a high level of management commitment and a robust governance structure, which can be supported by the COBIT framework. Only by pursuing a systematic and iterative strategy can companies fully exploit the advantages of integrating BYOD into the IT BSC while effectively managing the associated risks. In this context, both the IT BSC and the COBIT framework provide valuable tools for the continuous monitoring and adaptation of IT strategy, helping to maintain the balance between operational efficiency and strategic agility.

In summary, this approach has the potential for a multi-dimensional optimisation of IT performance, which is manifested by various key figures in the IT BSC. This ranges from increased efficiency in IT infrastructure and processes to increased effectiveness in the provision of IT services that better meet the needs of end users. Furthermore, the integration of BYOD into this system provides an effective platform for meeting compliance standards, particularly in light of the governance guidelines provided by the COBIT 2019 framework. Taking compliance metrics into account in the IT BSC not only promotes improved risk minimisation, but also contributes to more responsible and transparent IT governance. This is particularly important in today's dynamically changing business world with complex regulatory requirements.

The synergetic effects of integrating BYOD into the IT BSC in the context of COBIT 2019 can ultimately have a significant impact on the company's overall success. These influences are measurable not only quantitatively, for example through cost reductions, but also qualitatively, for example by strengthening the strategic alignment and adaptability of the IT organisation. However, the successful implementation of this integration is not a foregone conclusion and requires careful planning, continuous monitoring and periodic adjustments. Only by taking a systematic approach can a company maximise the opportunities and minimise the risks associated with such a strategic initiative. In this respect, the integration of BYOD into the IT-BSC management system in the COBIT 2019 context not only offers a number of advantages, but also the opportunity for a sustainable improvement in corporate success.

4 Empirical Research on BYOD Integration Into IT-BSC Systems

The empirical research, which is the focus of this study, was mainly conducted via an online survey. By surveying a sample of randomly selected companies, an analysis of the implementation status as well as the successes and failures in the implementation of BYOD and the link with management systems with international standards such as IT-BSC and COBIT 2019 in the group of companies was carried out. A strictly structured online questionnaire was selected as the survey method to ensure the broadest possible accessibility of companies (cf. Dillman, 2000, pp. 11). This procedure had the advantage of reducing costs and enabled the selection of the sample without parameters such as the geographical distribution of the respondents having an influence. As described in Chap. 1, technical possibilities for online participation should be available in all relevant companies (cf. J. Harris et al., 2012, 23–27).

When creating the strictly structured online questionnaire, social science guidelines according to Dillman (2000) were followed, such as neutral and precise wording. The range of answers was chosen to be so broad that ambiguity or no response was avoided. To avoid premature termination of the questionnaire, an attempt was made to keep it as short as possible. Since, according to SCHNELL, there is no theory of questioning, the questionnaire was extensively tested in advance (cf. Schnell, 1991, pp. 28).

The advantages of the Internet-based survey, in addition to the negligible costs of data collection, are the speed of implementation and the possibility of dispensing with a personal interviewer. This also makes it possible to effectively avoid errors in data collection. However, the lack of an interviewer is also a disadvantage of this method, since the respondent cannot be assisted if there are any comprehension problems. The survey period was deliberately set at three weeks in order to receive as many responses as possible with the help of an additional email reminder.

M. Groß, *Managing IT in the Age of BYOD and Remote Work*,
https://doi.org/10.1007/978-3-658-51216-3_4

4.1 Sample Selection

For the empirical study to be carried out, it was crucial to define the population, which in this case is the total number of all companies worldwide. Given the high number of these companies, which, depending on the definition, can be over 500 million, a complete survey was not possible (cf. on Trade and Development, 2021, p. 3). The original plan was to obtain a sample, including contact details, from central public-law organisations such as the World Trade Organization (WTO), the Organisation for Economic Co-operation and Development (OECD) or the United Nations (UN). However, since no such comprehensive and centralised data collection was available in the required timeframe, a pragmatic alternative had to be found. Instead of a public institution, a sample was therefore purchased from a private, commercial database that collects company data worldwide. Although this data does not come from a public institution, it was assumed to be sufficiently representative for the research questions.

The selection of companies was created using equally distributed filter criteria. The aim was also to achieve a balanced distribution across industries and geographic regions, and to exclude companies that belong to related groups or corporate groups, as this could distort the results by redundant identical statements (cf. Schnell et al., 2008, pp. 43). If possible, persons in management or with a leadership role should be addressed personally, as the author assumed that this would lead to more meaningful results. The weighted random sample for this study comprised 5000 participants, who were sent the internet address (URL) for the questionnaire by email. The large number of companies contacted was deemed necessary based on experience from similar surveys, which often had a response rate of less than 20%. To achieve a high response rate, participants were assured of anonymous questioning, and the survey software was set up to prevent multiple responses from the same participants (cf. Schnell et al., 2008, pp. 45 f.).

4.2 Questionnaire Design Empirical Survey

In order to translate the conceptual model presented in Sect. 3.2 into a quantifiable form, it is necessary to identify suitable variables and define the potential characteristics of these features for their evaluation. The classification for the developed model is described below. This classification requires a precise selection of the variables that are to represent the conceptual model. The variables must be selected in such a way that they represent the model in its entirety without unnecessarily increasing complexity. The possible characteristics of the features must then be carefully defined to enable an objective assessment. These steps are crucial for the empirical analysis of the model and help to convert the concepts and theories into measurable variables.

4.2.1 Main Classification

This chapter discusses the relevant questions for a basic classification of the participating companies. As shown in Table 4.1, the question of the type of company and its affiliation to a particular industry plays an important role in clarifying the research question. This is because different industries have different IT requirements and challenges, which can be well classified and distinguished by the ISIC standard (cf. Division, 2023, n.pag.). Using the international ISIC standard for classification provides a harmonised and unified basis for identifying different industries worldwide, which is essential for global comparative studies. A deep understanding of the industry can help to understand the context of the IT organisation, its strategic direction and the efficiency of its processes. Possible answers to this question allow conclusions to be drawn about how different industries incorporate BYOD integration into their IT BSC and how they perform within the COBIT framework.

Table 4.1 Type of Company by ISIC Section

Response	Type of Company
A: Agriculture, forestry and fishing	Specializes in agricultural, forestry, or fishing activities.
B: Mining and quarrying	Engages in extracting minerals or quarrying.
C: Manufacturing	Produces goods on a large scale.
D: Electricity, gas, steam and air conditioning supply	Provides essential utilities such as electricity and gas.
E: Water supply; sewerage, waste management and remediation activities	Manages water supply, waste treatment, or environmental remediation.
F: Construction	Undertakes construction projects.
G: Wholesale and retail trade; repair of motor vehicles and motorcycles	Deals in wholesale, retail, or vehicle repair services.
H: Transportation and storage	Offers logistical solutions including transport and storage.

(Continued)

Table 4.1 (Continued)

Response	Type of Company
I: Accommodation and food service activities	Provides lodging or dining services.
J: Information and communication	Operates in the tech or media landscapes.
K: Financial and insurance activities	Offers financial or insurance services.
L: Real estate activities	Deals in property transactions or management.
M: Professional, scientific and technical activities	Provides specialized professional or technical services.
N: Administrative and support service activities	Offers back-office and operational support.
O: Public administration and defence; compulsory social security	Engages in government functions or defense operations.
P: Education	Engages in educational services or institutions.
Q: Human health and social work activities	Provides healthcare or social work services.
R: Arts, entertainment and recreation	Specializes in cultural, recreational, or entertainment activities.
S: Other service activities	Operates in various other services not listed above.
T: Activities of households as employers; undifferentiated goods- and services-producing activities of households for own use	Falls under household employment or undifferentiated activities for personal use.
U: Activities of extraterritorial organizations and bodies	Operates under international jurisdiction or as an extraterritorial entity.

For example, companies in the finance and banking sector might have stricter security protocols that influence the integration of BYOD, while educational institutions might be more flexible. Therefore, the way in which the main hypothesis and the sub-hypotheses are confirmed or refuted in the real world is influenced by the type of company and the specific industry to which it belongs.

The question of the legal form (as presented in Table 4.2) of the company is important in the empirical study because it determines the legal, organisational and operational framework of the company. Different legal forms have different IT strategies and resources, access rights and security protocols, which in turn can influence the integration of BYOD. The type of legal structure can indicate how a company operates, what kind of IT resources it uses and how it implements its IT strategy. For example, sole proprietorships might have more flexible BYOD policies, while corporations might have more restrictive approaches due to stricter compliance and security requirements.

Table 4.2 Legal form of the Company

Response	Legal form of the Company
Sole proprietorship	The company is registered as a sole proprietorship.
Partnership (e.g. LLC, general partnership)	The company operates as a partnership, such as LLC or general partnership.
Corporate entity (e.g. Ltd., Inc.)	The company is structured as a corporation, such as Ltd. or Inc.
Cooperative	The company is organized as a cooperative.
Others	The company's legal form falls under "Others."

Overall, an understanding of the legal form of the company helps to clarify the context and the specific challenges and opportunities that could arise from integrating BYOD into the management system of an IT balanced scorecard within the COBIT framework.

The question in Table 4.3 about the size of the company, classified according to the criteria of the European Commission Recommendation 2003/ 361/EC is crucial to understanding the dimension and context of IT strategy and resources, particularly with regard to BYOD integration. Using this standardised classification scheme provides a harmonised view and makes it easier to compare the IT strategies and resources of different companies at the European level.

Micro, small and medium-sized enterprises (SME) could each take different approaches to BYOD integration, depending on the specific challenges and resources available to them. For example, medium-sized companies may have sufficient resources to implement an effective BYOD strategy that adheres to COBIT best practices, while micro-businesses may adopt more flexible but less structured approaches (cf. Commission, 2003, n.pag.). Understanding the size of the company therefore helps to clarify the specific context and the specific requirements and challenges that arise from integrating BYOD into the management system of an IT-BSC. It also helps to put the results of the study into context and to understand how different company sizes may react differently to BYOD integration.

Table 4.3 Size of the Company according to Commission Recommendation 2003/361/EC

Response	Size of the Company (according to Commission Recommendation 2003/361/EC)
1–9	The company is considered a "micro" enterprise, with 1 to 9 employees.
10–49	The company falls under the "small" enterprise category, employing between 10 and 49 individuals.
50–249	The company is classified as a "medium-sized" enterprise, with a workforce ranging from 50 to 249 employees.
250–1000	The company is beyond the "medium-sized" enterprise criteria but employs less than 1000 individuals.
Over 1000	The company's workforce consists of over 1000 employees, greatly exceeding the criteria for a "medium-sized" enterprise according to the recommendation.

The question in Table 4.4 about the company's international operations is relevant because it provides insight into the complexity and scope of the IT infrastructure and services. International companies may face additional challenges, such as the need to adapt to different regulatory standards and cultural preferences in different countries. This may impact how BYOD practices are integrated and managed, particularly in terms of security policies and user experiences. For example, if a company has offices in multiple countries, incorporating BYOD could require additional considerations in terms of data access, network connections and compliance in the various regions. Companies that export or import goods or services face additional challenges related to data transfers and security.

Table 4.4 International Activity of the Company

Response	International Activity of the Company
Yes, we have branches in multiple countries.	The company operates internationally with branches in multiple countries.
Yes, we export/import goods or services.	The company engages in international trade by exporting/importing goods or services.
No, we operate exclusively on a national level.	The company operates solely on a national level without international presence.

A company operating only nationally faces less complex challenges in terms of legal and cultural differences, but still has to ensure that BYOD practices are efficient and secure. Understanding a company's international footprint can therefore help clarify the specific requirements and contexts for BYOD integration and how these may affect the efficiency, effectiveness and strategic direction of IT.

The question about the respondent's position in the company is of central importance in order to understand the perspective and context of the answers (Table 4.5). Depending on their position, the respondent may have different insights and opinions regarding the integration of BYOD and its impact on IT performance.

Table 4.5 Position of the Respondent within the Company

Response	Position within the Company
CEO/Managing Director	You hold the position of CEO/Managing Director within the company.
CTO/CIO (Technology Leader)	You are the CTO/CIO (Technology/Information Leader) within the company.
Department Head	You are a Department Head within the company.
Project Manager	You are a Project Manager within the company.
Manager (other)	You have a Management position (not mentioned above)
Employee	You are an Employee within the company.
Other (please specify)	Please specify your position within the company.

1. **CEO/Managing Director**: This person has a broad view of the company and its strategy. Their views on BYOD integration show how it fits into the larger business context.
2. **CTO/CIO**: As technology or information leaders, these individuals are directly involved in decisions and implementations of IT strategies and systems. They provide detailed information on how BYOD is integrated into the IT infrastructure and the challenges and benefits they see.
3. **Department Head/Project Manager/Manager (other)**: These roles often have direct experience in executing projects and managing teams. They provide insights into the actual application and use of BYOD in their departments or projects.
4. **Employee**: General employees are the end users of most IT systems and services. Their perspective can provide valuable insights into the day-to-day experiences and challenges with BYOD.

5. **Other**: Individuals in other roles may provide unique perspectives not captured in the above categories.

Understanding who the responses are coming from will help to interpret the data correctly and understand the context of the responses, particularly when it comes to judging the efficiency, effectiveness, and strategic alignment of BYOD in relation to IT performance.

The question in Table 4.6 about the duration of employment in the current position is important because it provides insights into the experience and possibly the knowledge of the respondent about the company, its IT practices and the integration of BYOD.

Table 4.6 Duration of Tenure in Current Position

Response	Duration of Tenure
Less than 1 year	You have been in your current position for less than 1 year.
1–3 years	You have been in your current position for 1 to 3 years.
4–6 years	You have been in your current position for 4 to 6 years.
7–10 years	You have been in your current position for 7 to 10 years.
More than 10 years	You have been in your current position for more than 10 years.

1. **Less than 1 year**: Respondents who have been in their role for less than a year may offer fresh perspectives and views influenced by external experiences or previous roles. However, they may be less familiar with the organisation's historical IT strategy.
2. **1–3 years**: This group is likely to have a good mix of understanding of current company practices and possible changes or developments in terms of BYOD.
3. **4–6 years and 7–10 years**: With this length of service, respondents have followed the development of IT strategies and the integration of technologies such as BYOD over a longer period of time. They can provide detailed insights into the effects and changes caused by such initiatives.
4. **More than 10 years**: These respondents have a deep knowledge of the company's history and its IT developments. Their opinions could be particularly valuable for understanding long-term trends and the impact of BYOD.

The categorisation of the answers helps to understand the different perspectives and experiences that the respondents have with regard to BYOD and its integration into the IT strategy. It also allows the answers to be interpreted in the context of the experience and knowledge of the respondent.

The question in Table 4.7 about involvement in IT decisions is of central importance to understanding the respondent's perspective and the depth of their understanding and influence on the company's IT strategy and implementation.

Table 4.7 Involvement in IT Decisions

Response	Extent of Involvement
Primarily responsible	You have the primary responsibility for IT decisions within your company.
Advisory	You provide advisory input and recommendations for IT decisions.
Partially involved	You are partially involved in IT decisions without primary responsibility.
Not involved	You are not involved in IT decisions within your company.

1. **Primary Responsibility**: Respondents who are primarily responsible for IT decision-making have direct influence over the direction and implementation of IT initiatives, including those related to BYOD. Their opinions can directly influence organisational strategy and direction in this area.
2. **Consultative**: Individuals in a consultative role have a deep understanding of IT strategy and practice, but are not necessarily the primary decision-makers. They provide valuable perspectives as they can combine both technical knowledge and business insights.
3. **Partial involvement**: This group may consist of people who are involved in IT projects or affected by IT decisions, but are not directly involved in the decision-making process. They can offer unique insights into the practical implementation and the impact of decisions on the ground. item **Non-involved**: Although these individuals are not directly involved in IT decisions, they can still provide valuable perspectives, particularly on how IT decisions affect employees and other stakeholders in the organisation.

The insights gained from this question help to understand the different perspectives and levels of influence of the respondents in the context of BYOD and its integration into the company's IT strategy. It also allows the answers to be interpreted in the light of the position and influence of the respondent in IT decisions.

The question of the length of time required to introduce BYOD initiatives or guidelines within a company is of central importance for the study, as it can reveal potential relationships between the length of BYOD implementation and perceived efficiency, effectiveness and strategic alignment (Table 4.8).

Table 4.8 Duration of BYOD Initiatives or Policies

Response	Duration of BYOD Initiatives or Policies
We do not have any BYOD policies.	Your company does not have any BYOD policies in place.
Introduced less than 1 year ago.	BYOD policies were introduced in your company less than 1 year ago.
1–3 years.	Your company has had BYOD policies for 1–3 years.
4–6 years.	BYOD policies have been in place in your company for 4–6 years.
More than 6 years.	Your company has had BYOD policies for more than 6 years.

1. **Maturity and experience**: Organisations that have been implementing BYOD policies for longer may have had sufficient time to refine the initiative, overcome obstacles, and establish best practices. Such organisations may report higher efficiency and effectiveness in their use of BYOD.
2. **Initial difficulties**: Organisations that have only recently introduced BYOD may still be facing challenges or have not yet reached full efficiency because they are still in the initial phase of implementation.
3. **No BYOD policies**: Organisations without BYOD policies may be in this position for a variety of reasons—possible security concerns, lack of resources or because they do not see the value in such policies. Their perspectives provide insights into why some companies are hesitant to adopt BYOD.

The answers to this question will help to better understand the impact and benefits of BYOD at different stages of its implementation. Using an IT-BSC as shown in Table 4.9 can have a significant impact on a company's integration of BYOD. The IT-BSC is a strategic planning and management system used to align business and IT operations.

Table 4.9 Previous Experience with IT-Balanced Scorecards

Response	Experience with IT-Balanced Scorecards
Yes, regularly.	Your company used an IT-Balanced Scorecard on a regular basis before implementing BYOD.
Yes, but not regularly.	Your company used an IT-Balanced Scorecard, but not on a regular basis, before implementing BYOD.
No.	Your company did not use an IT-Balanced Scorecard before implementing BYOD.
Not known	Status is not known.

1. **Preparedness and Foundation**: Organisations that already use an IT BSC regularly have a firmer foundation and are better prepared to effectively integrate BYOD. They may also have the necessary processes and systems in place to effectively measure and manage the performance of BYOD.
2. **Volatile usage**—Organisations that use an IT BSC infrequently have recognised some of the benefits, but they may struggle to consistently apply and incorporate BYOD into their system.
3. **No experience**—Organisations that have not used an IT BSC before implementing BYOD have a larger learning curve. Implementing BYOD without an established method for measuring performance could lead to mixed results.

Overall, the answer to this question helps to better understand how a company's previous experience with IT BSC affects its ability to effectively integrate BYOD and maximise the resulting benefits.

4.2.2 Specific Classification BYOD-Homeoffice

In the following, an analysis of the specific criteria and metrics of the COBIT framework in relation to BYOD and home office is carried out. The aim of this analysis is to assess the impact of BYOD and home office on IT compliance. The question (Table 4.10) about the introduction of home office before the COVID-19 pandemic provides valuable insights into an organisation's organisational readiness and adaptability in terms of remote working and technology. Here is how the possible answers can be related to the research hypotheses:

Table 4.10 Introduction to Remote Working

Response	Frequency of Remote Work Before COVID-19
Daily	You or your employees worked from home on a daily basis before the COVID-19 pandemic.
Several times per week	You or your employees worked from home several times per week before the COVID-19 pandemic.
Once per week	You or your employees worked from home once per week before the COVID-19 pandemic.
Once per month	You or your employees worked from home once per month before the COVID-19 pandemic.
Never	You or your employees never worked from home before the COVID-19 pandemic.

1. **Daily/Multiple times per week**: Organisations that were already regularly practising home office before the pandemic have a culture and infrastructure that supports BYOD. This indicates greater efficiency and effectiveness, as they probably have experience with remote IT processes and services.
2. **Once a week/Once a month**: These responses indicate that the organisation has adopted a mixed strategy that allows for some flexibility but may not be fully aligned with remote technologies. Here, the integration of BYOD could present both opportunities and challenges.
3. **Never**: Organisations that never practised home office before the pandemic are struggling to implement BYOD and remote technologies. This indicates a lack of strategic direction and potential challenges in terms of efficiency and effectiveness.

This question helps to understand the context in which BYOD is being implemented in an organisation and contributes to the assessment of an organisation's ability to use technology efficiently and effectively in line with business objectives.

The question about changing the frequency of home office during the peak periods of the COVID-19 pandemic is crucial to understanding how companies respond to unforeseen events and how flexibly they can adapt their IT strategies (Table 4.11).

Table 4.11 Perception of Productivity During the Pandemic

Response	Development of Perception of Productivity in Remote Work
Significantly increased	The perception of productivity has significantly increased during remote work.
Slightly increased	The perception of productivity has slightly increased during remote work.
Unchanged	There has been no change in the perception of productivity during remote work.
Slightly decreased	The perception of productivity has slightly decreased during remote work.
Significantly decreased	The perception of productivity has significantly decreased during remote work.

1. **Significantly increased / Slightly increased**—Organisations that have seen an increase in home office frequency demonstrate an adaptability associated with sub-hypothesis H3. They may have quickly implemented BYOD practices and adapted their IT BSC to ensure efficiency and effectiveness.
2. **Unchanged**: Organisations that report no changes in home office frequency may have already had a strong remote working culture or may have found it difficult to adapt quickly to the new work reality.
3. **Slightly decreased / Significantly decreased**: A decrease in home office frequency indicates that the organisation has had difficulty supporting an effective remote working culture. This points to challenges in implementing BYOD and a lack of strategic direction.

This question therefore helps to assess an organisation's ability to respond to rapid changes in the business environment and provides insights into how the integration of BYOD into the management system can affect the IT organisation in such a context.

The question about the technological adjustments that were introduced or used more intensively during the pandemic to support remote working is of central importance for the investigation of the integration of BYOD into the management system of an IT BSC in the context of COBIT. It contributes to the research hypotheses by highlighting the following aspects:

1. **Efficiency (H1):** The introduction or intensive use of certain technologies increases the efficiency of IT resources. For example, the use of video con-

ferencing software and collaboration tools results in reduced travel costs and more efficient communication.
2. **Item Effectiveness (H2)**: Implementing VPN access and cloud storage solutions shows an effort to adapt processes to ensure that end-user requirements are met effectively.
3. **Strategic Alignment (H3):** The selection and introduction of new technologies reflects an organisation's strategic direction in order to quickly cope with changes in the business environment, such as the sudden need for home office.

The technologies and tools listed in Table 4.12 provide insight into the way a company responds to sudden changes in the work environment. It helps assess how well a company can adapt its IT strategy to the changes and how the integration of BYOD practices into the management process can influence those adaptations.

Table 4.12 Technological Adaptations During the Pandemic

Response	Description
Video conferencing software (e.g., Zoom, Teams)	Tools for virtual face-to-face meetings and collaboration.
Collaboration tools (e.g., Slack, Trello)	Platforms to enhance teamwork and communication.
VPN access	Virtual Private Network for secure remote access to internal networks.
Cloud storage solutions	Online storage for data accessibility and sharing.
Others	Additional technologies or tools adopted during the pandemic.

The question of how productivity is perceived in the home office compared to office work during the pandemic is particularly relevant for the main hypothesis and sub-hypotheses of the work. The possible answers and their classification are explained below:

1. **Efficiency (H1):** An increase in perceived productivity indicates that the integration of BYOD into the management system enables more efficient use of IT resources. This could be achieved, for example, by reducing IT costs through the use of private devices.

2. **Effectiveness (H2):** If productivity is perceived as unchanged or increased, it means that the introduction of BYOD practices has not negatively affected IT services and processes and may have even allowed for improved alignment with end-user requirements.
3. **Strategic Alignment (H3):** The perception of productivity also serves as an indicator of the IT organisation's ability to adapt its strategy to changes in the business environment (such as the switch to home office). An increase or maintenance of productivity indicates a successful strategic alignment supported by the integration of BYOD.

In summary, the question shown in Table 4.13 helps to assess the effect of BYOD on the efficiency, effectiveness and strategic alignment of the IT organisation in the context of the COBIT framework. It provides important insights into the impact of BYOD integration on the way employees work from home and how well they perform.

Table 4.13 Perception of Productivity During the Pandemic

Response	Development of Perception of Productivity in Remote Work
Significantly increased	The perception of productivity has significantly increased during remote work.
Slightly increased	The perception of productivity has slightly increased during remote work.
Unchanged	There has been no change in the perception of productivity during remote work.
Slightly decreased	The perception of productivity has slightly decreased during remote work.
Significantly decreased	The perception of productivity has significantly decreased during remote work.

The question presented in Table 4.14 provides valuable information on how team dynamics and collaboration have changed during the pandemic. These changes are directly linked to the hypotheses of the work:

Table 4.14 Effects on Team Dynamics During the Pandemic

Response	Change in Team Dynamics and Collaboration During Remote Work
Positively improved	The team dynamics and collaboration improved significantly during remote work.
Slightly improved	The team dynamics and collaboration showed slight improvement during remote work.
Unchanged	There was no change in team dynamics and collaboration during remote work.
Slightly worsened	The team dynamics and collaboration slightly worsened during remote work.
Significantly worsened	The team dynamics and collaboration worsened significantly during remote work.

1. **Efficiency (H1):** If team dynamics and collaboration have improved, this indicates a more efficient use of technology and the successful integration of BYOD. However, if these aspects have deteriorated, it is an indication that the system has not been optimally implemented.
2. **Effectiveness (H2):** An improvement in team dynamics indicates more effectively managed IT services and processes, while a deterioration signals potential problems within the COBIT framework.
3. **Strategic Alignment (H3):** The change in team dynamics is also an indicator of the strategic alignment between business and IT objectives. A positive change indicates a successful strategic integration of BYOD, while a negative change points to possible grievances in the alignment with business goals.

Overall, the question contributes to the clarification of the research question by examining the effects of the integration of BYOD on human aspects such as teamwork and communication. This provides a more holistic perspective on the effect of BYOD in the context of the COBIT framework.

The question presented in Table 4.15 examines the challenges that employees have experienced while working from home during the pandemic. The findings from this question are directly related to the main and sub-hypotheses of the work:

Table 4.15 Challenges of Remote Work During the Pandemic

Response	Challenges of Remote Work During the Pandemic
Technical issues	Significant technical challenges were faced during remote work.
Lack of separation between work and private life	The boundary between work and personal life became blurred during remote work.
Lack of communication with colleagues	Communication with colleagues became challenging during remote work.
Distractions at home	Various distractions at home hindered productivity during remote work.
Other	Other significant challenges not mentioned above were experienced.

1. **Efficiency (H1):** Technical issues are an obstacle to the efficient use of IT resources. Identifying these challenges helps to improve the integration of BYOD into IT-BSC.
2. **Effectiveness (H2):** Challenges such as a lack of communication with colleagues and distractions at home affect the effectiveness of IT services and processes. Analysing these factors provides revealing insights into the requirements of end users in the context of COBIT.
3. **Strategic Alignment (H3):** The lack of work-life separation indicates an imbalance between business and IT objectives. The integration of BYOD must therefore be carefully planned to promote better strategic alignment.

In summary, this question helps to understand the challenges that need to be considered when integrating BYOD into an IT BSC. This helps to support the hypotheses and recommendations for the successful implementation of BYOD in the context of COBIT.

The question, presented in Table 4.16, aims to understand the future plans of companies regarding the home office policy after the COVID-19 pandemic. This is relevant in relation to the research hypotheses of the work:

Table 4.16 Future Remote Work Policy After COVID-19 Pandemic

Response	Future Remote Work Policy After COVID-19 Pandemic
Fully remote	The company plans to adopt a fully remote work policy after the COVID-19 pandemic.
Hybrid model (mix of office and remote work)	The company intends to implement a hybrid work model that combines office and remote work.
Primarily in the office, but with occasional remote work days	The company's policy is to have employees primarily work from the office, but with the option for occasional remote work days.
Return to full office work	The company's policy is to return to full office work with no remote work options.
Still undecided	The company has not yet finalized its future remote work policy.

1. **Efficiency (H1):** Plans for home office policies have an impact on IT resource utilisation. For example, a full remote model could increase or decrease IT costs, depending on how it is implemented.
2. **Effectiveness (H2):** Different models of home office policy influence the effectiveness of IT services and processes. For example, a hybrid model could enable better alignment with the needs of end users.
3. **Strategic Alignment (H3)**: The decision on the home office policy could also influence the strategic alignment between business and IT objectives. The integration of BYOD must be in line with the chosen policy in order to position the IT organisation within the COBIT framework.

Overall, this question contributes to research into the possible effects of home office policies on the integration of BYOD. It helps to understand the challenges and opportunities associated with different remote working models, thus supporting the main research objectives in the context of efficiency, effectiveness and strategic alignment.

The question presented in Table 4.17 examines companies' long-term investment plans to support remote work. The question is crucial in terms of the research hypotheses of the work:

Table 4.17 Long-term Investments for Remote Work Support

Response	Long-term Investments for Remote Work Support After the Pandemic
Technology and software	The company plans to invest in technology and software to better support remote work in the long term.
Training and further education for employees	The company intends to allocate resources for training and further education to enhance remote work capabilities among employees.
Equipment and furniture for employees	The company is considering providing necessary equipment and ergonomic furniture to support comfortable remote work setups.
Expansion of IT security	The company plans to invest in enhancing IT security measures for sustained remote work arrangements.
None	The company does not have plans for specific long-term investments in remote work support.

1. **Efficiency (H1):** Investments in technology and software contribute to the efficiency of IT resource utilisation. Appropriate training and education could also improve employees' ability to use technology efficiently.
2. **Effectiveness (H2):** Investment in equipment and furniture helps employees to work more effectively, while enhancing IT security could help to ensure the integrity and reliability of IT services.
3. **Strategic Alignment (H3):** The long-term investment plans reflect the strategic direction of the organisation. Investing in certain areas could facilitate the integration of BYOD and promote better alignment between business and IT objectives within the COBIT framework.

In summary, this question contributes to research into the long-term strategy that companies are pursuing to support remote working in the wake of the pandemic. The answers to this question provide important insights into how companies are preparing for the long-term integration of BYOD and how these plans could help improve the efficiency, effectiveness and strategic alignment of IT organisations.

The question presented in Table 4.18 aims to identify the key lessons that companies have learned from the experience of remote working. This question is crucial to clarify the research hypotheses of the work:

Table 4.18 Important Lessons Learned from Remote Work

Response	Important Lessons Learned from Remote Work During the COVID-19 Pandemic
Flexibility is essential	The experience of remote work has highlighted the importance of being adaptable and flexible in work arrangements.
Good communication is crucial	Effective communication, especially in virtual environments, has been recognized as a critical factor for successful remote work.
Technology is key	The pandemic has underscored the significance of having the right technological tools and infrastructure for seamless remote collaboration.
Work-life balance is more important than ever	Remote work has brought attention to the need for maintaining a healthy balance between work and personal life.
Other	Additional insights and lessons learned from remote work during the pandemic.

1. **Efficiency (H1):** The importance of flexibility and technology has a direct impact on efficiency, as it facilitates adaptability to change and optimal use of IT resources.
2. **Effectiveness (H2):** Good communication and technology are crucial for the effective management of IT services and processes. They help to better meet the needs of end users.
3. **Strategic Alignment (H3)**: The highlighted lessons promote strategic alignment between business and IT objectives. For example, recognising the importance of work-life balance could facilitate a strategic focus on employee satisfaction and retention.

Overall, the question provides insights into the critical factors that organisations have identified in response to the challenges of remote working. Understanding these factors helps to inform and improve practices for integrating BYOD into the management system in the context of COBIT, thereby improving the efficiency, effectiveness and strategic alignment of IT organisations.

The question presented in Table 4.19 is of crucial importance in the context of the work, as it targets the long-term perspective of the home office and associated BYOD practices. The possible answers contribute to the clarification of the research hypotheses as follows:

Table 4.19 Future Vision of Remote Work Five Years After the Pandemic

Response	Future Vision of Remote Work Five Years After the Pandemic
Dominant and the new norm	Remote work becomes the dominant and standard mode of work for most employees.
A regular part, but not dominant	Remote work is a common practice, but traditional office work still holds significance.
Occasional, depending on the need	Remote work is practiced on occasion, based on specific job requirements and circumstances.
Rare or only in special circumstances	Remote work is limited to exceptional situations and special cases.
No longer practiced	Remote work is no longer a part of the work culture and has ceased to be practiced.

1. **Efficiency (H1)**: The permanent role of home office is likely to influence the way IT resources are used. A dominant or regular role could increase the need to efficiently integrate BYOD practices to reduce IT costs.
2. **Effectiveness (H2)**: The implementation of home office in various graduations has a direct impact on the control of IT services and processes. Understanding the future role of the home office helps to align IT services to effectively meet the needs of end users.
3. **Strategic Alignment (H3)**: The long-term vision of the role of the home office provides insights into the strategic planning of IT and business. Depending on the future perspective, the integration of BYOD could be adapted to strategic goals and changes in the business environment.

Overall, this question enables a strategic view of BYOD integration in the context of home office and provides insights into long-term planning that can be important for both scientific research and practice. It supports the research hypotheses by showing how BYOD and home office will interact in the future to improve the efficiency, effectiveness, and strategic alignment of IT organisations within the COBIT framework.

4.2.3 Specific Research COBIT 2019 Usage

In the following, the specific criteria and metrics in relation to the use of the COBIT framework will be analysed and examined in order to analyse them in the context of the research question. The question to assess the basic understanding and knowledge of COBIT 2019, as presented in Table 4.20, serves as a key element to understand the participants' baseline regarding the COBIT guidelines. This question contributes to the clarification of the research question in several ways:

Table 4.20 Assessment of Basic Knowledge of COBIT 2019

Response	Understanding of COBIT 2019
Very well informed	You have a comprehensive understanding of COBIT 2019 and its principles.
Well informed	You are well acquainted with the concepts and principles of COBIT 2019.
Basic knowledge present	You possess a foundational understanding of COBIT 2019.
Minimal knowledge present	You have minimal familiarity with COBIT 2019.
No knowledge present	You lack any knowledge of COBIT 2019.

1. **Efficiency (H1)**: A deeper understanding of COBIT indicates a better ability to efficiently integrate BYOD practices to optimise the use of IT resources and reduce costs.
2. **Effectiveness (H2)**: Knowledge of COBIT influences effectiveness in controlling IT services and processes by helping to plan and implement the integration of BYOD in accordance with best practices.
3. **Strategic Alignment (H3)**: A good understanding of COBIT is fundamental to the strategic alignment between business and IT objectives. Knowledge of this framework could improve the ability to align BYOD strategies with business objectives and changes in the business environment.

The possible answers to this question provide insight into the preparation and awareness of the participants for COBIT, a key element in the context of the work. This helps to understand the diversity of the respondents and how their knowledge of COBIT could influence the integration of BYOD. It provides valuable data that can be used to interpret the results of the empirical study in relation to the research hypotheses.

The question regarding the use of COBIT 2019 in the company, as listed in Table 4.21, provides crucial information to support the investigation of hypotheses H1, H2 and H3. The answers to this question can be categorised as follows:

Table 4.21 Usage of COBIT 2019 in the Company

Response	Utilization of COBIT 2019
As the primary framework for IT governance and management	COBIT 2019 is the main framework used for IT governance and management in the company.
As a supplement to other frameworks/methods	COBIT 2019 is used alongside other frameworks/methods to enhance IT governance and management practices.
It is used in specific projects or departments	COBIT 2019 is applied in certain projects or departments for targeted governance and management improvements.
It is known but not actively used	The company is aware of COBIT 2019, but it is not actively utilized for governance and management.
It is not known/not used	The company has no knowledge of or does not use COBIT 2019 for governance and management purposes.

1. **As main framework (Efficiency, Effectiveness, Strategic Alignment)**: If COBIT is used as the main framework, this indicates a stronger integration of BYOD that improves efficiency, effectiveness and strategic alignment.
2. **As a supplement to other frameworks (Efficiency, Effectiveness)**: If COBIT is used as a supplement, this indicates that the integration of BYOD is taking place, but may not be fully integrated into the company's IT strategy.
3. **In specific projects or departments (Efficiency)**: This indicates a partial integration of BYOD that could lead to efficiency gains in certain areas, but does not necessarily improve effectiveness or strategic alignment at the company level.
4. **Not actively used/Not known (Strategic alignment)**: If COBIT is not actively used or is not known, this could indicate that the integration of BYOD may not be optimal to support the strategic goals of the company.

The question provides important insights into how COBIT is implemented in the context of the company and helps to better understand the company's response to the integration of BYOD. It provides a solid foundation for analysing how the use of COBIT affects an organisation's ability to integrate BYOD into its IT BSC in order to achieve the stated goals in the hypotheses.

The question regarding training and further education on COBIT 2019, presented in Table 4.22, contributes significantly to the research hypothesis by shedding light on the understanding and acceptance of COBIT in the context of the integration of BYOD.

Table 4.22 Trainings and Further Education on COBIT 2019

Response	Participation in Training on COBIT 2019
Yes, in several	I have participated in multiple training sessions on COBIT 2019.
Yes, in one	I have attended at least one training session on COBIT 2019.
No, but I plan to in the near future	I have not taken any COBIT 2019 training yet, but I intend to do so soon.
No, and I currently have no plans in this direction	I have not participated in COBIT 2019 training, and I currently do not have plans to do so.

1. **Yes, on several (Efficiency, Effectiveness, Strategic Alignment)**: Multiple training courses indicate a deep integration of BYOD and promote efficiency, effectiveness and strategic alignment.
2. **Yes, at one (efficiency, effectiveness)**: This indicates a basic commitment to BYOD integration that supports efficiency and effectiveness, but may not cover the entire strategic direction.
3. **No, but I'm planning to do so in the near future (efficiency)**: This could indicate a growing interest in BYOD that could lead to efficiency improvements in the future, but may not currently influence all aspects of the integration.
4. **No and I have no current plans in this direction (strategic alignment)**: This could indicate that the integration of BYOD in the organisation may not be optimal to support the strategic goals of the company.

This question thus provides insights into organisational readiness and commitment to implementing COBIT, including staff training. It helps to understand how well the organisation is prepared to integrate BYOD into its IT BSC to achieve the objectives set out in the hypotheses.

The question shown in Table 4.23 on the influence of COBIT 2019 on IT decisions is of crucial importance for the research hypothesis. Here are the possible classifications:

Table 4.23 Influence of COBIT 2019 on IT Decisions

Response	Influence of COBIT 2019 on IT Decisions
To a very high extent	COBIT 2019 has a very significant influence on our IT decisions.
To a high extent	COBIT 2019 strongly influences our IT decisions.
Partly	COBIT 2019 has some influence on our IT decisions.
To a low extent	COBIT 2019 has a minor influence on our IT decisions.
Not at all	COBIT 2019 does not influence our IT decisions.

1. **To a very high degree (efficiency, effectiveness, strategic alignment)**: This shows that the company regards COBIT as a decisive guide for IT decisions. It indicates a high potential for integrating BYOD efficiently and effectively and supports strategic alignment.
2. **To a high degree (efficiency, effectiveness)**: This indicates that COBIT has a significant, but perhaps not dominant, influence on IT decisions. There may be room for improvement in terms of strategic alignment.
3. **Partly (efficiency)**: This indicates that COBIT is partially incorporated into IT decision-making, but other factors are also at play. This could support efficiency, but effectiveness and strategic alignment could be compromised.
4. **To a small extent/Not at all (strategic alignment)**: These responses could indicate a lack of integration of COBIT into IT decision-making, which raises questions about the strategic alignment of the integration of BYOD.

Overall, this question helps to understand the extent to which COBIT 2019 influences IT decisions in the organisation and provides important information on how well the organisation is positioned to integrate BYOD in line with the objectives set out in the hypotheses.

The question regarding the relevance of COBIT 2019 compared to previous versions, as shown in Table 4.24, helps to assess how the introduction of the latest version can influence the integration of BYOD into the management system. The possible answers can be categorised as follows:

Table 4.24 Relevance of COBIT 2019 Compared to Previous Versions

Response	Relevance of COBIT 2019 Compared to Previous Versions
Much more relevant	COBIT 2019 is much more relevant than previous versions.
Slightly more relevant	COBIT 2019 is slightly more relevant than previous versions.
Equally relevant	COBIT 2019 is equally relevant as previous versions.
Less relevant	COBIT 2019 is less relevant than previous versions.
Not relevant at all	COBIT 2019 is not relevant at all compared to previous versions.

1. **Much more relevant (Efficiency, Effectiveness, Strategic alignment)**: This indicates that COBIT 2019 has significant improvements over previous versions that are beneficial to the integration of BYOD and better positions the organisation within the COBIT framework.
2. **Somewhat more relevant (Efficiency, Effectiveness)**: This suggests that COBIT 2019 offers some improvements that may support the efficiency and effectiveness of BYOD integration, but do not significantly influence strategic alignment.
3. **Consistently relevant (strategic alignment)**: This could indicate that COBIT 2019 has not significantly changed from previous versions in a way that is specifically relevant to BYOD integration.
4. **Less relevant/Not relevant at all (Strategic Alignment)**: These responses may indicate that COBIT 2019 does not provide any enhancements compared to previous versions or is even less suitable for supporting the integration of BYOD.

Overall, this question helps to deepen the understanding of how the latest version of COBIT can influence the integration of BYOD and provides insights into the areas in which improvements have been made or where challenges may exist.

The question regarding the challenges of implementing COBIT, as presented in Table 4.25, contributes significantly to the research of the main hypothesis by examining the practical aspects of integrating COBIT in the context of BYOD. The possible answers can be categorised as follows:

Table 4.25 Challenges in Implementing COBIT 2019

Response	Challenges in Implementing COBIT 2019
The implementation was/is straightforward and without significant obstacles.	The implementation of COBIT 2019 was or is straightforward, with no major obstacles.
There were/are some challenges, but these were/are overcome.	While there were or are some challenges in implementing COBIT 2019, they have been or are being overcome.
There were/are significant challenges that affect the implementation.	Significant challenges have been or are being encountered that impact the implementation of COBIT 2019.
We have avoided implementing COBIT 2019 so far due to perceived challenges.	We have refrained from implementing COBIT 2019 due to challenges that we perceive.
Not applicable/Unsure	The question is not applicable to our situation, or we are unsure of the challenges in implementing COBIT 2019.

1. **Uncomplicated and without significant obstacles (efficiency)**: A smooth implementation suggests that COBIT can easily work with the integration of BYOD, improving the efficiency of the IT organisation.
2. **Some challenges, but manageable (Effectiveness)**: This response suggests potential obstacles, but that these can be overcome. It emphasises the need for adjustments to effectively implement COBIT, especially with regard to BYOD.
3. **Significant challenges, hindering implementation (Strategic Alignment)**: This response could indicate deep-seated issues that require an adjustment of business or IT strategy to incorporate COBIT with BYOD.
4. **Avoid due to perceived challenges (Strategic Alignment)**: This could indicate serious concerns or a lack of resources or expertise that inhibits adoption of COBIT.
5. **Not applicable/Unsure (Efficiency, Effectiveness, Strategic Alignment)**: This response could indicate that the organisation is unsure how COBIT would interact with BYOD, or that it is not relevant. It may require more detailed analysis.

Overall, this question helps to understand the reality of implementing COBIT in the context of BYOD and provides insights that are important for analysing the main hypothesis and sub-hypotheses.

This specific question aims to identify the COBIT components that contribute most to the positive integration of BYOD. The analysis of this question is of great importance in the context of the research:

1. **Efficiency (H1):** The selection of processes and organisational structures indicates the application of COBIT best practices, which enable a more efficient use of IT resources.
2. **Effectiveness (H2):** The mention of governance and management objectives, information flow and processes shows that the organisation has a clear focus on improving IT services and processes.
3. **Strategic Alignment (H3):** The choice of culture and behaviour, together with governance and management objectives, indicates a strategic alignment in which BYOD integration is embedded in the overarching business objectives.

The COBIT components listed in Table 4.26 provide a basis for examining how various aspects of the COBIT framework influence the integration of BYOD. The answer to this question provides important insights into how an organisation successfully integrates BYOD using COBIT. This contributes to the testing of the main and sub-hypotheses by revealing the components that are crucial for supporting BYOD integration within IT strategy and implementation. It also allows for better adaptation and application of the COBIT guidelines in relation to the IT-BSC.

Table 4.26 COBIT Components Contributing to Positive Integration of BYOD

Response	COBIT Components Contributing to Positive Integration of BYOD
Governance and Management Objectives	The governance and management objectives outlined in COBIT 2019 have contributed to a positive integration of BYOD (Bring Your Own Device) in our organization.
Processes	COBIT 2019 processes have played a role in successfully integrating BYOD practices in our IT operations.
Organizational Structures	The organizational structures recommended by COBIT 2019 have facilitated the smooth incorporation of BYOD initiatives.
Information Flow	COBIT's guidelines for information flow have supported the effective integration of BYOD while maintaining security.
Culture and Behavior	COBIT 2019's focus on promoting a positive culture and behavior aligns with our BYOD integration strategy.

The above question is crucial to the study of efficiency in the context of BYOD integration, using the COBIT framework. The answer to this question will directly contribute to the verification of sub-hypothesis H1, which concerns the relationship between the integration of BYOD and the efficiency of IT processes.

1. **Significantly improved**: This strengthens the thesis that the use of COBIT in the implementation of BYOD contributes significantly to improving efficiency. It also points to a successful application of COBIT processes and practices aimed at reducing IT costs and using IT resources efficiently.
2. **Slightly improved/unchanged**: This indicates that the COBIT framework has some, but limited, effect on efficiency, which calls for further research or adjustments to the strategy
3. **Slightly/significantly worsened**: This is an indicator that the application of COBIT was not successful in this specific context, which provides important insights for further research and practice.

The analysis of the responses in Table 4.27 allows to evaluate how the COBIT framework is applied in the real world to improve the processes related to BYOD. It helps to identify strengths or weaknesses in the existing application of COBIT that need to be considered in further research or in the adaptation of implementation strategies. The question asked is of great importance for understanding the strategic alignment in the integration of BYOD in the context of the COBIT framework. It is directly aligned with sub-hypothesis H3, which examines the strategic alignment between business and IT objectives.

Table 4.27 COBIT Framework's Contribution to Efficiency in BYOD Processes

Response	Impact on Efficiency in BYOD Processes
Significantly improved	The implementation of the COBIT framework has led to a significant improvement in efficiency in our BYOD processes.
Slightly improved	We have observed a slight improvement in efficiency in our BYOD processes due to the COBIT framework.
Unchanged	The COBIT framework has not had a noticeable impact on the efficiency of our BYOD processes.
Slightly worsened	The efficiency of our BYOD processes has slightly worsened since implementing the COBIT framework.
Significantly worsened	We have experienced a significant worsening of efficiency in our BYOD processes after adopting the COBIT framework.

1. **To a very high degree/To a high degree**: These responses suggest that the application of COBIT best practices when integrating BYOD contributes significantly to the strategic alignment between business and IT objectives. It highlights the relevance of the COBIT framework in supporting strategic decisions in the context of BYOD.
2. **Neutral**: A neutral response suggests that the COBIT framework contributes neither positively nor negatively to strategic alignment, which could raise the need for further research or adjusted practices.
3. **To a small extent/Not at all**: These answers suggest that the COBIT framework has not been successful in strategically aligning BYOD. This would be an important finding for both academic research and practitioners.

The analysis of the responses shown in Table 4.28 allows specific insights to be gained into the effectiveness of the COBIT framework in the strategic integration of BYOD. It provides important information for IT decision-makers to determine whether the application of COBIT best practices is appropriate for achieving strategic business objectives, and serves as a basis for further research in this area.

Table 4.28 Contribution of COBIT Best Practices to Strategic Alignment of BYOD

Response	Assessment of Contribution to Strategic Alignment of BYOD
To a very high extent	The COBIT best practices have contributed significantly to the strategic alignment of our BYOD initiatives.
To a high extent	The COBIT best practices have contributed to a great extent to the strategic alignment of our BYOD initiatives.
Neutral	The COBIT best practices have neither significantly contributed nor hindered the strategic alignment of our BYOD initiatives.
To a low extent	The COBIT best practices have contributed to a small extent to the strategic alignment of our BYOD initiatives.
Not at all	The COBIT best practices have not contributed at all to the strategic alignment of our BYOD initiatives.

The question of how effectively the COBIT framework has helped companies identify and manage the risks associated with BYOD is crucial to evaluating sub-hypothesis H2. It focuses on the role of the COBIT framework in effectively managing IT services and processes, specifically with regard to BYOD risks.

1. **Very effective/effective**: These responses suggest that the COBIT framework plays an important role in identifying and managing risks associated with BYOD. They support the hypothesis that COBIT increases the effectiveness of the IT organisation.
2. **Neutral**: This response suggests that the COBIT framework is neither particularly helpful nor a hindrance in identifying and managing risks. This could indicate a potential gap in the implementation or adaptation of COBIT in the context of BYOD.
3. **Not very effective/Not effective at all**: This indicates that the COBIT framework is not effective at identifying and managing risks. This could raise the need for additional research or a review of the implementation methods.

The analysis of the responses shown in Table 4.29 provides direct insight into the effectiveness of the COBIT framework in relation to BYOD risks. These assessments are crucial to deepening the understanding of the role of COBIT in risk management in the context of BYOD and to strengthening the theoretical and practical contribution to improving IT governance.

Table 4.29 Effectiveness of COBIT Framework in Identifying and Managing BYOD Risks

Response	Assessment of Effectiveness in Identifying and Managing BYOD Risks
Very effectively	The COBIT framework has been very effective in identifying and managing risks associated with BYOD.
Effectively	The COBIT framework has been effective in identifying and managing risks associated with BYOD.
Neutral	The COBIT framework's effectiveness in identifying and managing risks associated with BYOD is neither significant nor lacking.
Slightly effectively	The COBIT framework has been slightly effective in identifying and managing risks associated with BYOD.
Not at all effectively	The COBIT framework has not been effective at all in identifying and managing risks associated with BYOD.

4.2.4 Design to Validate the Main Hypothesis (MH)

BYOD integration improves the efficiency, effectiveness and strategic alignment of IT organisations within the COBIT framework. The question of how BYOD integration has affected the overall performance of the IT department is shown in Table 4.30. It provides a clear insight into the effects of implementing BYOD practices on various aspects of IT management, particularly in the context of COBIT. The possible answers can be interpreted in terms of relevant COBIT processes and instruments as follows:

Table 4.30 Impact of BYOD Integration on Overall IT Performance

Response	Impact of BYOD Integration on Overall IT Performance
Significantly improved	The integration of BYOD has significantly improved the overall IT performance.
Slightly improved	The integration of BYOD has slightly improved the overall IT performance.
Unchanged	The integration of BYOD has not caused any significant change in the overall IT performance.
Slightly worsened	The integration of BYOD has slightly worsened the overall IT performance.
Significantly worsened	The integration of BYOD has significantly worsened the overall IT performance.

1. **Greatly improved**: This indicates significant improvements in key processes such as APO01 (Manage the IT Management Framework), BAI01 (Manage Programmes and Projects) and DSS06 (Manage Business Process Controls).
2. **Slightly improved**: A small improvement can be observed in processes such as APO05 (managing the portfolio) and BAI07 (managing change).
3. **No change**: This answer indicates that the implementation of BYOD has had no visible impact on existing COBIT 2019 processes.
4. **Slightly worse**: Slight deterioration may occur in aspects such as DSS02 (Managing the service request and incident management), where BYOD has increased complexity.
5. **Significantly Deteriorated**: This response indicates serious issues in key areas such as APO13 (Manage Security) and DSS05 (Manage Security Services).

The specific insights gained from this question are particularly relevant for the sub-hypotheses relating to efficiency (H1), effectiveness (H2) and strategic alignment (H3). The detailed analysis of the influences on the respective COBIT processes makes it possible to draw specific conclusions about the effects of BYOD integration on the IT organisation that are directly linked to the main research hypothesis H0.

The question of the alignment of the IT strategy with the COBIT framework since the BYOD integration, as shown in Table 4.31, is crucial for evaluating the strategic orientation of the IT organisation, especially with regard to an IT-BSC.

Table 4.31 Alignment of IT Strategy with COBIT Framework Since BYOD Integration

Response	Alignment of IT Strategy with COBIT Framework Since BYOD Integration
Complete alignment	The IT strategy has been completely aligned with the COBIT framework since the integration of BYOD.
Major alignment	The IT strategy has been mostly aligned with the COBIT framework since the integration of BYOD.
Partial alignment	The IT strategy has been partially aligned with the COBIT framework since the integration of BYOD.
Minor alignment	The IT strategy has been slightly aligned with the COBIT framework since the integration of BYOD.
No alignment	There has been no alignment of the IT strategy with the COBIT framework since the integration of BYOD.

The possible answers can be interpreted as follows with regard to relevant COBIT processes, instruments and the connection to an IT-BSC:

1. **Complete agreement**: Here, the answer indicates a successful integration of BYOD that fully considers all relevant COBIT processes such as APO02 (Managing Strategy) and APO03 (Managing Enterprise Architecture). The IT BSC can also show comprehensive metrics for efficiency, effectiveness and strategic alignment.
2. **High alignment**: This may signal a high, but not complete alignment in processes such as APO04 (Managing innovation) and APO06 (Managing budget and cost), with the IT BSC still showing strong alignment.
3. **Partial alignment**: Here, alignment could be found in some, but not all, relevant COBIT processes. The IT-BSC might show gaps in areas such as effectiveness or strategic alignment.

4. **Low alignment**: This could indicate significant deficiencies in BYOD integration that have compromised the IT-BSC in key areas such as efficiency and strategic alignment.
5. **No alignment**: This response indicates a complete failure of BYOD integration in line with COBIT processes and tools. The IT-BSC would likely show poor performance in all main categories.

The interpretation of these answers makes it possible to carry out a detailed analysis of the alignment of IT strategy and COBIT through BYOD integration, which directly targets efficiency (H1), effectiveness (H2) and strategic alignment (H3). The selection of relevant COBIT processes and instruments, as well as the link to an inferred IT BSC, provides a robust framework for analysing and supporting the main research hypothesis MH.

The question of the extent to which the introduction of BYOD has contributed to a more efficient implementation of an organisation's IT strategy (Table 4.32) helps to clarify sub-hypothesis H1, which relates to efficiency.

Table 4.32 Perceived Efficiency Contribution of BYOD in IT Strategy Implementation

Response	Contribution of BYOD to Efficiency in IT Strategy
To a very great extent	BYOD contributes to efficiency in IT strategy to a very great extent.
To a great extent	BYOD contributes to efficiency in IT strategy to a great extent.
Neutral	BYOD has a neutral contribution to efficiency in IT strategy.
To a small extent	BYOD contributes to efficiency in IT strategy to a small extent.
Not at all	BYOD does not contribute to efficiency in IT strategy at all.

1. **To a very high degree/To a high degree**: These answers suggest that the implementation of BYOD is in line with certain COBIT2019 processes that aim at efficiency, such as APO10 (Managing Technology) and APO11 (Managing Quality). It supports the assumption that BYOD integration enables more efficient use of IT resources and reduces IT costs in the context of COBIT.
2. **Neutral**: This response shows that BYOD integration had no significant impact on efficiency, which would require a more detailed analysis of the relevant COBIT processes and IT-BSC measurements.
3. **To a small extent/Not at all**: These answers could indicate that the BYOD integration has not led to the expected increase in efficiency. This could require an

analysis of whether the BYOD integration was aligned with the right COBIT processes or whether there may have been obstacles that have hindered its effective implementation.

Linking this question to the selection of relevant COBIT processes and instruments and embedding it in an inferred IT-BSC allows for a detailed analysis of how BYOD integration contributes to the efficiency of an organisation's IT strategy. By understanding the relationship between BYOD integration, the COBIT framework and IT-BSC, this question can provide important insights that may confirm or challenge the main research hypothesis.

The question about the role of BYOD in the IT-BSC (Table 4.33) is crucial to understanding the integration of BYOD into the management system and how this contributes to the main research hypothesis.

Table 4.33 Role of BYOD in IT-Balanced Scorecard

Response	Description of BYOD's Role
Central and indispensable	BYOD is central and indispensable to the IT-BSC.
Important but not critical	BYOD plays an important role, but it's not considered critical.
Supplementary	BYOD is supplementary to the IT-BSC.
Minimal role	BYOD has a minimal role in the context of the IT-BSC.
No role	BYOD doesn't have any role in the IT-BSC.

1. **Central and indispensable**: This answer means that BYOD integration is closely linked to core processes in the COBIT2019 framework such as APO01 (Managing the IT Management Frameworks) and APO07 (Managing Human Resources). The IT-BSC should have a clear focus on BYOD as a strategic tool.
2. **Important but not critical**: This indicates that BYOD is important within certain aspects of the COBIT2019 framework, but not central to the overall strategy. Processes such as BAI01 (managing programmes and projects) could be affected.
3. **Supplementary/Minimal role/No role**: These responses may indicate a lack of integration or strategic importance of BYOD within IT-BSC. They also indicate that the link with the relevant COBIT2019 processes is missing or that BYOD is not considered a strategic tool within the IT organisation.

The insights from this question enable an understanding of how BYOD is integrated into the strategy and performance management process and help to assess efficiency, effectiveness and strategic alignment according to sub-hypotheses H1, H2 and H3. It is also helpful to identify which specific COBIT processes or tools are relevant or could be modified to better support BYOD integration within the IT-BSC.

The question of how the overall impact of BYOD on the effectiveness of IT strategy and implementation is assessed (Table 4.34) is central to testing hypothesis H2 and also contributes to clarifying the main research hypothesis MH.

Table 4.34 Overall Impact of BYOD on IT Strategy Effectiveness

Response	Overall Impact of BYOD
Very positive	BYOD integration has had a highly positive impact on the effectiveness of our IT strategy.
Positive	BYOD integration has contributed positively to the overall effectiveness of our IT strategy.
Neutral	The impact of BYOD integration on the effectiveness of our IT strategy is neither positive nor negative.
Negative	BYOD integration has negatively affected the overall effectiveness of our IT strategy.
Very negative	The integration of BYOD has significantly and adversely impacted the effectiveness of our IT strategy.

1. **Very positive/Positive**: This rating indicates that the integration of BYOD practices significantly contributes to the effectiveness of the IT strategy. The COBIT2019 processes most relevant here include APO03 (Managing the Enterprise Architecture) and BAI01 (Managing Programmes and Projects).
2. **Neutral**: This response suggests that BYOD contributes neither positively nor negatively to IT strategy effectiveness, which warrants a review of the link between BYOD and COBIT processes such as APO05 (Managing Portfolio) and BAI07 (Managing Change).
3. **Negative/Very negative**: These responses may indicate a problem with the integration or execution of BYOD within the IT strategy and implementation. This requires investigation of specific COBIT processes that negatively impact effectiveness, such as EDM03 (ensuring risk management) or APO13 (managing security).

The insights gained from this question are used to determine the extent to which BYOD practices contribute to the effectiveness of the IT strategy and how they are linked to the relevant COBIT processes and tools. Furthermore, it enables the identification of areas where improvements or adjustments may be needed to improve the effectiveness of IT strategy and implementation in the context of the COBIT framework.

4.2.5 Design to Validate the Sub-Hypothesis 1 (H1)

The integration of BYOD positively influences the customer perspective and business process perspective of the IT-BSC. The question regarding the change in the average IT budget effort since the integration of BYOD (Table 4.35) contributes significantly to the clarification of hypothesis H1, which focuses on efficiency in terms of the use of IT resources and the reduction of IT costs.

Table 4.35 Changes in IT Budget Expenditure Since BYOD Integration

Response	Change in IT Budget
Significantly reduced	The IT budget has been significantly reduced after the integration of BYOD due to decreased hardware and infrastructure costs.
Slightly reduced	There has been a minor reduction in the IT budget following BYOD integration, with some cost savings in hardware and support.
Unchanged	The IT budget remains unchanged after BYOD integration, as any savings from reduced hardware expenses are offset by other factors.
Slightly increased	There has been a slight increase in the IT budget after BYOD integration, possibly due to additional expenses for security measures and support.
Significantly increased	The IT budget has seen a significant increase after the integration of BYOD, possibly due to higher security and management costs.

1. **Significantly reduced/Slightly reduced**: This is a confirmation of hypothesis H1 that the integration of BYOD leads to a more efficient use of IT resources. COBIT2019 processes such as APO02 (Managing Strategy) and APO07 (Managing Human Resources) are relevant here.
2. **No change**: No change in budget spending indicates that BYOD has no impact on efficiency. This requires a closer examination of processes such as APO06 (Managing Budget and Costs) to understand the reasons.

3. **Slightly increased/Significantly increased**: An increase in the IT budget indicates that the integration of BYOD has not led to the expected efficiency and may require an examination of the implementation and the associated COBIT2019 processes such as APO01 (Manage IT Administration) and APO11 (Manage Quality).

This question helps to understand the impact of BYOD on IT budget spending and allows an analysis of how the integration of BYOD is linked to the relevant COBIT processes and instruments. This may also help to understand how BYOD is positioned within an inferred IT BSC and how it contributes to the strategic alignment set out in hypothesis H3.

The question regarding the utilisation of IT staff since the introduction of BYOD (Table 4.36) is of great importance for the research hypothesis and in particular for sub-hypotheses H1 and H2.

Table 4.36 Change in IT Staff Utilization since BYOD Integration

Response	Change in IT Staff Utilization
Significantly reduced	The utilization of IT staff has been significantly reduced since the integration of BYOD.
Slightly reduced	There has been a slight reduction in the utilization of IT staff since the integration of BYOD.
Unchanged	The utilization of IT staff has remained unchanged since the integration of BYOD.
Slightly increased	There has been a slight increase in the utilization of IT staff since the integration of BYOD.
Significantly increased	The utilization of IT staff has significantly increased since the integration of BYOD.

1. **Significantly reduced/Slightly reduced**: If the utilisation of IT staff has been reduced since the BYOD integration, this is an indicator of increased efficiency in the management of IT resources (H1). It is also relevant to check COBIT processes such as APO07 (Managing Human Resources) to ensure that this change is positive.
2. em **Unchanged**: This response indicates that BYOD integration is neither improving efficiency nor better meeting end-user needs (H2). This requires a detailed review of the implementation and associated COBIT processes.

3. **Slightly increased/Significantly increased**: An increase in utilisation is an indicator of more effective control of IT services and processes to meet the needs of end users (H2). At the same time, a significant increase is a sign of overloading, which could affect efficiency.

The selection of relevant COBIT processes and instruments, as well as the link to the IT-BSC, should be carefully aligned with the specific organisation and its objectives. Addressing this question will provide deep insight into the human resource management aspects of the IT organisation and how BYOD integration affects them, in order to foster stronger strategic alignment in line with business objectives (H3).

The study of customer satisfaction in the context of BYOD integration (Table 4.37) contributes significantly to the research question, as it is directly linked to the effectiveness (H2) and strategic alignment (H3) of IT organisations within the COBIT framework.

Table 4.37 Influence of BYOD Integration on Customer Satisfaction

Response	Influence on Customer Satisfaction
Significantly improved	The integration of BYOD has led to a significant improvement in customer satisfaction.
Slightly improved	There has been a slight improvement in customer satisfaction since the integration of BYOD.
Unchanged	Customer satisfaction has remained unchanged since the integration of BYOD.
Slightly worsened	There has been a slight decrease in customer satisfaction since the integration of BYOD.
Significantly worsened	The integration of BYOD has led to a significant decrease in customer satisfaction.

1. **Significantly improved/Slightly improved**: These answers support sub-hypothesis H2 that BYOD integration makes IT services and processes more effective and more likely to meet end-user requirements. This is supported by COBIT processes such as DSS01 (Manage Operations) and DSS05 (Manage Security Services) to increase the efficiency and effectiveness of IT services.
2. **Unchanged**: If customer satisfaction remains unchanged, this indicates that BYOD integration is not sufficiently aligned with COBIT best practices or that other factors are affecting customer satisfaction.

3. **Slightly deteriorated/Significantly deteriorated**: Deterioration of customer satisfaction is a serious warning sign and requires a review of the implementation of BYOD, the IT Balanced Scorecard and relevant COBIT2019 processes such as APO01 (Manage the IT Management Framework).

The link to the derived IT BSC includes how the BYOD integration fits into the overarching business objectives and how it contributes to the achievement of specific IT objectives in line with the IT BSC. This requires careful selection and alignment with relevant COBIT processes and tools to ensure that the BYOD integration is not only technically successful but also delivers business value and promotes strategic alignment (H3).

The question about Business Process Optimization (BPO) through BYOD (Table 4.38) is directly relevant for testing the sub-hypotheses H1, H2, and H3. It helps clarify how the integration of BYOD affects efficiency, effectiveness, and strategic alignment by evaluating the impact on business processes.

Table 4.38 Extent of BYOD Contribution to IT-Related BPO

Response	Extent of Contribution
To a very high extent	BYOD has contributed significantly to the optimization of IT-related business processes.
To a high extent	The integration of BYOD has had a substantial contribution to the optimization of IT-related business processes.
Neutral	There has been no significant impact on the optimization of IT-related business processes due to BYOD integration.
To a low extent	The contribution of BYOD to the optimization of IT-related business processes is minor.
Not at all	BYOD integration has not contributed to the optimization of IT-related business processes.

1. **To a very high degree/To a high degree**: These answers show support for H1 and H2, as they indicate that the integration of BYOD leads to a more efficient use of IT resources and makes IT services and processes more effective. Relevant COBIT processes include APO03 (Alignment of Strategy and Plans), BAI04 (Manage Availability and Capacity) and DSS02 (Managed Service Requests and Incidents).
2. **Neutral**: A neutral response indicates that BYOD integration has no discernible effect, which could indicate a possible discrepancy in implementation or incompatibility with existing business processes.

3. **To a small extent/Not at all**: These responses require a serious review of the BYOD strategy and implementation, as they are not delivering the desired improvements. This is a sign that a realignment of the COBIT processes, e.g. APO06 (Manage Budget and Costs) and BAI01 (Manage Programs), is necessary.

The link to the derived IT-BSC includes how the BYOD integration is aligned with the specific business objectives, and emphasises the strategic direction to ensure that BYOD effectively supports business processes. The integration of BYOD should be closely aligned with COBIT processes and tools to fully realise the optimisation of IT-related business processes.

The question regarding the impact of BYOD integration on responsiveness and adaptability (Table 4.39) is essential for investigating sub-hypotheses H2 and H3. It enables a detailed examination of how the integration of BYOD influences the effectiveness and strategic alignment of IT services.

Table 4.39 Effect of BYOD Integration on Response Time and Adaptability

Response	Effect on Response and Adaptability
Significantly accelerated/ improved	The integration of BYOD has led to a substantial improvement in response time and adaptability.
Slightly accelerated/ improved	There is a slight improvement in response time and adaptability due to BYOD integration.
Unchanged	The response time and adaptability have remained unchanged following BYOD integration.
Slightly slowed/ deteriorated	There is a slight decline in response time and adaptability after BYOD integration.
Significantly slowed/deteriorated	BYOD integration has significantly impacted response time and adaptability negatively.

1. **Significantly accelerated/improved**: This is a strong indication of support for H2 and shows that BYOD better meets the requirements of end users. COBIT2019 processes such as DSS01 (Manage Operations) and DSS05 (Manage Security Services) are particularly relevant.
2. **Slightly accelerated/improved**: This response also supports H2, but a need for further optimisation indicates that processes such as APO05 (Manage Portfolio) need to be examined.

3. **Unchanged**: This indicates that BYOD has not caused any significant changes, which could challenge the hypotheses. It requires a review of the implementation and an adjustment of the COBIT processes.
4. **Slightly slowed/deteriorated**: This response challenges the hypotheses, which require a detailed examination of processes such as APO07 (Manage Human Resources).
5. **Significantly slowed down/deteriorated**: This is a serious indication that BYOD integration has failed. A thorough review of processes such as APO10 (Manage Suppliers) is essential.

The connection to an IT-BSC derived emphasises the evaluation of the BYOD integration in relation to specific business objectives, with a focus on adaptability and response time. The correct alignment of the BYOD integration with COBIT processes and tools is critical to meeting business objectives and should be considered in detail to ensure effective implementation.

4.2.6 Design to Validate the Sub-Hypothesis 2 (H2)

The integration of BYOD leads to a stronger alignment between IT and business objectives within the IT-BSC. The question regarding the impact of BYOD integration on end-user satisfaction with IT services (Table 4.40) is particularly important to shed light on sub-hypothesis H2 and to understand the relationship with COBIT and IT-BSC.

Table 4.40 Influence of BYOD Integration on End-User Satisfaction

Response	Effect on End-User Satisfaction
Significantly improved	The integration of BYOD has led to a substantial improvement in end-user satisfaction with IT services.
Slightly improved	There is a slight improvement in end-user satisfaction with IT services due to BYOD integration.
Unchanged	End-user satisfaction with IT services has remained unchanged following BYOD integration.
Slightly deteriorated	There is a slight decline in end-user satisfaction with IT services after BYOD integration.
Significantly deteriorated	BYOD integration has significantly impacted end-user satisfaction with IT services negatively.

1. **Significantly improved**: This is a strong indicator that BYOD integration has increased the effectiveness of IT services, particularly with regard to COBIT processes such as DSS01 (Manage Operations) and DSS05 (Manage Security Services). Aligning BYOD with these processes serves as a model for other areas.
2. **Slightly improved**: This answer also supports H2, but suggests that improvements are needed in other areas. Processes such as APO05 (Manage Portfolio) play a role here.
3. **Unchanged**: This suggests that the BYOD integration has had no significant impact. A review of the integration with COBIT processes such as APO07 (Manage Human Resources) is necessary.
4. **Slightly Deteriorated**: This indicates a warning that certain aspects of the BYOD integration are not optimal. A detailed analysis of the COBIT processes such as APO10 (Manage Suppliers) indicates problems.
5. **Significantly Deteriorated**: This response indicates a serious deficiency in the BYOD integration that requires immediate review of processes such as BAI01 (Manage Programmes and Projects).

The connection to an IT-BSC derived from the ITIL framework emphasises the evaluation of the BYOD integration in terms of the specific satisfaction of the end users. This is done by adjusting KPIs in the IT-BSC system that are closely linked to the relevant COBIT processes. Through this investigation and analysis, a deeper understanding of the impact of BYOD integration on end-user satisfaction is achieved in the context of the COBIT framework. It enables targeted improvement and optimisation to achieve the goals of effectiveness within the IT organisation.

The investigation of which IT services have become more effective through BYOD integration contributes directly to the investigation of the sub-hypotheses H2 and establishes a link to the effective control of IT processes in line with COBIT best practices.

1. **Helpdesk Support**: The effectiveness of this service can be linked to COBIT processes such as DSS02 (Service Request and Incident Management). An increase in effectiveness indicates improved response time and customer care.
2. **Network access**: This is associated with processes such as DSS03 (Manage Problems) and APO09 (Manage Service Agreements). An increase in effectiveness indicates improved accessibility and reliability of the network.
3. **Software Deployment**: This is linked to processes such as BAI07 (Manage Change) and APO03 (Manage Enterprise Architecture). More effective software deployment can improve the alignment of IT with business strategy.

4. **Data Access and Security**: The relationship with processes such as DSS05 (Manage Security Services) is obvious. Improving this area emphasises the importance of data security across the enterprise.
5. **Other**: This allows the investigation of other services that may be relevant and may be tailored to COBIT processes not covered in the above services.

Connecting these services to an inferred IT-BSC requires the identification and integration of KPIs that measure the effectiveness of these services in the context of BYOD integration and COBIT processes (Table 4.41). The results of this research are used to further refine the alignment of IT strategy to support both business objectives and the effectiveness and efficiency of IT services within the COBIT framework.

Table 4.41 IT Services Made More Effective Through BYOD Integration

Response	Effective IT Services Through BYOD
Helpdesk Support	The integration of BYOD has enhanced the effectiveness of helpdesk support services for end-users.
Network Access	BYOD integration has improved the efficiency and accessibility of network access services.
Software Deployment	There is a positive impact on the deployment of software to devices due to BYOD integration.
Data Access and Security	BYOD integration has contributed to better data access and security measures for end-users.
Others	Other IT services have become more effective through the integration of BYOD, as indicated by respondents.

The question of how BYOD integration has affected response times to IT requests is a key indicator of the efficiency and effectiveness of IT services and is directly related to sub-hypotheses H1 and H2.

1. **Significantly reduced/slightly reduced**: A reduction in response time is an indicator that IT organisations have become more efficient as a result of BYOD integration. This is associated with COBIT processes such as DSS02 (Service Request and Incident Management), which aim to ensure the efficient processing of IT requests.
2. **Unchanged**: An unchanged response time indicates that BYOD integration has no significant impact on performance, neither positive nor negative.

3. **Slightly increased/significantly increased**: An increase in response time indicates that BYOD integration brings additional challenges that could negatively impact efficiency. This could be the subject of further research to identify the causes.

In terms of linking to an IT-derived BSC, response time can be considered as a KPI in the 'Internal Business Processes' perspective. By measuring and analysing response time (Table 4.42), IT organisations can better understand how BYOD integration affects their ability to respond to IT requests in a timely and effective manner. This question thus provides valuable insights into the efficiency and effectiveness of BYOD integration and helps to identify areas for improvement in order to optimise IT performance in line with the COBIT frameworks.

Table 4.42 Impact of BYOD Integration on IT Request Response Time

Response	BYOD Impact on Response Time
Significantly shortened	The integration of BYOD has led to a significant reduction in IT request response time.
Slightly shortened	A minor reduction in IT request response time is observed due to BYOD integration.
Unchanged	There is no significant change in IT request response time after the integration of BYOD.
Slightly lengthened	IT request response time has slightly increased following BYOD integration.
Significantly lengthened	The integration of BYOD has resulted in a substantial increase in IT request response time.

The question regarding the impact of BYOD on the alignment of IT and business objectives is closely linked to sub-hypothesis H3, which concerns strategic alignment within the organisation.

1. **Significantly contributed/slightly contributed**: Positive responses in these categories suggest that BYOD contributes to improving alignment between IT and business objectives. In terms of COBIT2019, this is consistent with processes such as APO02 (Manage Strategy) and APO11 (Manage Quality), which aim to integrate business and IT strategies.
2. **Neutral**: A neutral response indicates that BYOD adoption has had no noticeable effect on IT business alignment.

3. **Slightly impeded/significantly impeded**: Negative responses in these categories indicate potential challenges or problems that have arisen as a result of BYOD adoption and that require further investigation and resolution.

From an IT-BSC perspective, this question is most relevant in the 'Strategic Alignment' or 'Business Value' dimension. The answers to this question (Table 4.43) provide important insights into how BYOD integration has helped or hindered the organisation to adapt to changing business requirements and how it promotes the integration of IT and business strategies. These insights are used to identify specific actions or adjustments that will enable the organisation to better leverage the potential of BYOD integration and improve strategic alignment in line with the COBIT framework.

Table 4.43 BYOD Contribution to the IT and Business Goals Alignment

Response	BYOD Impact on Alignment
Significantly contributed	The integration of BYOD has played a significant role in aligning IT and business goals.
Slightly contributed	BYOD integration has contributed to some extent in aligning IT and business goals.
Neutral	There is no notable impact on the alignment of IT and business goals after BYOD integration.
Slightly hindered	Some hindrance in the alignment of IT and business goals is observed due to BYOD integration.
Significantly hindered	The integration of BYOD has significantly hindered the alignment of IT and business goals.

The question of the role of BYOD in the prioritisation of IT projects and initiatives is central to understanding how BYOD is integrated into IT strategic planning and alignment. This particularly affects sub-hypotheses H1 and H3, which deal with efficiency and strategic alignment.

1. **Central role/important role**: If BYOD plays a central or important role, this indicates that it actively contributes to aligning IT projects with business objectives. In the COBIT context, this is associated with processes such as BAI01 (Manage Programmes and Projects) and APO05 (Manage Portfolio).
2. **Complementary role**: A complementary role of BYOD indicates a supporting contribution, but not a leading influence in the prioritisation of projects.

3. **Minimal role/No role**: This answer indicates a lack of integration of BYOD in the decision-making process and calls for a critical review of the strategy.

In the IT-BSC, this question is particularly relevant for the 'strategic alignment' and possibly the 'efficiency' of the IT functions. The Table 4.44 serves as a starting point for a more detailed analysis of how BYOD is integrated into planning and prioritisation and how it can affect the efficiency and strategic alignment of the IT organisation within the COBIT framework. By exploring this question, organisations can better understand the role of BYOD in their prioritisation process and identify possible strengths or weaknesses in their current strategy. This, in turn, can help them to use BYOD more effectively to align IT projects and initiatives and thus add value to the business.

Table 4.44 Role of BYOD in Prioritizing IT Projects

Response	Role of BYOD in IT Prioritization
Central role	BYOD plays a central and critical role in prioritizing IT projects and initiatives.
Important role	BYOD has an important role in influencing the prioritization of IT projects and initiatives.
Supplementary role	BYOD plays a supplementary role in IT project and initiative prioritization.
Minimal role	The role of BYOD in prioritizing IT projects and initiatives is minimal.
No role	BYOD does not have any role in the prioritization of IT projects and initiatives.

The question regarding the impact of BYOD integration on communication between IT and business teams relates to a critical aspect of an organisation's strategic direction and effectiveness. In particular, sub-hypotheses H2 and H3 regarding effectiveness and strategic direction are addressed here. In the IT-BSC, this question can be particularly related to 'customer satisfaction' and 'internal business processes'.

1. **To a very high degree/To a high degree**: These responses indicate that BYOD is acting as a key enabler for improved communication and collaboration between IT and the business. In the COBIT context, this can be correlated with pro-

cesses such as APO08 (Manage Relationships) and BAI03 (Manage Solution Identification and Build).
2. **Neutral/To a small extent/To no extent**: These categories indicate little or no effect of BYOD integration on communication, which requires detailed investigation to identify potential barriers or challenges.

The detailed analysis of this question, as presented in Table 4.45, enables the organisation to evaluate the role of BYOD in the communication process and to understand how it promotes or hinders interaction and collaboration between IT and business teams. This in turn can provide important insights for improving strategies and processes in the context of the COBIT framework and helps to optimise the integration of BYOD into the communication and business strategy.

Table 4.45 Impact of BYOD Integration on Communication

Response	Extent of BYOD Integration Impact
High extent	BYOD integration has a very high impact on communication between IT and business teams.
To a high extent	BYOD integration has a high impact on communication between IT and business teams.
Neutral	The impact of BYOD integration on communication between IT and business teams is neutral.
To a small extent	BYOD integration has a small impact on communication between IT and business teams.
Not at all	BYOD integration has no impact on communication between IT and business teams.

4.2.7 Design to Validate the Sub-Hypothesis 3 (H3)

Risk assessment and control in the context of BYOD is a critical factor for the success of IT-BSC. The question regarding BYOD integration and its impact on the strategic alignment of IT initiatives with business objectives directly addresses sub-hypothesis H3. It examines how BYOD influences the alignment between IT and business objectives. Within the IT-BSC, this question is linked to the 'strategic alignment' or 'learning and growth' perspective.

1. **Greatly improved/Slightly improved**: These responses indicate strong support for BYOD integration as part of the company's strategic direction. COBIT pro-

cesses such as APO02 (Manage Strategy) and APO05 (Manage Portfolio) are seen here as key instruments for this integration.
2. **No Change**: A No Change result indicates that there are no challenges or barriers preventing the BYOD integration from fully realising its strategic benefits.
3. **Slightly Worsened/Significantly Worsened**: These categories are a sign that BYOD integration is not well aligned with existing business goals and that changes or adjustments are needed.

By analysing this question in detail, as shown in Table 4.46, the company can measure the impact of BYOD on strategic alignment. This can help identify the most effective ways to integrate BYOD while understanding the challenges and risks that could be associated with implementation. Ultimately, this analysis helps to verify the main research hypothesis HM and develop the strategies and tactics necessary to optimally integrate BYOD in the context of COBIT and IT-BSC.

Table 4.46 Influence of BYOD Integration on the Strategic Alignment

Response	Effect of BYOD Integration on Strategic Alignment
Significantly improved	BYOD integration has significantly improved the strategic alignment of IT initiatives with business objectives.
Slightly improved	BYOD integration has slightly improved the strategic alignment of IT initiatives with business objectives.
Unchanged	The strategic alignment of IT initiatives with business objectives is unchanged by BYOD integration.
Slightly deteriorated	BYOD integration has slightly deteriorated the strategic alignment of IT initiatives with business objectives.
Significantly deteriorated	BYOD integration has significantly deteriorated the strategic alignment of IT initiatives with business objectives.

This specific question in Table 4.47 addresses several aspects of the main research hypothesis, including efficiency, effectiveness, and strategic alignment. It serves to understand which business goals are specifically supported by the integration of BYOD.

Table 4.47 Business Goals Supported by BYOD Integration

Response	Business Goals Supported by BYOD Integration
Increased employee productivity	BYOD integration supports the business goal of increasing employee productivity.
More flexible work style	BYOD integration supports the business goal of enabling a more flexible work style for employees.
Cost reduction	BYOD integration supports the business goal of reducing operational costs.
Expanded customer/client service	BYOD integration supports the business goal of enhancing customer or client service.
Other	BYOD integration supports other business goals not listed above.

1. **Increased employee productivity**: This correlates directly with the efficiency of the IT organisation, as a more productive workforce often leads to better results. The link to COBIT can be established via the BAI07 (Manage Change) process.
2. **More flexible working style**: This goal is closely related to the strategic direction and adaptation to changes in the business environment, as mentioned in H3. Processes such as APO03 (Manage Enterprise Architecture) and APO04 (Manage Innovation) are relevant here.
3. **Cost reduction**: This addresses sub-hypothesis H1 directly, which relates to efficiency and the reduction of IT costs. The selection of the appropriate COBIT process is APO06 (Manage Budget and Costs).
4. **Enhanced customer/client service**: This goal is aligned with effectiveness as it satisfies the end users' requirements. The link to COBIT is established through the process DSS01 (Manage Operations).
5. **Others**: This option allows the investigation of aspects that may not have been foreseen and could provide additional insights into the implementation and adaptation of BYOD.

The connection to an IT-BSC derived could span multiple perspectives, including 'Customer Focus', 'Internal Business Processes' and 'Learning and Growth'. Analysing this question and connecting it to the Table 4.47 allows the specific business goals supported by BYOD to be identified and how this integration can be implemented within the COBIT framework and IT-BSC. This contributes significantly to the testing and refinement of the research hypotheses by showing the specific ways in which BYOD supports and improves business goals.

The question of the frequency of risk assessments in the context of BYOD plays a crucial role in assessing the efficiency and effectiveness of the integration of BYOD into the IT BSC system.

1. **Efficiency (H1):** The regularity of risk assessment indicates proactive monitoring of IT resources and rapid response to potential risks. This will link to COBIT processes such as APO12 (Manage Risk) and DSS05 (Manage Security Services).
2. **Effectiveness (H2)**: The effectiveness of the risk management processes related to BYOD improves the security and reliability of IT systems, which in turn meets the requirements of the end users. The relevant COBIT process is EDM03 (Ensure Risk Optimisation).
3. **Strategic alignment (H3)**: Regular risk assessment ensures that the IT organisation remains flexible and can respond to changes in the business environment. This supports the strategic alignment between business and IT objectives. The COBIT process APO05 (Manage Portfolio) is relevant here.

The question supports the IT-BSC in the perspectives of 'internal business processes' and 'risk management'. It helps to get a clearer picture of risk appetite and control over BYOD integration. Analysing this question, in conjunction with the Table 4.48, not only helps to understand how BYOD risks are managed within the organisation, but also how these risk management practices are integrated within the COBIT framework and the IT BSC. It is essential to understand the overall impact of BYOD integration on the IT organisation and to test the main research hypothesis.

This question is directed at the sub-hypotheses on effectiveness (H2) and also provides insights into efficiency (H1) and strategic alignment (H3).

1. Effectiveness **(H2)**: Assessing the effectiveness of risk control activities associated with BYOD provides insight into how well the IT organisation is controlling its risks in line with COBIT best practices. This is associated with COBIT processes such as EDM03 (Ensure Risk Optimisation) and APO12 (Manage Risk).
2. **Efficiency (H1):** A high level of effectiveness of risk control measures could also indicate an efficient use of IT resources by minimising potential losses. The DSS05 (Manage Security Services) process is relevant here.
3. **Strategic Alignment (H3):** The ability to manage risks effectively is also critical to the strategic direction of the IT organisation, as it influences the organisation's

Table 4.48 Frequency of Risk Assessments Related to BYOD

Response	Frequency of Risk Assessments Related to BYOD
Weekly	Risk assessments related to BYOD are conducted on a weekly basis.
Monthly	Risk assessments related to BYOD are conducted on a monthly basis.
Quarterly	Risk assessments related to BYOD are conducted on a quarterly basis.
Semi-annually	Risk assessments related to BYOD are conducted semi-annually (twice a year).
Annually or less often	Risk assessments related to BYOD are conducted annually or less frequently.

ability to respond to changes in the business environment. The APO05 (Manage Portfolio) process thus applies here.

This question can also be linked to the IT-BSC perspectives 'Internal Business Process' and 'Risk Management'. It helps to understand how effective the control measures are in managing risks related to BYOD integration. The detailed analysis of the answers to this question in conjunction with the Table 4.49 provides a deeper insight into the effectiveness of BYOD risk control measures. This directly contributes to the verification of the research hypothesis and helps to understand

Table 4.49 Effectiveness of Current Risk Control Measures in Connection with BYOD

Response	Effectiveness of Current Risk Control Measures in Connection with BYOD
Very effective	The current risk control measures in connection with BYOD are highly effective in mitigating risks.
Effective	The current risk control measures in connection with BYOD are effective in mitigating risks.
Neutral	The current risk control measures in connection with BYOD have a neutral impact on risk mitigation.
Slightly effective	The current risk control measures in connection with BYOD are somewhat effective in mitigating risks.
Not effective at all	The current risk control measures in connection with BYOD are not effective in mitigating risks.

the overall impact of BYOD integration on the IT organisation within the COBIT framework and the IT-BSC.

This specific question in Table 4.50 examines how the company prioritises the risk assessment in relation to BYOD within its IT BSC. Placing this question in the context of the research requires a thorough analysis:

Table 4.50 Importance of Risk Assessment in Connection with BYOD in the IT-BSC

Response	Importance of Risk Assessment in Connection with BYOD in the IT Balanced Scorecard
Very high importance	Risk assessment in connection with BYOD is of utmost importance in the IT Balanced Scorecard.
High importance	Risk assessment in connection with BYOD is highly important in the IT Balanced Scorecard.
Neutral	Risk assessment in connection with BYOD has a neutral level of importance in the IT Balanced Scorecard.
Low importance	Risk assessment in connection with BYOD is of relatively low importance in the IT Balanced Scorecard.
No importance	Risk assessment in connection with BYOD is not important at all in the IT Balanced Scorecard.

1. **Efficiency (H1):** The importance of risk assessment indicates a careful use of IT resources. The IT organisation focuses on risk management to avoid unexpected costs or loss of resources. This correlates with the COBIT process APO12 (Manage Risk).
2. **Effectiveness (H2):** A high importance of risk assessment indicates that the IT organisation is proactively working to identify and mitigate risks in order to make its processes and services more effective. The APO13 (Manage Security) process is relevant here.
3. **Strategic alignment (H3):** The risk assessment in the IT-BSC also indicates that the company regards the risks associated with BYOD as a strategic factor. The COBIT process APO05 (Manage Portfolio) is a suitable indicator for strategic alignment.

Assessing the importance of risk assessment in relation to BYOD can be directly linked to the internal business process perspective of the IT-BSC, especially if the company considers risk management to be an important part of its performance indicators. Investigating this question contributes significantly to answering the research question by revealing how the company prioritises risk assessment in the context of BYOD within its IT-BSC. Analysing the responses, along the structure shown in Table 4.50, allows a detailed insight into the role of risk assessment in the IT organisation's performance measurement and management, in line with the COBIT processes and IT BSC.

4.3 Analysis of the Empirical Survey

For the statistical analysis of the survey, it was necessary to implement the answers according to a defined scheme. This coding of the items was already planned when the questionnaire was created and was carried out automatically by the web-based survey tool. After the survey was completed, the results could be exported to a file. The actual further processing of the collected data was carried out using the statistical program SPSS developed at Stanford University (cf. Raab-Steiner and Benesch, 2010, pp. 64 f.). In addition to determining absolute and relative frequency distributions, further descriptive statistical methods are used. To obtain insights into the average values of relevant statements, arithmetic means and medians are calculated.

To identify dependencies between the measured variables, the probability of this relationship is determined using Pearson's correlation coefficient. This correlation coefficient is a measure of the strength of a linear relationship and is in the range of ± 1. If the coefficient is exactly plus or minus one, all points lie on a straight line and the factors would be fully dependent. This can be quantitatively evaluated as the confirmation of a hypothesis. If the coefficient is virtually zero, it is referred to as uncorrelated. Uncorrelated only means that there is no linear relationship, which does not exclude the possibility of other relationships. From a purely quantitative point of view, this would refute a hypothesis. In line with HAIDER, the parameters

Table 4.51 Correlation of Measurement Variables

Coefficient r	Interpretation
0 or close to 0	No relationship between the variables
> 0 to 0.2	Very low/weak correlation
> 0.2 to 0.5	Moderate correlation
> 0.5 to 0.7	High/strong correlation
> 0.7 to 0.9	Very high/very strong correlation
> 0.9 to 1.0	Extremely high correlation to functional relationship

listed in Table 4.51 should apply here (cf. Haider, 2000, pp. 44 f.). In the context of the evaluation, the determination of the correlation is considered in particular in the context of the characteristic 'compliance implementation'. This should provide information on the use and necessity of COBIT structures in the control of BYOD measures, which are integrated into a holistic management system of an IT-BSC. This allows conclusions to be drawn about the research hypotheses that have been formulated.

In order to be able to exclude the possibility that differences between measured variables have occurred only by chance, i.e. by the selection of the sample or the returns, their significance (p-value) is calculated. If there is a significance, it is statistically concluded that there is actually a relevant difference between the respondents. According to Fischer, the significance level of $\alpha = 5\%$ ($p < 0.05$) is used for this evaluation (cf. Raab-Steiner and Benesch, 2010, pp. 111 f).

In order to test the research hypotheses regarding the efficiency, effectiveness and strategic orientation of IT organisations in the context of the COBIT framework for their general validity, several levels of analysis were carried out. First, a comprehensive investigation was conducted to determine whether there were significant relationships between specific company characteristics and the responses received. Of particular interest were the company's size, the industry in which it operated, and the role of the respondents within the company (e.g., their position, length of service, and decision-making authority with regard to IT projects). This helped to better understand the context in which IT strategies were being implemented and to assess the generalisability of the research findings. Second, statistical analyses were conducted to identify correlations between the maturity levels of IT organisations and various aspects of their IT strategies, including the implementation of BYOD, the use of home offices and the application of the COBIT framework. The aim was to investigate whether companies with advanced maturity levels also tended to pursue more complex or effective IT strategies. Thirdly, dependencies and indices were examined to determine whether companies with higher IT maturity levels also tended to implement certain IT BSC structures. This could indicate a more mature approach to performance measurement and management, which in turn could have influenced the efficiency and effectiveness of the IT organisation. Finally, each of these points was developed qualitatively to contextualise the statistical results and to shed light on possible cause-and-effect relationships or other interpretative aspects. The qualitative analysis served as an additional method to validate the results and develop a more comprehensive understanding of the topic. Overall, this multi-level, mixed approach allowed for an in-depth assessment of the factors influencing the effectiveness of BYOD strategies in the context of COBIT, and contributed to the robustness and relevance of the research results.

In the present study, a total of 5,000 companies were contacted to complete a questionnaire on the topic of integrating BYOD, taking into account the IT-BSC and the COBIT framework. With a gross response rate of 1,091 completed questionnaires, this study proves to be the most extensive in this particular field of research that the author is aware of to date. Particularly noteworthy is the high participation rate of almost 22%, which indicates that the topic is of considerable interest to companies. This high figure is certainly partly due to the careful selection of the sample, which minimised wastage. When considering the net response rate, 1023 participants actually took part in the survey. However, 68 participants did not complete the questionnaire in full and were therefore not included in the final analysis. Interestingly, the dropout rate was particularly high in the section concerning the specific evaluation of research hypothesis 1 (page 6 of the questionnaire), where it was almost 30%. This could indicate that the questions in this area were possibly complex or misleading. An on-site interviewer could probably have helped to clarify any comprehension problems here. Furthermore, the average response time for the questionnaire was 10 minutes and 23 seconds. This result confirms the previous assessment from the pre-test, according to which the questionnaire was logically structured and easy for the participants to understand. Finally, the high participation rate and the depth of the collected data provide a solid foundation for further analysis and interpretation of the research results, although the need for future improvements, particularly in the area of the questions to evaluate the hypotheses, has also become clear.

4.3.1 Classification of Survey Participants

First, the survey participants were classified according to the identified metrics of industry, number of employees, functional profile, decision-making authority, and basic experience in COBIT and home office/BYOD relevance. The question regarding the industry of the participating companies showed the distribution shown in Fig. 4.1. With 22% (225 in absolute terms), the group from the 'Information and communication' sector represented the largest group of respondents. Contrary to the assumption often expressed in the literature, the 'Manufacturing' sector only comes in second place with 7.6% (78 in absolute terms), followed by 'Professional, scientific and technical activities' with almost 6.5% (66 in absolute terms) and 'Wholesale and retail trade' and 'Financial and insurance activities' with 5.9% each (60 in absolute terms). The remaining 15 sectors according to the ISIC scheme account for between 5% (51 in absolute terms) and 1.8% (18 in absolute terms) of the survey participants. No significant frequency distribution could be determined for the other sectors surveyed. This is an indication of the high quality of the survey results, since not only IT-related sectors responded. The data collected provides a solid foundation for analysing the effects of integrating BYOD using COBIT on the IT-BSC in companies. Particularly interesting is the high level of participation from companies in the 'Information and communication' sector, which highlights the relevance of IT-related strategies in this sector. The comparatively low participation of the manufacturing sector indicates different priorities in IT governance. These sector-specific differences are relevant for the adaptation of COBIT guidelines for the integration of BYOD into the IT-BSC. Furthermore, this is seen as a confirmation of the main research hypothesis MH that the research topic is relevant for all organisations today.

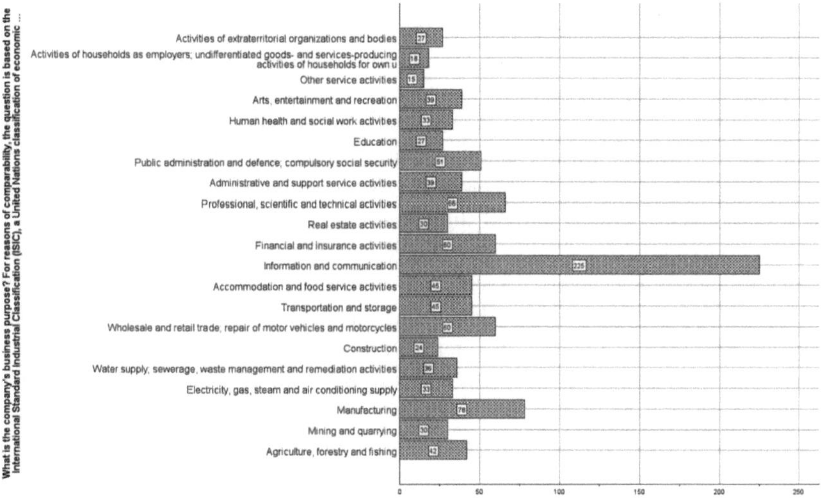

Fig. 4.1 Industry distribution according to ISIC classification

There are some contradictory data from the variables on the legal form of the respondent's company and the number of employees in the company. For example, 42.2% (432 in absolute terms) state that they work in a sole proprietorship. By contrast, only 35.5% (363 in absolute terms) work in a corporation such as a GmbH or AG, and 18.5% (189 in absolute terms) work in a partnership such as a KG or general partnership. In contrast, only 1.5% (15 in absolute terms) responded that the number of employees was between 1 and 10. The vast majority, 44.9% (459 in absolute terms), work in companies with between 51 and 200 employees, and 20.8% (213 in absolute terms) work in companies with between 11 and 50 employees. Companies with 250-1000 employees account for 17.3% (177 in absolute terms), while companies with over 1000 employees account for 15.5% (159 in absolute terms) of the participants. Whether this discrepancy is due to a misunderstanding in the design of the question cannot be clarified without personal interviews. However, this assumption was confirmed by the statements on the internationality of the participating companies, with 44.9% (459 in absolute terms) stating that they have branches in several countries and 42.8% (438 in absolute terms) that they trade in goods or services internationally. Only 12.3% (126 in absolute terms) operate purely nationally. The heterogeneity of company sizes and forms, which emerges from the survey data, shows that a flexible application of COBIT guidelines is necessary to effectively integrate BYOD strategies. In particular, for smaller companies, which make up a high proportion of the survey, the IT-BSC must be adapted to their specific needs and capacities. This is crucial to improve the efficiency and effectiveness of IT structures in these companies.

An important aspect for the further survey is the classification of the respondents according to their position and operational affiliation in the company, as well as their decision-making authority for IT projects. As the author expected, the vast majority of participants in the empirical study are in a position that allows them a good strategic overview of decisions in their respective companies. 30.5% (312 in absolute terms) are department heads, 23.8% (243 in absolute terms) are CEOs/managing directors and 22.8% (231 in absolute terms) are CTOs/CIOs. The remaining participants are 13.2% (135 in absolute terms) project managers, 7.3% (75 in absolute terms) other managers and only 1.8% (18 in absolute terms) normal employees. All this speaks for the high quality of the survey results in terms of evaluating and analysing strategic decisions. This view is strengthened by the fact that the participants have been in their current job positions for a long time. Thus, 37.8% (387 in absolute terms) have been in this position for 7 to 10 years, 29.6% (303 in absolute terms) have held the position for 4 to 6 years, and 26.4% (270 in absolute terms) have been in their current role for over 10 years. Only 4.7% (48 in absolute terms) stated that they had been in their current role for between one and three years, and just 1.5% (15 in absolute terms) had been in the role for less than a year. The strategic dimension of the responses is further supported by the decision-making authority with regard to IT decisions. Thus, 43.4% (444 in absolute terms) state that they are primarily responsible for such decisions. 41.3% (423 in absolute terms) are involved in an advisory capacity and 12.5% (129 in absolute terms) are still partially involved. Only 2.6% (27 in absolute terms) state that they have no authority whatsoever with regard to IT direction in the company. The high level of participation by decision-makers in the survey, particularly CEOs and CTOs/CIOs, highlights the strategic importance of IT governance. Their decision-making authority with regard to IT projects and the length of time they have been in their current positions suggest that the survey results offer a deep insight into the practical challenges and potential of integrating BYOD strategies into IT BSC using COBIT.

The Fig. 4.2 shows that companies that regularly use an IT-BSC have generally implemented longer-standing and more stable BYOD initiatives. With a median value of around 3.5, these organisations indicate a medium-term and consistent implementation of BYOD, which suggests that the IT BSC is used effectively as a tool to measure and evaluate BYOD deployment. Organisations that use the IT BSC infrequently show a similar median value of just under 4, indicating that even occasional use indicates some consistency in BYOD implementation, albeit with less rigour and consistency than regular use. In the group of companies that do not use an IT-BSC, the median for the duration of BYOD is significantly lower, at around 2. This suggests that without the structural advantages of an IT-BSC, the implementation of BYOD tends to be short-term and less consistent. The greater dispersion in this group indicates a greater variance in implementation and possibly a lack of strategic direction. The greatest dispersion is seen in companies that cannot provide any clear information on the use of the IT BSC, with a median value of around 4. This suggests that these companies are pursuing very different approaches

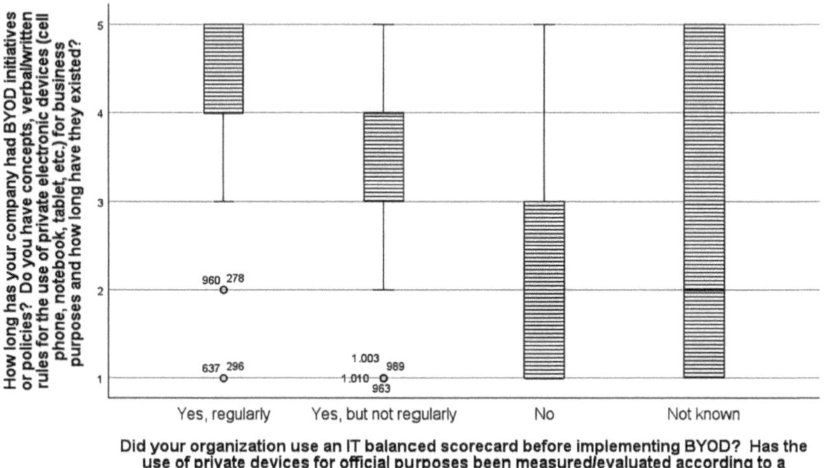

Fig. 4.2 Insufficient BYOD control through IT-BSC

to implementing BYOD, which could be heavily dependent on individual company factors rather than on the systematic use of the IT BSC.

The high level of experience of the survey participants with BYOD initiatives can be seen from the duration of the implementation of corresponding initiatives. 44.3 (453 in absolute terms) of the participants stated that corresponding initiatives have been in place for between four and six years, and for 21.4% (219 in absolute terms) it has been more than six years. For 20.2% (207 in absolute terms), it is still one to three years, for 6.2% (63 in absolute terms) less than a year, whereas 7.9% (81 in absolute terms) state that they have not introduced any BYOD initiatives. The use and control of an IT-BSC in the company is seen as an initial indicator of adequate control of the BYOD initiative. In this context, 45.7% (468 in absolute terms) state that they use an IT BSC regularly and 43.1% (441 in absolute terms) that they check the IT BSC irregularly. A cumulative total of 11.1% (114 in absolute terms) state that they do not use an IT BSC or do not know whether they use one. When considering the two parameters, it is striking that a Pearson correlation is only found at $r = 0.463$, i.e. a medium correlation. Despite the high degree of implementation of an IT BSC in the participating companies, it is apparently only used to a limited extent for controlling the equally intensively used BYOD initiatives. This is an initial validation for the main research hypothesis MH.

4.3.2 Classification According to COBIT Experience

The analysis of the survey results on the use and knowledge of COBIT 2019 in companies provides valuable insights with regard to the research hypothesis that the integration of BYOD into the IT-BSC system using COBIT optimises the efficiency, effectiveness and strategic alignment of IT structures in companies. The following is intended to determine the level of maturity in dealing with and knowledge of COBIT 2019, the international best practice for IT governance. For example, 42.8% (438 in absolute terms) state that they are well informed about COBIT and a further 41.1% (420 in absolute terms) are very well informed. As many as 10% (102 in absolute terms) have basic knowledge and only 6.1% in total (63 in absolute terms) have little or no knowledge of COBIT. This is consistent with the information on the use and application of COBIT in the respective companies of the participants. For 43.7% (447 in absolute terms), COBIT is used as a supplement to other frameworks, and for a further 35.2% (360 in absolute terms), COBIT is the primary framework for IT governance, which underlines its central role in the IT strategy of many organisations. This widespread use of COBIT is an indicator of its effectiveness in managing and monitoring IT processes and policies, particularly in the context of BYOD strategies. In 12.9% (132 in absolute terms) of cases, COBIT is used in individual projects or departments. It is not used in just 5.6% (57 in absolute terms), while 2.6% (27 in absolute terms) state that they are aware of the framework but do not actively use it. This is supported by the information on training and education in the area of COBIT. Thus, 52.5% (437 in absolute terms) have received several training courses on COBIT and a further 36.7% (375 in absolute terms) have received training on the framework. Of the remaining participants, 7.9% (81 in absolute terms) are planning training in the area. Only 2.9% (30 in absolute terms) stated that they have not yet attended a seminar and have no plans to do so. This is particularly relevant for the implementation of BYOD, since a sound knowledge of COBIT guidelines and practices is crucial for the effective integration of BYOD into the IT strategy.

When asked about the influence of COBIT 2019 on IT decisions in the company, a majority of 48.1% (492 in absolute terms) stated that this best practice framework has a very high influence on IT decisions. In addition, a further 40.8% (417 in absolute terms) stated that COBIT has a high influence on such decisions. Only 6.2% (63 in absolute terms) see no influence on information technology. Nevertheless, 5% (51 in absolute terms) still state that COBIT has a minor or partial influence. It is interesting to note that 51.3% (525 in absolute terms) state that COBIT 2019 is significantly more relevant than earlier versions of COBIT (e.g. COBIT 5 or COBIT 4.1). A further 34.5% (354 in absolute terms) consider COBIT to be even more relevant than earlier versions. In contrast, 7% (72 in absolute terms) consider the relevance to be unchanged. For 6.2% (63 in absolute terms), COBIT is no more relevant than before, and only 0.9% (9 in absolute terms) state that this framework is not relevant at all. This indicates a verification of research hypothesis MH. This is also supported by the strong correlation of $r = 0.618$ between COBIT implementation and relevance of the current version, and supports the assumption that COBIT 2019 plays a crucial role in optimising IT structures.

The Fig. 4.3 illustrates the influence of COBIT 2019 on IT decisions in organisations in relation to the perceived relevance of this version compared to previous versions such as COBIT 5. It is noticeable that the distribution of the data points is scattered across the entire spectrum, indicating a wide variance in the perception and use of COBIT 2019. The low relevance category (value 1 on the X-axis) contains data points that indicate a low to moderate influence on IT decisions (values 1 to 3 on the Y-axis). This suggests that companies that consider COBIT 2019 to be less relevant also incorporate this framework less into their IT decision-making processes. For the higher relevance values (values 4 and 5 on the X-axis), the data points tend to show a stronger alignment with COBIT 2019 in IT decisions, indicating that companies that consider the new version to be relevant also integrate it more strongly into their strategic IT decisions. This confirms the assumption that the perceived relevance of COBIT 2019 correlates directly with its influence on IT governance and strategy. However, the dispersion of the data points shows that even among those who consider COBIT 2019 to be relevant, the degree of integration into IT decisions varies, indicating different implementation strategies and possibly different needs and priorities within companies. This discrepancy could be due to factors such as different organisation sizes, industry requirements or the maturity level of IT governance structures.

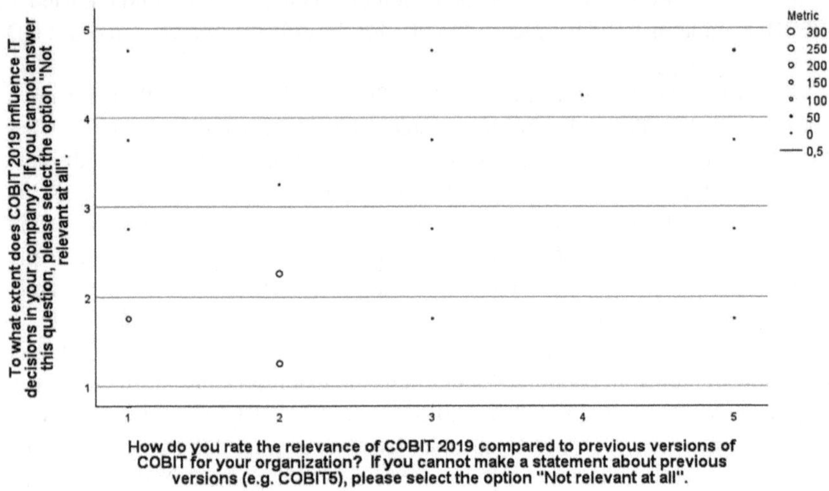

Fig. 4.3 COBIT relevance for IT decisions

Furthermore, the survey also looked at the extent to which there were challenges in implementing the current version of COBIT in the company. A large majority of 40.8% (417 in absolute terms) stated that there were few challenges and that the implementation went according to plan. Furthermore, 37% (378 in absolute terms) faced some challenges during implementation, but were able to overcome them. This indicates a high level of maturity in IT strategy and the necessary processes. Only 11.4% (117 in absolute terms) spoke of major challenges that had an impact on implementation. Only 1.8% (18 in absolute terms) have refrained from implementing it so far because of feared obstacles and 9.1% (93 in absolute terms) are unable to make a statement. Overall, the survey results confirm research hypothesis MH that integrating BYOD into the IT-BSC system using COBIT improves the efficiency, effectiveness and strategic alignment of IT structures in organisations. The widespread knowledge and application of COBIT 2019, the high level of participation in relevant training and education, and the significant influence of the framework on IT decisions show that COBIT is an effective tool for integrating and managing BYOD strategies.

4.3.3 Classification According to BYOD Experience

The evaluation of the data on the use of home offices and BYOD during the COVID 19 pandemic provides revealing insights with regard to the research hypothesis. It shows that the integration of BYOD into the IT-BSC system using COBIT plays a crucial role in optimising IT structures in companies. In the wake of the COVID-19 pandemic, the use of home offices and thus the use of BYOD has increased massively. Therefore, it was investigated to what extent home offices have already been institutionalised and what the associated prospects for the future are. Even before the pandemic, 56.3% (576 in absolute terms) stated that they had used some form of BYOD in their home office once a week, and for a further 33.7% (345 in absolute terms) this was even the case several times a week. For 6.2% (63 in absolute terms), working from home only occurred once a month, whereas 2.6% (27 in absolute terms) stated that they worked with their own devices every day. Only 1.2% (12 in absolute terms) could not report any private use. The increase in home office in the wake of the COVID-19 pandemic is confirmed by the statement that 69.2% (708 in absolute terms) report having used it more. For 27% (276 in absolute terms), there has even been a significant increase in BYOD use. For 3.5% (36 in absolute terms), there was no change, and 0.3% (3 in absolute terms) stated that use had decreased. The data suggests that there was already significant use of BYOD in the home office before the pandemic, which indicates a certain familiarity and acceptance of this way of working in the corporate landscape. The significant increase in BYOD use during the pandemic, with 69.2% of respondents reporting increased use, illustrates the flexibility and adaptability of companies to changing working conditions. This adaptability is a key element for the strategic alignment and effectiveness of IT structures.

The statements on the change in productivity due to the increase in BYOD and home office use are also interesting when evaluating the measures. The vast majority (75.7%, 774 in absolute terms) of the survey participants stated that productivity had generally increased and a further 13.2% (135 in absolute terms) even spoke of a significant increase in productivity. For 10.3% (105 in absolute terms), there have been no changes, whereas 0.9% (9 in absolute terms) speak of a slight to significant reduction. These statements are supported by the information on how collaboration has been affected by the increased use of BYOD during the pandemic. Despite greater physical distance, 60.4% (618 in absolute terms) reported a slight improvement in collaboration, and a further 27.3% (279 in absolute terms) reported a significant improvement. For 6.2% (63 in absolute terms), there are no changes, while 5.9% (60 in absolute terms) and 0.3% (3 in absolute terms) expect a slight to significant deterioration. Problems with remote working using BYOD arose in 15.8% (162 in absolute terms) due to technical obstacles, 40.8% (417 in absolute terms) due to a lack of separation between private and professional life, 42.5% (435 in absolute terms) cited a lack of communication with colleagues, and 31.7% (324 in absolute terms) mentioned distractions at home. Only 4.4% (43 in absolute terms) stated that there were no challenges or problems at all with the use of BYOD. The observation that 75.7% of the survey participants noticed an increase in productivity due to the increased use of BYOD and home office underscores the potential of these technologies for increasing efficiency. This insight is particularly relevant for IT BSC, as it shows that BYOD strategies, properly integrated and managed, can contribute to improved performance. The improvement in collaboration despite physical distance, as reported by 60.4% of respondents, speaks to the effective use of communication technologies and the strategic importance of a well-thought-out IT infrastructure. The challenges posed by remote working, such as technical obstacles and the separation of private and professional life, emphasise the need for a well-thought-out implementation and training in the area of BYOD, which in turn underlines the importance of COBIT in this process.

The Fig. 4.4 illustrates the influence of the BYOD experience on the long-term design of working models, with the shift towards hybrid and flexible working structures being strongly influenced by the experiences gained during the pandemic. Organisations that have experienced greater flexibility in IT and work organisation as a result of BYOD are more likely to maintain or expand this flexibility, which is visible in the adoption of hybrid working models after the pandemic. This tendency can be seen as confirmation of the hypothesis that the introduction of BYOD contributes to lasting change in corporate structures by increasing adaptability and breaking down traditional work patterns. The strong transitions to hybrid models underscore the increasing importance of flexibility and mobility in the modern world of work, which is significantly supported by BYOD. The results suggest that companies that have adopted BYOD have not only responded to the challenges of the pandemic in the short term, but are moving to a more sustainable and adaptable long-term working structure, which can be seen as a strategic adaptation to the new demands of work. These changes are relevant in the context of IT governance and strategy because they suggest that BYOD experiences have influenced strategic direction and IT policy towards greater flexibility and decentralisation.

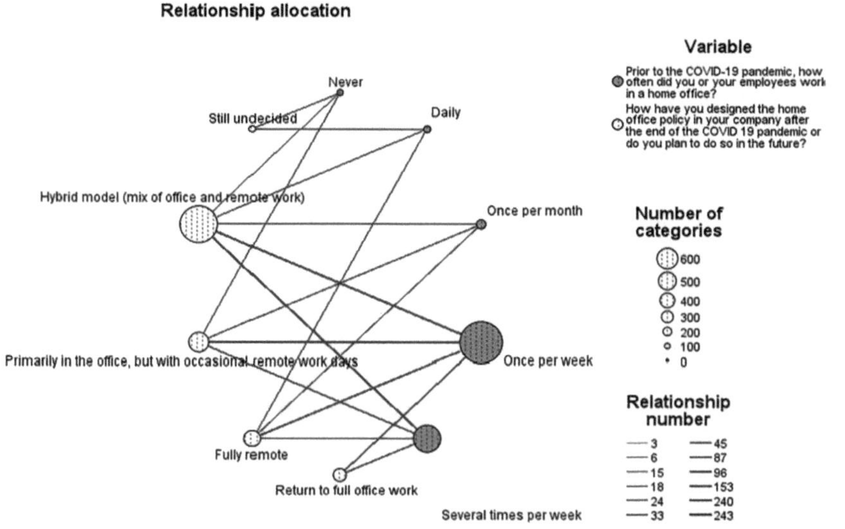

Fig. 4.4 Frequency relationship allocation

The largely positive experiences with home office use should also be relevant for planned future implementation. Therefore, after the pandemic ends, 49.6% (507 in absolute terms) want to continue using a hybrid model, i.e. a combination of physical and home offices. For 22.3% (228 in absolute terms), the plan is to use an office as their primary base with the occasional home office option. By contrast, 15.8% (162 in absolute terms) want to aim for full remote working. In contrast, only 11.7% (120 in absolute terms) plan to return to the office full-time and 0.6% (6 in absolute terms) are still undecided. It is clear from this that companies that have previously offered remote working on a regular basis (at least once a week) want to offer significantly more flexible models in the future. The companies plan to invest in technology and software (25.5%, or 261 in absolute terms), training (44.9%, or 459 in absolute terms), better employee resources (32.6%, or 333 in absolute terms), and IT security measures (only 25.8%, or 264 in absolute terms). The plans for the future, with 49.6% of companies aiming for a hybrid model, show that the experiences from the pandemic will lead to lasting changes in the organisation of work. The investment plans in technology, training and IT security make it clear that companies recognise the importance of a robust IT infrastructure and are willing to invest in it to maximise the benefits of BYOD and home offices.

The biggest learning experiences and positive teachers from the increase in home office and BYOD during the pandemic were, for 51% (522 in absolute terms), that good communication is crucial, for 16. 7% (171 in absolute terms) consider work-life balance to be a crucial factor and 16.4% (150 in absolute terms) see flexibility of work as essential. Therefore, for 55.1% (564 in absolute terms), the use of BYOD and home offices will be a regular, but not dominant, part of the future, and for a further 23.2% (237 in absolute terms), it will be the new norm. For 20.8% (213 in absolute terms), this will be used on a situational basis, and only 0.9% (9 in absolute terms) state that it is unlikely to be used and only under special circumstances. The lessons learned from the pandemic, particularly the importance of communication and work-life balance, show that the optimal integration of BYOD into corporate culture and IT strategy is crucial for success. The fact that for 55.1% of respondents, the use of BYOD and home offices will become a regular part of the way they work indicates that the integration of these technologies into the IT-BSC will be crucial to optimising the efficiency, effectiveness and strategic alignment of IT structures.

These data confirm the research hypothesis HM that incorporating BYOD into the IT BSC system using COBIT will optimise the efficiency, effectiveness and strategic alignment of IT structures in organisations. The pandemic has acted as a catalyst for accelerating the adoption and adaptation of BYOD strategies, providing valuable insights into the future design of corporate IT landscapes.

4.3.4 Evaluation of the Validation of Main Hypothesis (MH)

The use of BYOD (home office) has a variety of effects on performance in the IT department of companies. For example, 46.9% (480 in absolute terms) state that the use of BYOD has slightly increased performance in IT, and for a further 42.8% (438 in absolute terms) there has even been a significant increase. For 9.4% (96 in absolute terms), the use has not resulted in any benefit at all, and for 0.9% (9 in absolute terms), there has been a slight reduction. The optimisation is supplemented by the question of the alignment of the IT strategy with the COBIT framework since the BYOD integration. Here, 37.5% (absolutely 384) indicate a very high level of alignment and 27.6% (absolutely 282) indicate complete alignment with the COBIT framework. For a further 26.1% (267 in absolute terms), there is a partial match, whereas a cumulative 7.8% (90 in absolute terms) indicate little or no match. The moderate correlation (Pearson correlation $r = 0.458$) between the alignment of the IT strategy with the COBIT framework and the increase in efficiency and effectiveness through BYOD is interesting. This suggests that a stronger alignment of the IT strategy with COBIT could further increase the positive effects of BYOD. The correlation confirms the main research hypothesis MH that a closer connection to COBIT enables optimised use of BYOD in the IT strategy.

Figure 4.5 shows the relationship between BYOD integration and the overall performance of the IT department in the context of alignment with the COBIT framework. In the categories 'Complete alignment' and 'Major alignment', the median value of IT performance is around 2, indicating that close strategic alignment with the COBIT framework tends to lead to stable and positive performance results. This suggests that incorporating BYOD in accordance with COBIT guidelines can create a solid basis for improved IT performance. For 'Partial alignment', the median also remains at 2, but the wider dispersion indicates that the results are less consistent when strategic alignment is only partially in place. The 'Minor alignment' category shows a significantly wider dispersion and a median of 3.5, indicating that minor alignment with COBIT tends to lead to more fluctuating and less positive results. Finally, the 'No alignment' category shows some outliers, suggesting that a lack of strategic alignment can potentially negatively impact IT performance. Overall, the graphic shows that a stronger alignment with COBIT in the context of BYOD can lead to more stable and better results, while a low or no alignment with the framework leads to less predictable IT performance.

The empirical data on the efficiency of IT strategy implementation through BYOD integration further emphasises this point. A large majority of 59.5% (609 in absolute terms) state that this introduction has contributed to a large extent, and a further 25.5% (261 in absolute terms) assume that it has made a very significant contribution. A neutral impact is assumed by 12.3% (126 in absolute terms), and only 2.7% (27 in absolute terms) cumulatively assume little or no influence. When asked about the role of BYOD in their IT BSC, the majority of 58.7% (600 in absolute terms) stated that it is important but not critical, supported by 24.6% (252 in absolute terms) who consider it to be central and indispensable. 16.1% (165 in absolute terms) stated that it plays no role at all, while only 7.6% (78 in absolute terms) believe it plays only a minor or supplementary role. The strong correlation ($r=0.571$) between the role of BYOD in the IT-BSC and the contribution to IT strategy implementation indicates that BYOD has a significant influence on the strategic orientation and effectiveness of IT structures. This also underlines the verification of the research hypothesis HM according to a strong strategic significance of COBIT for the control of BYOD implementation in an IT-BSC. This statement is further strengthened when specifically asked about the overall influence of BYOD on the effectiveness of IT strategy and implementation, as 46.3 (474 in absolute

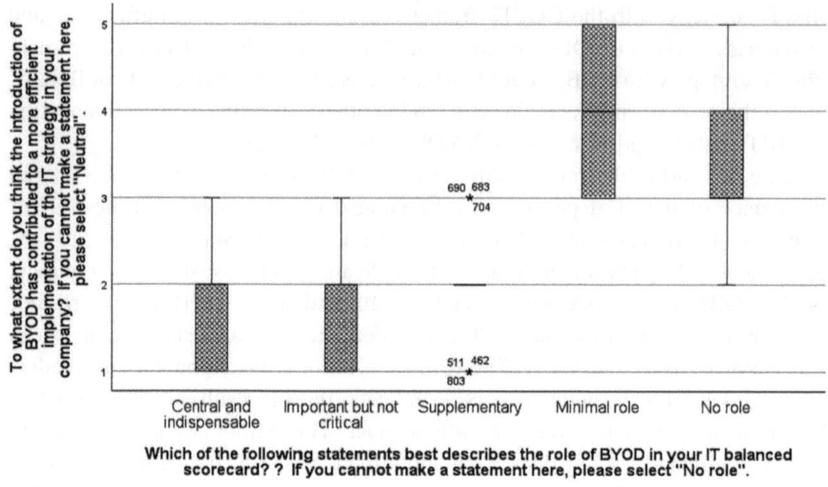

Fig. 4.5 Role in strategy development through BYOD implementation

terms) assume a positive and a further 36.4% (372 in absolute terms) a very positive influence on the impact of the strategy. A total of 16.1% (165 respondents) gave a neutral response, while only 1.2% (12 respondents) gave a negative or very negative response. This perception shows that BYOD is seen as a significant factor in IT strategy, but not as the only one.

The evaluation in Fig. 4.6 analyses the relationship between the importance of risk assessment in connection with BYOD and the perceived effectiveness of risk management measures in the IT-BSC. In the categories 'Very high importance' and 'High importance', the median value of the effectiveness of the risk management measures remains at around 2, indicating that despite the high priority given to risk assessment, the measures to mitigate risk are only considered to be averagely effective. This could indicate that challenges remain in practice to fully optimise the effectiveness of risk management strategies, even when the importance of risk assessment is highly rated. In the 'neutral' category, the median also remains at 2, indicating that a neutral attitude towards risk assessment does not result in a significant change in perceived effectiveness. In the 'low importance' and 'no importance' categories, the dispersion of ratings increases, with 'no importance' showing a median of around 3.5. This suggests that in environments where risk assessment is considered less important, the effectiveness of risk management measures is paradoxically perceived as higher, possibly due to a simpler and clearer structure of

IT risks. This graphic suggests that the perceived effectiveness of risk management measures is not necessarily proportional to the importance of risk assessment, especially in less complex IT environments.

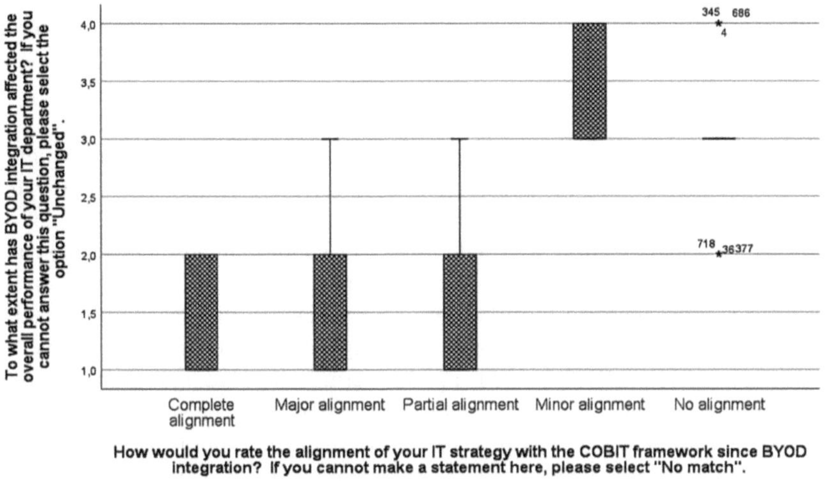

Fig. 4.6 Strategic impact of COBIT utilisation for BYOD implementation

Thus, the evaluation of the empirical study on the main research hypothesis MH shows that this is largely covered by the participants in the study, that the integration of BYOD using COBIT into the IT-BSC system optimises the efficiency, effectiveness and strategic alignment of IT structures in companies. This result thus proves that the integration of BYOD into the management system of an IT BSC enables a substantial increase in the efficiency, effectiveness and strategic coherence of IT structures within the established COBIT framework.

4.3.5 Evaluation of the Validation of Sub-Hypothesis 1 (H1)

The question of how IT budget expenditure has changed since the integration of BYOD is an essential indicator for evaluating the change in costs that can be achieved through the implementation of BYOD. The majority of participants (51.9%, or 531 in absolute terms) state that costs have increased slightly, while for a further 14.7% (150 in absolute terms) there has even been a large increase as a result of the use of

BYOD. Only 12% (123 in absolute terms) saw a slight reduction and 11.7% (120 in absolute terms) saw a large reduction in the budget. About 10% (99 in absolute terms) see no change at all. This was not expected by the author, since the statements of the evaluated experts and literature always speak of a significant reduction in costs. The evaluation of the data on BYOD integration in companies reveals a differentiated picture with regard to the effects on resource allocation and cost reduction within the COBIT framework. Contrary to the expectation that BYOD generally leads to cost reductions, the survey shows that 51.9% of the participants report a slight and 14.7% a large increase in costs. This indicates that the introduction of BYOD may be associated with additional investments, such as for security solutions and training. However, these initial costs could be offset in the long term by efficiency gains and improved resource utilisation. This trend is also evident in the utilisation of IT staff since the introduction of BYOD. Thus, 39.3% (402 in absolute terms) state that the burden has increased significantly, while 27.9% (285 in absolute terms) speak of a slight increase in utilisation. This statement also speaks for a better allocation of resources among employees. A slight reduction is seen in 12.3% (126 in absolute terms). For 10.3% (105 in absolute terms), there is a significant reduction in utilisation, and for 10.3% (105 in absolute terms), there is no change at all. The utilisation of IT employees has also changed since the integration of BYOD. While 39.3% of respondents report a significant increase and 27.9% a slight increase in workload, the results also suggest a possible improvement in resource allocation. A slight or significant reduction in workload for 22.6% of participants could indicate a more efficient use of employee resources. This provides a conditional confirmation of sub-hypothesis H1.

A significant improvement in operational efficiency can be seen in terms of customer satisfaction in the context of IT services through BYOD integration. Here, the vast majority of 63.3% report a slight improvement and a further 20.2% (207 in absolute terms) report a strong improvement. The situation remains unchanged for 16.4% (168 in absolute terms). It is remarkable that no one saw a deterioration, which is a clear correlation for operational efficiency and a verification for sub-hypothesis H1.

The question of optimising IT-related business processes in the company was also largely answered by the BYOD implementation. A majority of 56.9% (582 in absolute terms) stated that business processes had been greatly improved by the introduction of BYOD. For 28.7% (294 in absolute terms), the improvement was even very strong. For 13.5% (138 in absolute terms), efficiency remained unchanged, and 0.9% (9 in absolute terms) stated that the optimisation was very low or non-existent. This is reinforced by the impact on the response time and adaptability of IT services in relation to customer requirements. Here, the majority of participants

(59.2%, 606 in absolute terms) state that the response time has been significantly accelerated or improved. For a further 28.7% (294 in absolute terms), a slight acceleration or improvement is still assumed. For 11.7% (120 in absolute terms), no change is seen and only 0.3% (3 in absolute terms) speak of a slight deterioration. These results underline the potential of BYOD strategies to positively influence operational efficiency and business process optimisation.

The analysis of Fig. 4.7 in relation to hypothesis H1, that the integration of BYOD strategies into IT management systems leads to improved resource allocation and cost reduction within the COBIT framework, shows differentiated results. In the category 'significantly reduced IT personnel utilisation', the IT budget is clearly in the area of reduction, which supports hypothesis H1. Here, BYOD could have led to efficiency gains that made it possible to reduce both personnel utilisation and the budget. A similar situation applies to the category 'Slightly reduced IT staff utilisation', where the IT budget also tends to be reduced, which also indicates an improvement in resource allocation. In the category 'Unchanged IT staff utilisation', the IT budget is distributed more broadly, with a median that remains at unchanged values. This suggests that BYOD has not caused significant cost reductions or additional costs in these cases. However, for 'Slightly increased IT staff utilisation', the boxplot shows a clear tendency towards an increase in the IT budget, with a median of around 4 on the budget scale. This could indicate that BYOD

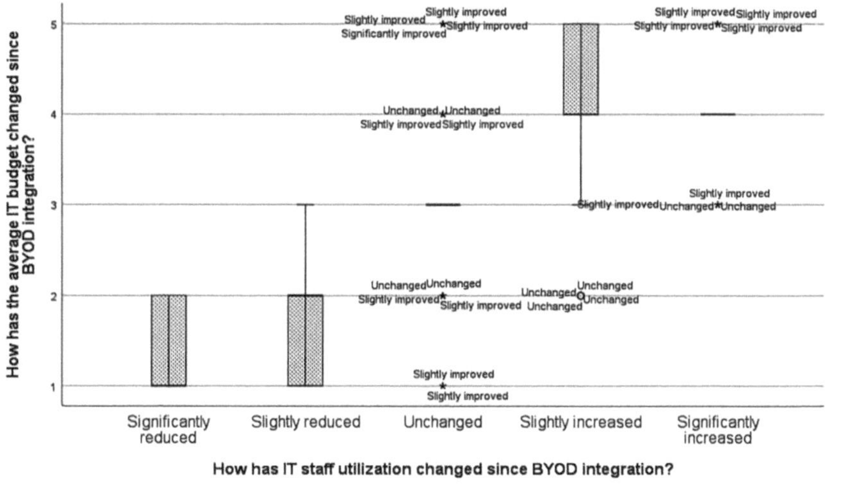

Fig. 4.7 IT budget change since BYOD integration

has required additional investment here, possibly to meet increased demands. In the category 'Significantly increased IT staff utilisation', this trend is even more pronounced, with the IT budget also increasing sharply, which clearly contradicts the hypothesis. This suggests that in these cases, the implementation of BYOD has required significant resources, possibly due to higher security requirements or complexities in integration.

The evaluation of the specific sub-questions for the evaluation of sub-hypothesis H1 shows that the integration of BYOD into the management system significantly leads to a more efficient use of resources in the IT area. The accelerated response time and improved adaptability of IT services, observed by 87.9% of the participants, shows that BYOD initiatives enable a fast and flexible response to customer requirements. This is an important factor for improving service quality and customer satisfaction. The result proves that the synergetic combination of BYOD initiatives and the IT-BSC contributes to a significant improvement in operational efficiency, thus increasing the potential for resource-optimised processes within the IT ecosystem. The original assumption of a cost reduction was only partially confirmed in the survey, which points to initial investments and implementation costs. In the long term, however, the potential for cost savings and resource-optimised processes within the IT ecosystem could be realised through the synergetic linking of BYOD initiatives and the IT BSC.

4.3.6 Evaluation of the Validation of Sub-Hypothesis 2 (H2)

The analysis of the data on the integration of BYOD strategies into IT management systems reveals insightful results with regard to the needs of end users and compliance with COBIT guidelines. When asked how end-user satisfaction with IT services has been affected by BYOD integration, the picture is very clear, with a significant improvement for the vast majority (56.9%, or 582 respondents). A further 25.5% (363 respondents) report that satisfaction has improved to some extent. 7.6% (78 in absolute terms) see no change at all. It is remarkable that no one reported a deterioration (slight or severe). The significant improvement in end-user satisfaction with IT services, reported by 56.9% of respondents, is a clear indicator of the success of BYOD integration. The fact that no deterioration in satisfaction is reported supports sub-hypothesis H2 that BYOD methods better meet the needs of end users. In contrast to this is the result of the question regarding the influence of BYOD integration on the response time to IT requests. Here, 53.7% (549 in absolute terms) state that this time has increased slightly. For 12.9% (132 in absolute terms), a slight reduction is indicated, and 12% (123 in absolute terms) speak of a significant slowdown. A significant reduction is seen by 11.1% (114 in absolute terms). According to 10.3 survey participants (105 in absolute terms), the response time is unchanged. The increase in response time to IT requests among more than half of the respondents (53.7%) could indicate initial challenges in implementing BYOD. However, it is noteworthy that 11.1% of the participants report a significant reduction in response time, which could indicate long-term benefits of BYOD strategies.

When asked how the BYOD strategy has helped align IT and business objectives in the company, the vast majority (59.2%, or 606) said that the strategy has helped to align these objectives to a slight extent. For a further 29.3% (300 in absolute terms), there was even a significant contribution to the alignment of objectives, confirming the assumption that BYOD contributes to a better alignment of IT services with corporate objectives. According to the survey participants, 11.1% (114 in absolute terms) reported no change and 0.3% (3 in absolute terms) reported a slight hindrance to alignment. It is noteworthy that there is only a weak correlation with the answer regarding competence in IT decisions ($r = 0.236$) and a very weak correlation with the management role of the respondents ($r = 0.165$). A much stronger correlation would have been expected from the author. The weak correlations between this answer and the competence for IT decisions and the management role of the respondents are surprising, but could indicate different perceptions in different company departments.

When asked about the role of BYOD in prioritising IT projects and initiatives in line with business objectives, a majority of 51.6% (528 in absolute terms) said it played an important role, and a further 23.5% (300 in absolute terms) said it played a central role. For a further 16.1% (165 in absolute terms), BYOD still plays a supplementary role, while for a cumulative 8.8% (90 in absolute terms), BYOD plays little or no role in the prioritisation of IT projects. This shows that BYOD is seen as a key factor in aligning IT activities with business objectives. Such an improvement is crucial to making IT services and processes more effective and better meeting the needs of end users. This result also verifies sub-hypothesis H2, as it means that user needs are being better met.

To clarify the question of the extent to which BYOD integration has led to clearer communication between IT and business teams, 55.7% (570 in absolute terms) stated that this has improved communication to a high degree. A further 32% (327 in absolute terms) even speak of a very high improvement. A neutral change is indicated by 10.9% (111 in absolute terms) of the participants, and cumulatively, 1.5% (15 in absolute terms) speak of a very small or no change. Thus, the answers to the sub-hypothesis H2 show that the increase in efficiency and the integration of BYOD into the IT management system represent a significant opportunity and substantially increase the value of the IT services provided. This finding indicates that the merging of BYOD practices with an IT-BSC system leads to improved management and governance of IT services. This, in turn, aims to optimise the benefits of the IT services provided and ensure enhanced fulfilment of end-user requirements in line with COBIT best practices.

Figure 4.8 shows that the integration of BYOD methods has a positive impact on end-user satisfaction, especially if IT services are improved as a result. In the 'significantly improved' category, the median satisfaction is around 2.5, indicating a high level of satisfaction when the responsiveness and adaptability of IT services have been greatly improved. For 'Slightly improved,' satisfaction also remains high, with a median just over 2, suggesting that even moderate improvements through BYOD are positively perceived. In the 'Unchanged' category, the median satisfaction score is around 2, meaning that even when IT services remain unchanged, end-user satisfaction remains relatively stable. This could indicate that the mere availability of BYOD options is meaningful to end users. For 'Slightly Deteriorated,' the median value is just below 2, showing that a slight deterioration in IT services does not result in a drastic decline in satisfaction. Overall, this supports hypothesis H2 that BYOD methods, when implemented according to COBIT guidelines, lead to improved fulfilment of end-user needs, with satisfaction being highest when IT services are improved. Even when IT services remain unchanged or deteriorate slightly, satisfaction remains relatively stable, indicating a certain acceptance of BYOD integration.

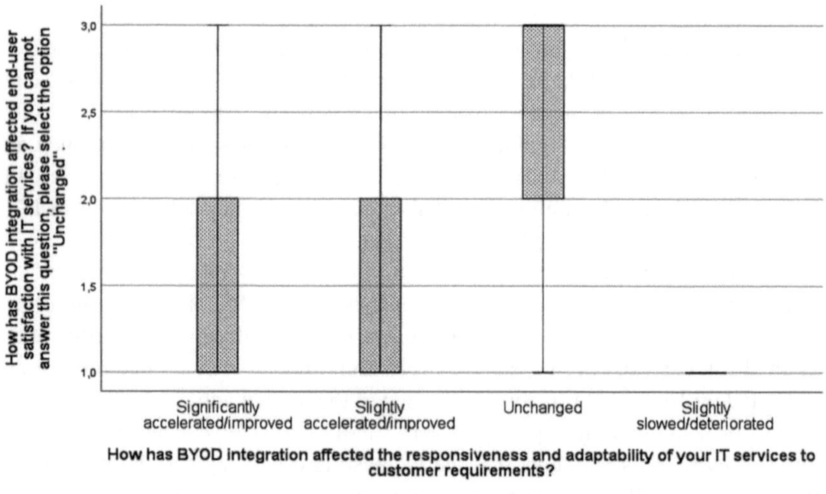

Fig. 4.8 End-user satisfaction with IT services after BYOD integration

Overall, these results prove that integrating BYOD into the IT-BSC system leads to more efficient control of IT services and processes and, in accordance with COBIT guidelines, better meets the needs of end users. Implementing BYOD methods thus appears to be a crucial step in optimising IT services and ensuring greater fulfilment of end-user requirements. These results confirm the research hypothesis H2 and show the potential of BYOD strategies in the modern IT landscape.

4.3.7 Evaluation of the Validation of Sub-Hypothesis 3 (H3)

The study of the integration of BYOD and its influence on the strategic alignment between business and IT objectives confirms sub-hypothesis H3. The majority of participants (52.2%, or 534 in absolute terms) state that this has been significantly strengthened. A further 26.4% (372 in absolute terms) still speak of a slight influence and 10.9% (111 in absolute terms) assume that there has been no change. Only 0.6% (6 in absolute terms) speak of a slight weakening. These results support the assumption that BYOD plays an important role in promoting closer alignment between business and IT goals. The observed improvements in employee productivity, workflow flexibility, cost reduction, and customer service quality show that BYOD can significantly increase the efficiency and effectiveness of IT strategies and infrastructures. This is the first validation of sub-hypothesis H3, which states that the integration of BYOD creates the basis for an optimised strategic alignment between corporate and IT objectives. Specifically, 20.8% (213 in absolute terms) of employee productivity was increased, 52.2% (534 in absolute terms) of the flexibility of workflows, 38.1% (390 in absolute terms) of cost reduction and 14.4% (147 in absolute terms) of an increase in customer service quality. These statements show that the increasing penetration of IT infrastructures with BYOD practices underscores the necessity for a closer strategic alignment of corporate goals and IT strategies and thus supports research hypothesis H3.

In response to the question of how often risk assessments are carried out in connection with BYOD in the company, 41.3% (423 in absolute terms) stated that they are reviewed on a monthly basis. A further 23.8% (243 in absolute terms) stated that they are reviewed on a quarterly basis and 17% (174 in absolute terms) stated that they are reviewed on an annual basis. For 11.1% (114 in absolute terms), the risk assessment is carried out every six months. For 6.7% (69 in absolute terms), the topic is so relevant that there is a weekly review, which shows that companies are taking the potential risks of BYOD seriously and actively taking risk management measures. In response to the emerging synergy between IT and business objectives, such relevance is also a clear sign of support for sub-hypothesis H3. This finding is reinforced by the effectiveness of current risk management measures in the context of BYOD. Here, 53.1% (543 in absolute terms) of participants state that effectiveness is being efficiently implemented. Another 33.1% (339 in absolute terms) even speak of a very high level of efficiency. This is followed by 12.6% (129 in absolute terms), who have a neutral view, and a cumulative 1.2% (12 in absolute terms), who speak of low or no efficiency.

The high priority of risk assessment in the context of BYOD in the IT BSC is indicated by 44.6% (456 in absolute terms), and a further 43.1% (441 in absolute terms) even speak of a very high priority, which shows that BYOD initiatives are seen as an integral part of IT governance and strategy. This reflects the growing realisation that integrating BYOD into the IT strategy is not just a question of technology, but also a strategic decision that improves the direction and responsiveness of the IT organisation. For 11.1% (114 in absolute terms), the perspective is neutral, whereas a cumulative 1.2% (12 in absolute terms) see no or only limited relevance here. This is based on the insight that combining BYOD initiatives with the principles of IT-BSC promotes greater flexibility and adaptability of the IT organisation to a changing business environment. Thus, it contributes to increasing the agility of IT structures and thus enables an improved positioning of the IT organisation within the COBIT framework.

The Fig. 4.9 shows that in the categories 'very high' and 'high importance' of risk assessment, the effectiveness of risk management measures is on average only at a median value of about 2. This shows that despite the high prioritisation of risk assessment, the measures to mitigate risk are rated as rather average. These results suggest that the integration of BYOD, although recognised as strategically important, still has room for improvement in its implementation in order to fully realise the desired improvement in strategic alignment between business and IT objectives. In the 'Neutral' category, the median effectiveness score is also 2, indicating that the neutral attitude towards risk assessment has no significant impact on the effectiveness of risk management measures. This could be due to the fact that in these cases there is less focus on the strategic integration of BYOD, which means that the effectiveness of the measures remains at a similar level to that of high importance. In the categories 'Low Importance' and 'No Importance', the assessment of effectiveness varies greatly. In particular, the category 'No Importance' shows a wide dispersion of values, with a median value of around 3.5. This could indicate that organisations that attach less importance to risk assessment may adopt simpler and less complex risk management strategies that are perceived as more effective in their specific environment.

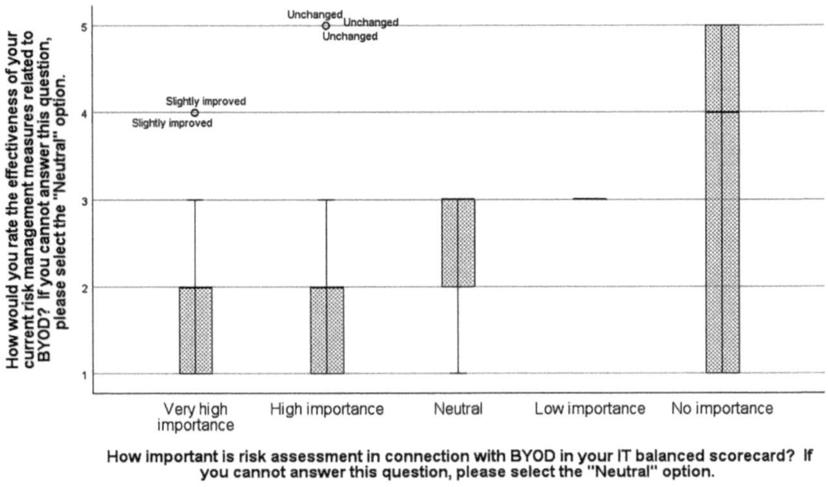

Fig. 4.9 Effectiveness of risk management after BYOD integration

The analysis of the responses to sub-hypothesis H3 clearly shows that the integration of BYOD strategies plays a key role in improving strategic alignment between business and IT objectives. Improving this alignment optimises the ability to respond to external changes and strengthens the IT organisation within the COBIT framework. This confirms research hypothesis H3 and illustrates the potential of BYOD strategies to promote effective business-IT alignment and to improve the agility and adaptability of IT structures in a constantly changing business environment.

4.4 Interpretation of the Research Hypotheses

According to the study, the integration of BYOD in companies has far-reaching effects on various aspects of IT strategy and efficiency. First of all, a strong increase in performance can be seen with the introduction of BYOD. Processes such as APO01 (management of IT management frameworks) and EDM01 (monitoring, evaluation and control of IT) benefit from the integration of BYOD, which in turn increases the overall efficiency and effectiveness of IT systems. This improvement in IT performance indicates that BYOD is an effective means of increasing IT efficiency and promoting the strategic alignment of IT with business objectives. Interestingly, contrary to the initial assumption of a cost reduction, BYOD leads to an increase in costs for a large proportion of respondents. These could be attributed to initial investments in security solutions and training. This observation suggests that careful planning and efficient resource allocation are of great importance within the COBIT processes, in particular APO04 (Resource Management) and EDM01 (Organisation's policies, plans and models). In the long term, the efficiency gains achieved through BYOD could offset these initial investments, with a positive impact on MEA03 (performance measurement) and APO06 (budget and cost management). Another important aspect is the significant improvement in end-user satisfaction through BYOD. This indicates an effective implementation of processes such as APO01 and MEA03, which in turn increases the value contribution of IT to the company's success. In addition, the initial challenges and subsequent improvement in response time to IT requests could indicate a learning curve in the implementation of BYOD. This is directly related to processes such as APO04 (Resource Management) and EDM03 (Realisation of Value Contribution). Finally, the strengthening of the strategic alignment between business and IT goals through BYOD is confirmed by 52.2

The integration of BYOD strategies into companies has a significant influence on customer satisfaction, which is reflected in the application of various COBIT processes. The study finds a moderate correlation between IT strategy alignment with COBIT and the efficiency gains achieved through BYOD. This suggests that a closer alignment with COBIT processes, particularly DSS01 (Service Delivery), could make service delivery more efficient and thus improve customer satisfaction. Efficient service delivery is a key factor in customer satisfaction and is supported by a stronger focus on COBIT guidelines. In addition, the study shows a significant improvement in customer satisfaction due to the implementation of BYOD. This progress is closely linked to the processes DSS01 (Service Delivery) and DSS06 (Incident and Problem Management), as BYOD enables a fast and flexible response to customer requirements. The improved communication between IT and business teams that BYOD promotes also plays an important role in increasing customer satisfaction. This improvement in communication falls under the processes DSS01 (Service Delivery) and DSS06 (Incident and Problem Management), which are responsible for effective service delivery and the management of incidents and problems. Finally, the improvement in service quality through BYOD has a direct impact on customer satisfaction. The positive results in this area confirm the effectiveness of processes such as DSS01 (Service Delivery) and MEA04 (Customer Satisfaction Management). BYOD enables an optimisation of service quality, which is directly reflected in increased customer satisfaction.

The integration of BYOD in companies has a significant influence on the areas of learning and development, which is reflected in the COBIT processes. The introduction of BYOD in the context of IT-BSC can be seen as a catalyst for continuous learning and development. In particular, BYOD offers new learning opportunities and methods that have a positive effect on the processes APO07 (Human Resource Management) and MEA01 (Performance Measurement). BYOD exposes employees to new technologies and ways of working, highlighting the need for training and efficient resource allocation. This is particularly relevant for Human Resource Management (APO07), as it aims to develop employees' skills and competencies in the use of new technologies. Furthermore, the different perceptions of IT and management roles with regard to BYOD could indicate a need for ongoing education and development. This can be addressed through processes such as APO07 and MEA01, by implementing targeted training and performance reviews to promote a coherent view and use of BYOD in different areas of the company. Another important aspect is the regular performance of risk assessments in connection with BYOD, which is directly linked to APO14 (Knowledge Management and Learning) and EDM05 (Risk Management). The efficient handling of these risks through appropriate management practices shows that organisations are able to master and learn from new challenges posed by BYOD. The continuous assessment and adaptation of risk management strategies in the context of BYOD illustrates the need for a dynamic learning and development process within the organisation.

The integration of BYOD in companies has a significant impact on the process perspective within the IT strategy. A strong correlation between the role of BYOD in the IT-BSC and the contribution to IT strategy implementation highlights the importance of BYOD for the process perspective. Processes such as BAI01 (Manage Programmes) and APO08 (Manage Relationships) could be made more effective by introducing BYOD, as it enables a more agile and risk-aware implementation of the IT strategy. This is reflected in improved adaptability and accelerated IT department response time to change, which is directly linked to APO02 (Manage Strategy) and APO05 (Manage Portfolio). These processes help make the IT department more agile and responsive. In addition, respondents report an improvement in IT-related business processes through BYOD, which can be attributed to processes such as BAI04 (Manage Availability and Capacity) and MEA02 (Monitor, Evaluate and Assess the System of Internal Control). These improvements in system performance and in the management of operational and service requirements are crucial to the efficiency and effectiveness of IT services. The role of BYOD in prioritising IT projects and initiatives also highlights the importance of processes such as APO05 (Manage Portfolio) and APO08 (Manage Relationships). BYOD is seen as a central factor influencing direction and prioritisation within IT portfolio management and risk management. Finally, BYOD is considered an integral part of IT governance and strategy in IT-BSC. This is reflected in processes such as APO02 (Manage Strategy) and BAI01 (Manage Programmes), which are responsible for managing strategy and programmes. BYOD contributes to the adaptability and agility of IT structures and is therefore an important factor in the strategic alignment and operational implementation of IT processes.

The study on the integration of BYOD strategies into the IT management system underlines their significant influence on the efficiency, effectiveness and strategic alignment of corporate IT structures. It is clear that the integration of BYOD into the COBIT framework and the IT-BSC is crucial for optimising these processes. A key factor for the success of BYOD is strengthening the link between IT strategy and COBIT processes. This not only leads to improved IT performance, but also increases customer satisfaction and supports continuous learning and development within the IT organisation. The study shows that BYOD strategies contribute to improved resource allocation and operational efficiency, but are initially associated with challenges in terms of costs and employee utilisation. In the long term, cost savings and optimised processes could be realised by linking BYOD initiatives with COBIT processes and the IT-BSC. These results emphasise the need for careful planning and implementation of BYOD strategies as part of IT management. The integration of BYOD leads to more efficient control of IT services and processes, which improves the needs of end users. Implementing BYOD helps to optimise IT services and ensures greater fulfilment of end-user requirements. These results confirm the research hypotheses and demonstrate the potential of BYOD strategies in the modern IT landscape, particularly in terms of improving IT service quality, making efficient use of resources, and promoting organisational adaptability.

In summary, the integration of BYOD plays a key role in improving the strategic alignment between business and IT objectives. Optimising this alignment improves the ability to respond to external changes, which strengthens the IT organisation within the COBIT framework. These results confirm the effectiveness of BYOD strategies in promoting effective business-IT alignment and in increasing the agility and adaptability of IT structures in an ever-changing business environment.

Conclusion and Recommendations from Chapter IV

The empirical survey of this study is primarily based on the application of an online questionnaire, which was developed according to strict social science criteria. This method of data collection was not chosen at random, but was favoured specifically for its cost efficiency and ability to reach a wide range of companies. It is a largely standardised survey technique that makes it possible to generate quantifiable and comparable data. The sample for the study consisted of companies from a variety of industry sectors and geographic locations, and was drawn from a commercially available database. This ensures broader representativeness of the results and allows for inferences that may be valid across individual sectors or markets.

Prior to widespread application of the questionnaire, it underwent extensive preliminary testing to ensure the reliability and validity of the questions. In addition, the questionnaire was iteratively adjusted and refined to maximise the quality of the data. The universe for this study includes the worldwide number of companies, a population of considerable size and complexity. Due to the practical impossibility of capturing this entire universe, a random sample of 5,000 companies was used for the study. The response rate for the questionnaire from this sample was a remarkable 22%. This high rate underscores the relevance of the topic and gives the study increased credibility and significance. The selection of this sample was carried out taking into account specific, evenly distributed criteria, including the affiliation to different industries and the geographical location of the companies. This methodological approach was used to ensure a representative sample that allows for robust and generally valid conclusions.

The design of the questionnaire was based on a conceptual model developed for this study. It included the selection and definition of relevant variables that contribute to answering the research questions and hypotheses. To ensure standardisation and quality of the collected data, the coding of the answers was automated using a web-based survey tool. This minimised the risk of human error and increased the reliability of the data. The data analysis was carried out using the statistical programme SPSS. This enabled a variety of statistical analyses to be conducted, providing both descriptive and inferential statistical insights. This analytical approach increases the scientific rigour of the study and enables an in-depth understanding of the phenomena under investigation. Overall, the methodology of the study provides a robust basis for investigating the influences of BYOD integration in IT-BSC in the context of the COBIT framework.

Pearson's correlation coefficient was used to enable an in-depth analysis of the relationships between the various variables. This statistical method is particularly suitable for measuring the linear relationship between two metric variables. This made it possible to quantify both the degree and the significance of the correlations between the variables examined. This quantified approach makes it possible to draw targeted conclusions about the research hypotheses formulated in the study. In particular, it substantiated the assessment of the efficiency, effectiveness and strategic orientation of IT organisations in the context of BYOD integration, IT-BSC and the COBIT framework. The statistical evaluation provided a differentiated picture of the relationships and interactive effects between the implementation of BYOD strategies and the established IT management systems. The complexity of the results became apparent from the fact that different degrees of correlation, from weak to strong dependencies, were identified. These gradual differences allowed a differentiated assessment of the main and sub-hypotheses. They thus provided a valuable basis for interpreting the complex interactions that characterise the integration of BYOD in IT-BSCs within the COBIT framework. Overall, the use of Pearson's correlation coefficient contributed to a well-founded, scientifically rigorous investigation. It allowed going beyond simple descriptive statistics and drawing inferential statistical conclusions, which are of central importance for answering the research questions.

In the empirical study conducted, the integration of BYOD in companies and its influence on IT structures and strategies was examined using the COBIT framework and the IT-BSC. The study provides insightful findings regarding the impact of BYOD on various aspects of IT strategy and efficiency. The classification of the survey participants was based on various parameters such as industry, number of employees, functional profile, decision-making authority, experience with COBIT and the relevance of home office/BYOD. The results show that the majority of the participants came from the 'Information and Communication' sector, followed by 'Manufacturing', 'Professional, Scientific and Technical Activities' and other industries according to the ISIC classification. This broad range of industries in the study shows the general relevance of BYOD across different sectors.

The data on the legal form of the companies and the number of employees reveals some contradictions, which may be due to ambiguities in the questionnaire design. Nevertheless, the heterogeneity of company sizes and forms highlights the need for a flexible application of COBIT guidelines to effectively integrate BYOD strategies, especially in smaller companies. The majority of the study participants held strategic positions such as department heads, CEOs/managing directors and CTOs/CIOs, which confirms the high quality of the survey results in terms of evaluating and analysing strategic decisions. The length of time spent in the aforementioned positions, as well as the decision-making authority in IT matters, makes it clear that the survey results offer in-depth insights into the challenges and potential of integrating BYOD strategies using COBIT. The results show that BYOD can improve the efficiency, effectiveness and strategic alignment of corporate IT structures when integrated into IT-BSC within the COBIT framework. Strengthening the link between IT strategy and COBIT processes is a key factor for success. The integration of BYOD leads to improved IT performance, increased customer satisfaction and supports continuous learning and development within the IT organisation.

The study confirms that the integration of BYOD strategies in companies has a significant influence on customer satisfaction, which is reflected in the application of various COBIT processes. The study finds a moderate correlation between IT strategy alignment with COBIT and the efficiency gains achieved through BYOD. This suggests that closer alignment with COBIT processes could make service delivery more efficient and thus improve customer satisfaction. The results confirm the research hypotheses and demonstrate the potential of BYOD strategies in the modern IT landscape, particularly with regard to improving IT service quality, making efficient use of resources and promoting organisational adaptability. Overall, the study shows that the integration of BYOD plays a key role in improving the strategic alignment between business and IT objectives. Optimising this alignment improves the ability to respond to external changes, which strengthens the IT organisation within the COBIT framework.

Conclusion and Recommendations

Finally, the collected findings and results of the extensive research will be summarised, which was started with the aim of developing a sustainable and efficient method for integrating BYOD initiatives into the management system of an IT BSC. This is all done in the context of the COBIT framework, as an international best practice collection for IT controlling, and further supported by the concept of IPM, which ensures consistent alignment between strategy, performance measurement, and operational execution.

First of all, it is important to emphasise the central point of the intended work: the creation of a comprehensive methodology specifically designed to support the design and implementation of an IT BSC. The goal is clearly defined—the methodology should make it possible to create rational and high-quality solutions for companies of various sizes by relying on the fundamentals of the COBIT framework and adapting them specifically for BYOD initiatives. This is an essential step in providing companies with a clear and effective path for implementing BYOD, taking into account the specific advantages and challenges of this technology, while embedding it within a broader, IPM-driven performance logic.

The comprehensive foundations that were developed in the course of this research work form the basis for the development of such an implementation model. They take into account the complex relationships and dependencies between the IT-BSC, the COBIT framework and BYOD initiatives. It is a multidimensional task that requires a thorough knowledge and understanding of the various dimensions addressed in the research hypotheses. In addition, the results of the empirical study, which formed an essential part of this dissertation, are an important reference point for the construction of the model. They have not only confirmed the relevance of the research hypothesis, but have also provided a wealth of data and insights that serve as a basis for the development of concrete and customised solutions.

M. Groß, *Managing IT in the Age of BYOD and Remote Work*,
https://doi.org/10.1007/978-3-658-51216-3

Based on the established premises and the empirically collected data, a recommendation for an implementation model is now being made. This model will include specific KPIs designed to enable measurable and effective deployment of BYOD in organisations, in line with the IT BSC system and the COBIT framework. By focusing on specific KPIs, it will be possible to create a clear and concise guideline that will enable companies to implement BYOD initiatives in a rational and informed manner. Particular attention will be paid to maintaining strategic alignment and optimising the efficiency and effectiveness of IT processes.

Furthermore, the implementation model will be conceptually embedded within an IPM, which plays a pivotal role in ensuring the strategic consistency and governance conformity of BYOD measures. In this context, the IPM is understood not merely as a technical construct, but as a strategic instrument that structures the relationships between performance indicators, strategic objectives, and data flows in a way that is both scalable and adaptable. It supports the semantic and functional integration of BYOD-relevant data into the IT BSC and facilitates dynamic, context-sensitive analyses of performance contributions across organisational units.

The integration of such an IPM into the IT BSC enables a systematic abstraction and visualisation of performance-critical information, thus ensuring the traceability and alignment of BYOD initiatives with overarching governance frameworks such as COBIT. As outlined in the research, this information-centric approach makes it possible to close the gap between strategic design and operational execution and promotes a continuous optimisation cycle based on real-time data and feedback mechanisms.

In this context, the IPM developed and conceptualised in the theoretical foundation of this work plays a critical role as a methodological backbone of the implementation model. Its integrative design provides not only a structural mapping of the interrelations between strategic objectives, performance indicators and control mechanisms, but also enables the translation of abstract governance requirements from COBIT into actionable and measurable constructs within the IT BSC framework. The IPM thus serves as both an analytical lens and an operational guide, ensuring that BYOD initiatives are systematically aligned with strategic priorities and continuously evaluated in terms of effectiveness, compliance, and value contribution. By embedding the IPM into the conclusion of this dissertation, its role as a central architectural element of the proposed solution framework is reaffirmed and elevated to its appropriate level of relevance.

In doing so, it contributes significantly to the transformation of IT performance management and sets a methodological benchmark for the integration of emerging technologies within structured governance architectures.

BYOD implementation concept in the management system, taking into account an IT-BSC with COBIT

The effective introduction of BYOD into a company's management system requires a carefully planned and structured approach that takes into account both the IT-BSC and the COBIT framework (Fig. A.1). The initial phase of the concept focuses on clearly defining the company vision, mission, and strategy, with the overarching goal of ensuring that the BYOD strategy is in harmony with the organisation's primary objectives and mission. The application of the COBIT framework serves as a supportive guide here, helping to precisely articulate the company values and take into account the necessary best practices during the integration phase.

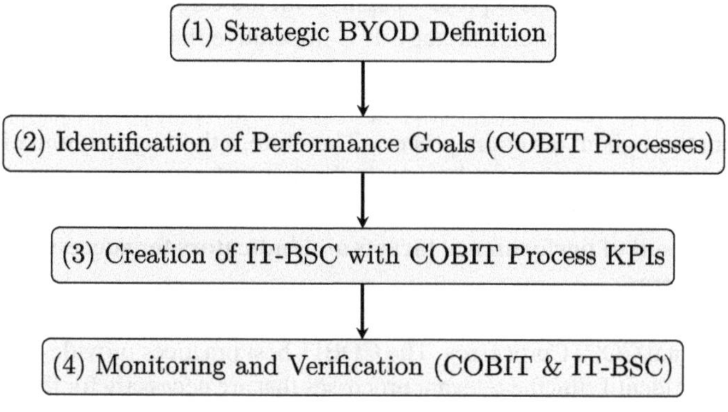

Fig. A.1 Process Diagram for BYOD Integration Using the COBIT Framework and IT-BSC. (Own illustration, 2024)

The next step in this process is to identify the essential COBIT processes that provide a basis for developing specific performance targets. This includes defining the characteristics of a successful management system, with a particular focus on flexibility, transparency and adaptability to the constantly changing IT landscape. Subsequently, the IT-BSC will be introduced as a central tool to measure the effectiveness of BYOD integration through the development and implementation of representative KPIs. These KPIs are an essential instrument for measuring the added value of the BYOD strategy and for supporting the strategic direction of the IT organisation.

Finally, the last phase involves continuous monitoring of current developments, followed by thorough validation and verification of the implemented strategies. This stage guarantees that the strategy is not only implemented but also monitored for effectiveness, enabling continuous improvements and ensuring the long-term success of BYOD integration. With this structured and well-thought-out approach, the concept creates a solid foundation for companies to successfully navigate BYOD integration and fully exploit the advantages of this strategy, with the principles of IT-BSC and the COBIT framework serving as supporting pillars. An essential integrative element in this context is the IPM, which provides the structural linkage between the phases outlined below. It ensures that strategy, governance and performance measurement are coherently connected throughout the implementation process:

1. **Definition of corporate vision, mission and strategy**
   The initiation of a BYOD project begins with the careful definition of the corporate vision, mission and strategy. It is imperative that the BYOD integration is aligned with the organisation's overall goals and mission. The COBIT framework serves as a guide here, ensuring that current best practices are taken into account throughout the entire process. Therefore, a thorough examination of the core corporate values and objectives is the first and crucial step.

2. **Development of performance targets and indicators for successful management systems**
   The next step is to define specific performance targets that are aligned with the fundamental COBIT processes. The COBIT best practices provide a solid foundation for identifying the relevant processes that are necessary for the successful integration of BYOD. In addition, it is important to emphasise the characteristics that a management system must fulfil in order to be considered successful, with aspects such as flexibility, transparency and adaptability to a dynamic IT landscape being given priority.

3. **Using the IT-BSC to measure BYOD effectiveness and develop representative KPIs**
   In this phase, the IT-BSC is a central instrument for developing and implementing representative KPIs. These KPIs, which are derived from the processes identified in phase 2, serve to measure the added value and effectiveness of the BYOD strategy and to derive strategic impulses for the IT organisation. The selection and alignment of these KPIs are supported by the IPM, which provides a unified model architecture to ensure that performance metrics remain consistent with strategic goals and governance requirements throughout the implementation.

4. **Monitoring current developments, validation and verification**
   The final phase involves continuous monitoring to keep an eye on developments and proactively address possible challenges. This requires both validation and verification of the implemented strategies to ensure that the defined goals are achieved and to continuously optimise the strategy within the framework of the COBIT framework and the IT-BSC. In this context, the IPM serves as a reference framework for assessing the coherence of implementation outcomes with predefined KPIs and governance objectives, thereby enabling traceable evaluation and targeted adjustments.

(1) Definition of the company's vision, mission and strategy
Before tackling the integration of BYOD, it is essential to have a well-founded corporate vision and a clear strategy for this area. It is essential that the introduction of BYOD is harmoniously aligned with the overarching goals and mission of the organisation, whereby an orientation towards the best practices of the COBIT framework provides a useful guideline. In this context, it is necessary that the performance indicators developed—which are at the centre of the IT-BSC—effectively support the strategic ambitions of the company. This not only creates a tangible framework for day-to-day work, but also enables employees to see and understand the relevance of their activities more clearly in the larger context of the company's objectives. To support this alignment between strategy and performance measurement, the IPM provides a formal structure for mapping strategic objectives to relevant KPIs. It ensures that all performance indicators embedded in the IT-BSC reflect not only operational realities but also overarching governance and business priorities.

The initial phase of this process requires a clear vision of where the organisation is headed in the near future. The goal should be ambitious, but not completely out of reach, in order to provide a motivating challenge while also remaining realistic. This strategic direction provides managers with the necessary basis for successfully and purposefully steering the organisation in what may be a highly competitive market environment. In terms of implementing BYOD, it is therefore important to ensure that it is fully aligned with the defined corporate strategy. This means that the use of BYOD must offer specific advantages for achieving the defined goals. This not only favours an efficient and effective IT organisation within the COBIT framework, but also promotes an improved strategic alignment between business and IT goals.

The integration of BYOD strategies into the management system of an IT BSC offers an opportunity to increase the efficiency, effectiveness and strategic alignment of IT organisations in the context of the COBIT framework. This chapter presents a detailed, step-by-step plan for the successful implementation of this integration.

The IPM serves as a methodological framework that spans all steps of this integration process. It enables the consistent translation of strategic goals into measurable results, ensuring semantic coherence across vision, process definitions, and control mechanisms.

1. **Introduction**

   - **Background:** Explains the significance of BYOD, COBIT, and the IT-BSC linked to IPM in modern IT management and why integrating all these aspects is relevant.
   - **Problem Statement:** Discusses the specific challenges and opportunities arising from the introduction of BYOD into an IT-BSC.
   - **Objective:** Clarifies how integrating BYOD into the IT-BSC can improve efficiency, effectiveness, and strategic alignment, considering the COBIT framework.

2. **Strategic Alignment**

   - **Company Vision, Mission, and Strategy:** Explains how the BYOD strategy aligns with company-wide goals and overall strategy.

3. **Foundations and Preparation**

   - **Definition of BYOD:** Establishes BYOD policies that consider both security aspects and user-friendliness.
   - **COBIT Framework:** Selects relevant COBIT processes and metrics that serve as the basis for performance measurement.
   - **IT-BSC:** Incorporates BYOD-related metrics and goals into the existing IT-BSC.

4. **Implementation**

   - **Pilot Phase:** Introduces BYOD policies in a small, controlled environment to identify potential issues early.
   - **Role and Responsibility Assignment:** Assigns roles for the implementation, management, and monitoring of the BYOD strategy.
   - **Technical Implementation:** Establishes the necessary technical measures, including network security and data management.

5. **Measurement and Adjustment**

- **Performance Monitoring:** Uses the IT-BSC to regularly monitor and analyze BYOD-related metrics.
- **Feedback Loops:** Implements feedback mechanisms for stakeholders to continuously improve the BYOD strategy.
- **Strategic Realignment:** Periodically reviews whether the BYOD strategy is still aligned with corporate goals and IT management. The IPM supports this realignment by offering a stable yet adaptable reference model for comparing current performance against strategic intent. It facilitates the identification of structural gaps and enables evidence-based adjustments in line with governance priorities.

6. **Review and Optimization**

- **Success Control:** Evaluates the achieved results compared to the originally set goals.
- **Optimization:** Makes adjustments based on the insights gained to further improve performance.
- **Scaling:** Expands the BYOD strategy to other business areas or the entire company if the pilot phase and initial implementation steps were successful.

A thorough examination of these key points makes it possible to draw well-founded conclusions about the impact of BYOD integration on performance measurement and management of IT organisations. The symbiosis of a clear strategic vision and well-considered BYOD integration can thus be a key driver in sustainably improving the efficiency, effectiveness and strategic alignment of the IT organisation.

(2) Development of performance targets and indicators of successful management systems

The detailing of clearly defined performance targets and measures for BYOD integration according to COBIT best practices is of central importance in order to be able to effectively evaluate both stakeholder satisfaction and the harmonisation of IT strategies with business processes. In this context, it is essential to define which specific performance targets the organisation must achieve in order to realise the developed vision. Suitable measures should be identified and implemented over an appropriate period of time—for example, three to five years. The complexity of this undertaking should not be underestimated, as various variables, such as the number of employees and their level of participation, influence this process.

One tool that plays a central role here is the BSC. It translates the corporate vision into a set of performance targets categorised under four perspectives: financial, customer, internal business processes, and learning and growth. This scorecard serves not only as a tool for measuring progress towards the vision, but also for evaluating the long-term drivers of the company's success. To ensure consistency between vision, measurement, and governance structures, the IPM provides a formal framework for embedding these performance targets within the IT-BSC. It links strategic objectives to performance indicators and maps them against COBIT control processes, enabling a traceable and semantically coherent implementation of BYOD strategies.

Creating effective performance measures requires a close tie to the strategic vision of the organisation. The measures established should be focused on the outcomes that are essential to achieving the vision and strategic objectives. It is essential to define each measure precisely, taking into account aspects such as the target group, the measurement methodology, the data sources and the measurement period. A useful approach is to integrate a balanced mix of quantitative and qualitative measures, with the former providing greater objectivity and making it possible to quantify savings achieved through the use of BYOD, for example.

Qualitative measures, on the other hand, relate more closely to subjective perceptions, such as employee satisfaction, and can provide valuable insights into performance and results, although they are less objective. Carefully selecting and defining measures helps to effectively guide the implementation of the company's vision, promoting both efficiency and effectiveness within the COBIT framework. The IPM supports this process by offering a structured logic for selecting and aligning performance indicators with governance-based control objectives and business outcomes. It ensures that both qualitative and quantitative metrics are not only valid and measurable, but also systematically embedded in a consistent performance architecture.

In assigning the COBIT processes to the four perspectives of the IT-BSC, a methodological approach was adopted that is based on the specific functions and effects of each process within an IT organisation, taking into account the core principles set out in the research hypotheses. Initially, an in-depth analysis of each COBIT process was carried out to understand the main functions and effects on an IT organisation. The focus was on the influence of each process on the efficiency, effectiveness and strategic alignment of IT organisations within the COBIT framework.

Subsequently, the four perspectives of the IT-BSC, IT value contribution, user satisfaction, internal processes, and learning and growth, served as a foundation for categorising the processes. These perspectives aim to optimise different facets of IT organisational performance. The IPM functions as an integrative model that bridges the structural dimensions of COBIT processes with the BSC perspectives. It facilitates the categorisation of processes by aligning their functional logic with strategic performance dimensions, thereby ensuring methodological consistency throughout the assignment.

1. **IT value contribution** focuses on the value added by IT investments and strategies.
2. **User Satisfaction** assesses the quality of IT services from the end-user's perspective.
3. **Internal Processes** focuses on the efficiency and effectiveness of internal processes and systems.
4. **Learning and Growth** is concerned with the further development and optimisation of the organisation through learning and improvement processes.

Each COBIT process was then mapped to the IT BSC perspective, as shown in Fig. A.2, that best represents the key functions and impacts of the process. For example,

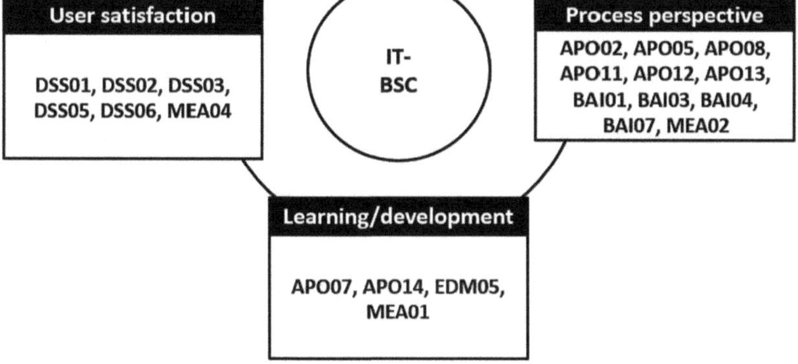

Fig. A.2 Full alignment of COBIT with the IT-DSC for BYOD. (Own illustration, 2024)

- **APO01 (Manage the IT Management Framework)** was categorised under the 'IT Value Contribution' category because it focuses on developing a structured IT management framework that contributes to the strategic alignment of IT organisations.
- **DSS01 (Manage Operations)** was categorised under 'user satisfaction' because it supports the continuous and efficient delivery of IT services, which in turn increases end-user satisfaction.

This approach enabled a systematic and conceptually sound assignment of the COBIT processes derived from the empirical study to the perspectives of the IT-BSC, always keeping in mind the objectives set out in the hypotheses.

The Table A.1 demonstrates the role of various COBIT processes in increasing **IT value contribution** by integrating BYOD strategies. Starting with APO01, who manages the IT management framework, this process facilitates the integration of BYOD, thereby promoting strategic adaptability. This enables organisations to respond quickly to changes in the technology sector and to adapt their IT strategies accordingly.

Table A.1 IT Value Contribution

COBIT Process	Process Description	Short Explanation of the Contribution
APO01	Manage the IT Management Framework	Aids BYOD integration for strategic adaptability.
APO03	Manage Enterprise Architecture	Aligns BYOD with enterprise architecture for efficiency.
APO04	Manage Innovation	Fosters innovative BYOD strategies for efficiency and effectiveness.
APO06	Manage Budget and Costs	Optimizes budget and costs via smart BYOD incorporation.
APO09	Manage IT Risk	Enhances resilience through BYOD risk management.
APO10	Manage Suppliers	Improves supplier efficiency considering BYOD dynamics.
EDM01	Ensure Governance Framework Setting and Maintenance	Sets a BYOD-friendly governance framework.
EDM03	Ensure Risk Optimization	Optimizes risk strategy for BYOD demands.
MEA03	Monitor, Evaluate, and Assess Compliance With External Requirements	Ensures compliance in BYOD settings per COBIT guidelines.

APO03, who is responsible for managing the enterprise architecture, supports the alignment of BYOD with the existing enterprise architecture. This helps to increase efficiency by ensuring that BYOD initiatives integrate seamlessly with the existing IT landscape. APO04 focuses on managing innovation and promotes innovative strategies in the context of BYOD. This process is critical to increasing efficiency and effectiveness because it helps to develop and implement new and advanced BYOD approaches. In managing budget and costs, represented by APO06, intelligent integration of BYOD optimises budget and costs. This process is important to ensure that BYOD solutions are implemented cost-effectively and achieve a positive ROI (return on investment). APO09 addresses the management of IT risks and strengthens resilience through targeted BYOD risk management. In a BYOD environment, it is crucial to identify and manage the risks associated with the use of personal devices. The APO10 process, which covers vendor management, improves vendor efficiency while taking into account the dynamics of BYOD. This may mean that vendor relationships need to be adapted to meet the specific requirements of BYOD.

EDM01 ensures that a BYOD-friendly governance framework is established and maintained. This is critical to ensuring a comprehensive and effective governance structure that takes BYOD into account. EDM03 aims to optimise the risk strategy for BYOD requirements. This involves developing and implementing risk management strategies specifically tailored to the challenges and opportunities of BYOD. Finally, MEA03 ensures compliance with external requirements in BYOD settings according to COBIT guidelines. This process is critical to ensuring compliance in a BYOD environment, which in turn strengthens stakeholder confidence.

The Table A.2 illustrates that the integration of BYOD strategies into IT management practices through COBIT processes can lead to improved **user satisfaction**. In the context of the DSS01 process, which ensures the improvement of IT operations management, service is enhanced, which in turn increases user satisfaction. The DSS02 and DSS03 processes complement this aspect by ensuring that service requests are processed efficiently and that proactive problem management is in place to improve overall service quality. The DSS05 process is particularly critical as it focuses on managing IT security services. In a BYOD environment, this process is crucial to ensure user trust and satisfaction, as personal devices often have different security profiles and risks. Stringent security mechanisms and controls can minimise risks and increase user trust.

Table A.2 User Satisfaction

COBIT Process	Process Description	Short Explanation of the Contribution
DSS01	Manage Operations	Enhances service delivery and user satisfaction with BYOD.
DSS02	Manage Service Requests and Incidents	Efficiently handles service issues in BYOD, boosting user satisfaction.
DSS03	Manage Problems	Reduces service interruptions in BYOD for improved user experience.
DSS05	Manage Security Services	Secures IT services in BYOD, building user trust.
DSS06	Manage Business Process Controls	Ensures business process effectiveness, increasing user satisfaction.
MEA04	Monitor, Evaluate, and Assess the Management of IT	Monitors IT services including BYOD impact, aligning with user expectations.

In addition, the COBIT MEA04 process, which is responsible for monitoring, evaluating and assessing IT performance and compliance, plays an important role in this context. MEA04 ensures that performance indicators are monitored and sets evaluation criteria to ensure that IT management practices, including the integration of BYOD, meet business objectives and user requirements. Through continuous performance and compliance monitoring, MEA04 can identify any deficiencies or deviations at an early stage. In a BYOD environment, this process helps to systematically monitor the performance of integrated personal devices in terms of security, quality of service and user satisfaction. Corrective action can therefore be initiated more quickly, contributing to improved user satisfaction.

Finally, the DSS06 process considers the management of business process controls. Here, attention is paid to improving the effectiveness of business processes, which also contributes to increased user satisfaction. The Table A.2 impressively shows how the careful integration of BYOD strategies into COBIT-supported IT management practices can contribute to increasing user satisfaction in various dimensions.

Table A.3 highlights the role of various COBIT processes in improving an IT organisation's **internal processes**, particularly in the context of BYOD integration and IT-BSC application. The strategy management processes (APO02, APO05, and APO08) are central to the design of an approach that aligns organisational goals with

BYOD initiatives. Particular emphasis is placed on the maintenance of relationships and strategic direction, which are essential to the success of BYOD strategies. The quality, risk and security management processes (APO11, APO12, and APO13) focus on establishing robust management strategies that ensure efficiency and security in BYOD environments, all in line with COBIT standards. The processes dealing with solution identification and creation, as well as availability and capacity management (BAI03 and BAI04), play a key role in ensuring that IT services meet the requirements of BYOD strategies and function optimally.

Table A.3 Internal Processes

COBIT Process	Process Description	Short Explanation of the Contribution
APO02	Manage Strategy	Fosters alignment and readiness for BYOD, enhancing strategic direction.
APO05	Manage Portfolio	Ensures BYOD strategies are well-represented in the IT portfolio.
APO08	Manage Relationships	Fosters partnerships beneficial in a BYOD environment.
APO11	Manage Quality	Ensures quality of BYOD strategies per COBIT standards.
APO12	Manage Risk	Focuses on risk management in BYOD settings.
APO13	Manage Security	Safeguards assets in BYOD settings per COBIT standards.
BAI01	Manage Programmes and Projects	Ensures proficient execution of BYOD initiatives.
BAI03	Manage Solutions Identification and Build	Facilitates BYOD integration through innovative solutions.
BAI04	Manage Availability and Capacity	Manages IT service availability essential in BYOD settings.
BAI07	Manage Change Acceptance and Transitioning	Smoothens transition and acceptance of BYOD-related changes.
MEA02	Monitor, Evaluate and Assess the System of Internal Control	Assesses internal controls, including BYOD, for compliance per COBIT.

The COBIT process MEA02, which focuses on monitoring and evaluating IT performance, also plays an important role. Through continuous monitoring and evaluation, MEA02 ensures that BYOD strategies are implemented both efficiently and effectively and achieve the specified goals. In this way, this process contributes to the continuous improvement and adaptability of the organisation, which is crucial for a successful BYOD implementation. Finally, the processes for managing programmes and projects, as well as change acceptance and transition (BAI01 and BAI07), emphasise the need for efficient execution of BYOD initiatives and smooth adoption of changes to ensure internal efficiency, all within the framework of COBIT recommendations.

Table A.4 presents various COBIT processes that are geared towards **learning and growth** in an IT organisation, particularly in the context of integrating BYOD while taking the IT-BSC into account. The processes for managing human resources and communication (APO07 and APO14) represent important aspects that influence the learning and growth perspective in an IT organisation. They place a strong emphasis on promoting learning and personal growth through the competent management of IT personnel and improving communication strategies to create a conducive environment for the integration of BYOD.

Table A.4 Learning and Growth

COBIT Process	Process Description	Short Explanation of the Contribution
APO07	Manage Human Resources	Manages IT staff for smooth BYOD implementation, fostering learning and growth.
APO14	Manage Communication	Enhances communication for BYOD integration, supporting learning and growth.
EDM05	Ensure Stakeholder Transparency	Ensures transparency in BYOD policies, aiding organizational learning and growth.
MEA01	Monitor, Evaluate and Assess Performance and Conformance	Monitors performance in BYOD, promoting learning and growth.

Process EDM05 aims to ensure transparency to all stakeholders, which is particularly important when implementing BYOD policies. This promotes organisational learning and growth by enabling clear communication and understanding of processes, all in line with the COBIT framework. The MEA01 process facilitates the monitoring and evaluation of performance and compliance, which is necessary in a BYOD environment to promote learning and support growth, using COBIT guidelines as a guide. This ensures that the organisation is able to learn and grow constantly by monitoring and evaluating performance, thus promoting continuous improvement. By embedding these COBIT processes within a unified performance architecture, the IPM ensures that learning and growth mechanisms are systematically captured, measured, and strategically directed. It thus contributes to a dynamic feedback loop between performance monitoring, organisational learning, and governance compliance.

(3) Empirical Insights and Information Modeling in Measuring BYOD Effectiveness with IT-BSC

The effective integration of BYOD into enterprise IT management systems, particularly within the COBIT framework, requires an evidence-based approach to performance measurement. This section connects the results of the empirical study with the conceptual structure of IPM and highlights the use of the IT-BSC as both a diagnostic and strategic tool. The integration is based on four iterative process dimensions: planning, collection, analysis, and adjustment. Each dimension is supported by targeted findings from the field and serves as a component in the development of representative and actionable KPIs.

1. **Planning**:

   - Establish a performance measurement framework tailored to the characteristics and challenges of BYOD.
   - Integrate stakeholder requirements and regulatory constraints early in the design.
   - Define strategic goals based on the dual focus of enabling mobility and safeguarding control.

2. **Collection**:

   - Design intelligent and privacy-aware data collection methods to monitor BYOD usage.
   - Implement automated logging of usage patterns, device diversity, and compliance incidents.
   - Capture both qualitative and quantitative dimensions (e.g., satisfaction, availability, data access behavior).

3. **Analysis**:
    - Ensure cross-functional interpretation of KPI results, involving IT, compliance, HR, and end users.
    - Analyze relationships between BYOD adoption and key success factors (e.g., productivity, user satisfaction, risk exposure).
    - Use visualization dashboards and trend analyses to support communication.

4. **Adjustment**:
    - Build in flexible update cycles for KPIs based on usage trends and feedback.
    - Create structured feedback loops with operational units.
    - Promote transparency by publishing metric outcomes and actions taken.

The structured derivation of KPIs from empirical insights and COBIT-aligned control mechanisms allows organizations to build a BYOD-sensitive IT-BSC that is both robust and adaptive. This alignment supports stakeholder satisfaction through the visibility of IT performance and risk management, enhances strategic agility, and fosters closer business-IT integration. By linking individual device usage to process optimization, and user preferences to service personalization, information modeling transforms BYOD data into actionable control elements. As such, IPM not only structures the flow of information but reinforces the strategic relevance of BYOD as a performance-enhancing and innovation-enabling element in the IT governance ecosystem.

The KPIs presented in Table A.5 provide important insights into the value added by BYOD initiatives. The KPIs suggest that integrating BYOD into IT systems could increase the return on IT investments, increase stakeholder satisfaction and help achieve defined goals. These findings indicate a positive influence of BYOD policies on an organisation's overall performance and goal achievement.

The KPIs in Table A.6 underscore the relevance of a well-thought-out enterprise architecture in the BYOD implementation. Taking BYOD policies into account in the current enterprise architecture will promote the integrity and security of business operations. Monitoring exceptions to the enterprise architecture standards could reveal potential security vulnerabilities and enable them to be closed. Finally, feedback on satisfaction with enterprise architecture management can be used to continuously optimise the BYOD guidelines and better align them with user expectations and organisational goals.

Table A.5 IT Value Contribution—APO01

KPI and Formula	Relevance to BYOD
ROI of IT Investments: $\frac{\text{Profit from IT investments - Cost of IT investments}}{\text{Cost of IT investments}} \times 100\%$	Integrating BYOD can potentially reduce the costs of providing devices, thereby possibly increasing the ROI of IT investments.
Stakeholder Satisfaction: Average rating on a scale of 1 to 5	The flexibility afforded by BYOD can lead to higher stakeholder satisfaction, as they can choose devices according to their preferences.
Degree of Goal Achievement: $\frac{\text{Number of goals achieved}}{\text{Total number of goals}} \times 100\%$	Implementing BYOD can assist in achieving certain IT goals more efficiently by enabling the use of personal, familiar devices.

Table A.6 IT Value Contribution—APO03

KPI and Formula	Relevance to BYOD
Percentage of business processes covered by current enterprise architecture: $\left(\frac{\text{\# business processes covered by current enterprise}}{\text{Total number of business processes}}\right) \times 100\%$	By considering the BYOD policies in the enterprise architecture, an organization can ensure that all the business processes adhere to BYOD guidelines, thereby enhancing the integrity and security of business operations.
Number of enterprise architecture standards exceptions: Count of instances where standards are not met	Keeping track of exceptions helps in identifying the gaps in adhering to BYOD policies, which can further assist in tightening the BYOD guidelines to avoid any potential breaches.
Satisfaction level with enterprise architecture management: Scale from 1 (not satisfied) to 5 (very satisfied)	Ensuring the satisfaction level through regular feedback can help in fine-tuning the BYOD policies to be more aligned with user expectations and organizational goals.

In Table A.7, the focus is on the constant maintenance and evaluation of the IT portfolio in order to meet the requirements of the BYOD initiatives. A harmonious portfolio composition that takes into account the concerns of all stakeholder groups plays a central role in finding a broad consensus and addressing the specific needs and security requirements that BYOD brings. Continuously updating the portfolio elements, including the BYOD guidelines, fosters an adaptive IT environment that keeps pace with the latest developments and challenges. Tracking satisfaction with the impact of new investments, particularly those related to BYOD technologies, enables IT strategies to be aligned with organisational goals.

Table A.7 IT Value Contribution—APO04

KPI and Formula	Relevance to BYOD
Percentage of stakeholder groups expressing satisfaction with portfolio composition: $\left(\frac{\text{Number of satisfied stakeholder groups}}{\text{Total number of stakeholder groups}}\right) \times 100\%$	Ensuring a well-balanced portfolio that includes BYOD policies can satisfy a larger group of stakeholders by addressing the needs and security concerns pertinent to BYOD.
Frequency of update of portfolio components: Number of updates in a specified period	Regular updates to the portfolio components, including the BYOD policies, can help in keeping the IT environment vibrant and in tune with the latest developments and requirements.
Satisfaction level with the outcome of new investments: Scale from 1 (not satisfied) to 5 (very satisfied)	Measuring satisfaction levels with new investments, including those in BYOD technologies, can help in aligning the IT strategies more closely with organizational objectives.

The Table A.8 focuses on the importance of the financial aspects of a BYOD strategy. It emphasises that a transparent presentation of the financial benefits and the return on investment of the BYOD strategy can significantly increase the satisfaction of the management. Furthermore, it is emphasised that close monitoring of any budget overruns is necessary to ensure the economic efficiency of the strategy, which could be affected by fluctuating numbers of participants. Finally, the importance of clearly communicating the financial principles of the BYOD initiative to stakeholders is discussed in order to promote a deeper understanding and support for the project.

Table A.8 IT Value Contribution—APO06

KPI and Formula	Relevance to BYOD
Level of satisfaction of business executives with the financial information provided: Scale from 1 (not satisfied) to 5 (very satisfied)	Enhancing the satisfaction level of business executives by providing financial details on the cost benefits and returns on investment from the BYOD strategy can be crucial.
Frequency of budget overruns: Number of overruns in a specified period	Keeping track of budget overruns is essential, especially when incorporating a BYOD strategy that might have fluctuating costs due to varying employee participation levels.
Percentage of stakeholders who understand the financial principles applied: $\left(\frac{\text{\# of stakeholders who understand the principles}}{\text{Total number of stakeholders}}\right) \times 100\%$	Illustrating the financial principles behind the BYOD strategy clearly can enhance stakeholder understanding and foster support for the initiative.

The integration of BYOD into a risk management programme can potentially expand the coverage of corporate risks and thus ensure a more comprehensive approach to mitigating those risks. In addition, the Table A.9 highlights the importance of constant monitoring of unidentified risk events in order to continuously optimise and refine risk assessment. Furthermore, the careful integration of BYOD into the risk profile can help to maintain or increase stakeholder satisfaction by demonstrating control and efficiency.

Transparent integration of BYOD strategies and guidelines will potentially increase stakeholder satisfaction by promoting a better understanding of IT costs and benefits. Furthermore, continuous monitoring of services that fall short of the targets will help to continuously improve BYOD strategies and align them with desired service levels (Table A.10).

By understanding and aligning BYOD strategies with IT governance, stakeholder satisfaction can potentially be increased, as this ensures a more strategic and structured approach to IT governance. Furthermore, a well-integrated BYOD

Table A.9 IT Value Contribution—APO09

KPI and Formula	Relevance to BYOD
Percentage of enterprise risk covered by the risk management program: $\left(\frac{\text{Enterprise risk covered}}{\text{Total enterprise risk}}\right) \times 100\%$	Incorporating BYOD into the risk management program can potentially expand the coverage of enterprise risks, ensuring a comprehensive approach to mitigating risks.
Number of risk events occurring that were not identified in risk assessments: Number of unidentified risk events	Keeping a tab on the risk events not identified initially can help in iterating the risk assessment process while incorporating BYOD to be more foresightful and effective.
Level of satisfaction of stakeholders with the risk profile: Scale from 1 (not satisfied) to 5 (very satisfied)	Satisfaction levels can be maintained or improved by presenting a well-balanced risk profile which includes the careful integration of BYOD, showcasing control and efficiency.

Table A.10 IT Value Contribution—APO10

KPI and Formula	Relevance to BYOD
Level of stakeholder satisfaction with the transparency and understanding of IT costs, benefits, strategy, policies and service levels: Scale from 1 (not satisfied) to 5 (very satisfied)	Stakeholder satisfaction can potentially be increased by transparently integrating BYOD strategies and policies, which might foster a better understanding of IT costs and benefits.
Number of services below target service levels: Number of services below target	Keeping a record of services that are below the target service levels can help in continuously improving and aligning the BYOD strategies to meet the desired service levels.

policy can facilitate a more dynamic and responsive IT strategy that can quickly respond to changes in business strategy, thereby increasing overall agility, as shown in Table A.11.

Table A.11 IT Value Contribution—EDM01

KPI and Formula	Relevance to BYOD
Stakeholder satisfaction with enterprise governance of IT arrangements: Scale from 1 (not satisfied) to 5 (very satisfied)	Understanding and aligning BYOD strategies with IT governance can potentially enhance stakeholder satisfaction by ensuring a more streamlined and strategic approach to IT governance.
Frequency of update of the IT strategy in response to business strategy changes: Number of updates in the last 12 months	A well-integrated BYOD policy can facilitate a more dynamic and responsive IT strategy, which can quickly adapt to changes in the business strategy, enhancing overall agility.

The implementation of BYOD will increase the realisation of benefits from optimising IT investments by enabling more flexible and efficient use of IT resources. In addition, integrating BYOD into the IT portfolio can ensure alignment with strategic priorities by promoting agility and responding to changing business needs and priorities, according to Table A.12.

Table A.12 IT Value Contribution—EDM03

KPI and Formula	Relevance to BYOD
Realisation of benefits from investments in IT-enabled change: % of defined benefits realised from IT-enabled investments	Implementing BYOD can potentially increase the realization of benefits by optimizing IT investments, as it allows for more flexible and efficient use of IT resources.
Alignment of portfolio with strategic priorities: % of IT investments that are directly aligned with business	BYOD integration into the IT portfolio can ensure alignment with strategic priorities by fostering agility and responsiveness to changing business needs and priorities.

The successful integration of BYOD has a positive effect on user satisfaction with IT services. If employees can use their preferred devices, this could generally increase satisfaction, as indicated by a high percentage of user satisfaction (see Table A.13). A reduced number of service complaints could also be an indicator of high user satisfaction with the IT services enabled by BYOD. Furthermore, a short average resolution time for service complaints can indicate efficient BYOD management practices that promote user satisfaction.

Table A.13 IT Value Contribution—EDM03

KPI and Formula	Relevance to BYOD
Percentage of user satisfaction with IT services: $\frac{\text{Number of satisfied users}}{\text{Total number of users}} \times 100\%$	A high percentage of user satisfaction could indicate successful integration of BYOD, where employees are able to use their preferred devices, generally increasing satisfaction.
Number of service complaints: Total number of filed complaints	A lower value in this KPI could indicate high user satisfaction with the IT services enabled by BYOD.
Average resolution time of service complaints: $\frac{\text{Total time taken to resolve all complaints}}{\text{Total number of resolved complaints}}$	A short average resolution time could indicate efficient BYOD management practices fostering user satisfaction.

Incorporating BYOD strategies helps to increase user satisfaction by improving the efficiency and effectiveness of the IT service desk. A high first contact resolution rate at the service desk could indicate that the IT service desk is well prepared to solve problems arising from the BYOD policy, thus ensuring user satisfaction (Table A.14). In addition, minimising the average downtime through competent BYOD management can increase user satisfaction by ensuring constant availability of the service.

Training users to effectively use BYOD systems can be a key tool for increasing user satisfaction (Table A.15). A high percentage of users who are satisfied with the IT training is an indicator that the familiarisation with the BYOD aspects has been successful, which in turn can increase overall satisfaction. Furthermore, an

Table A.14 User Satisfaction—DSS02

KPI and Formula	Relevance to BYOD
Service desk first-contact resolution rate: $\frac{\text{Number of incidents resolved on first contact}}{\text{Total number of incidents reported}} \times 100\%$	A high first-contact resolution rate might indicate that the IT service desk is well-equipped to handle issues arising from the BYOD policy, thus ensuring user satisfaction.
Average downtime of services: $\frac{\text{Total downtime in hours}}{\text{Total number of incidents}}$	Minimizing the average downtime through proficient BYOD management can elevate user satisfaction by ensuring consistent service availability.

Table A.15 User Satisfaction—DSS03

KPI and Formula	Relevance to BYOD
Percentage of users satisfied with IT training: $\frac{\text{Number of satisfied users}}{\text{Total number of users surveyed}} \times 100\%$	Enhancing IT training to encompass aspects of BYOD can help in increasing the satisfaction levels among the users.
Average time to deliver a training session: $\frac{\text{Total time taken for all sessions}}{\text{Number of sessions}}$	Streamlining the training process by incorporating BYOD aspects can potentially reduce the time required to deliver each session, thereby improving satisfaction levels.

optimised training procedure that takes BYOD aspects into account can potentially reduce the time required for each session, which can have a positive effect on satisfaction levels.

A shorter mean time to fulfil end-user service requests is an indication that the implementation of BYOD strategies accelerates the response time to fulfil end-user service requests, which in turn improves user satisfaction, as listed in Table A.16. Furthermore, the integration of BYOD into the IT structure could enable a more efficient solution, increasing the proportion of requests resolved on the first attempt and thus increasing user satisfaction.

Table A.16 User Satisfaction—DSS05

KPI and Formula	Relevance to BYOD
Average time to satisfy end-user service requests: $\frac{\text{Total time to satisfy requests}}{\text{Number of requests}}$	Utilizing BYOD strategies can potentially expedite the response time to satisfy end-user service requests, thereby improving the user satisfaction.
Percentage of service requests with first-time resolution: $\frac{\text{Number of service requests resolved on the first attempt}}{\text{Total number of service requests}} \times 100\%$	Integrating BYOD can foster a more efficient resolution process, increasing the proportion of requests resolved at the first attempt, hence improving user satisfaction.

Developing a structured BYOD policy increases user satisfaction by enabling IT services to be made more responsive and personalised. This can be measured by the KPI 'user satisfaction with the IT service management process', where users can rate their satisfaction on a scale of 1 (not satisfied) to 5 (very satisfied) (see Table A.17). Furthermore, a well-implemented BYOD strategy fosters a culture of continuous improvement in which end users are encouraged to suggest improvements. This will further optimise the system and is measurable by the number of end-user suggested improvements in a given period.

Table A.17 User Satisfaction—DSS06

KPI and Formula	Relevance to BYOD
User satisfaction with the IT service management process: Scale from 1 (not satisfied) to 5 (very satisfied)	Developing a structured BYOD policy may improve user satisfaction by potentially allowing IT services to be more responsive and tailored to individual needs.
Number of improvements suggested by end users: Total number of improvements suggested in a given period	A well-implemented BYOD strategy could foster a culture of continuous improvement where end-users are encouraged to suggest improvements, thereby enhancing the system further.

Aligning the BYOD strategy with the overall IT strategy can ensure coherent planning and could lead to a more synergistic approach to achieving organisational goals. This is measurable by the alignment of the IT strategic plan with the business strategic plan, using a scale of 1 (not aligned) to 5 (fully aligned) as shown in Table A.18.

Table A.18 Internal Processes—APO02

KPI and Formula	Relevance to BYOD
Alignment of the strategic IT plan with the enterprise strategic plan: Scale from 1 (not aligned) to 5 (fully aligned)	Aligning BYOD strategy with the overall IT strategy can ensure cohesive planning and may result in a more synergized approach towards achieving organizational goals.
Level of satisfaction of business executives with the contribution of IT to the achievement of the business strategy: Scale from 1 (not satisfied) to 5 (very satisfied)	BYOD policies that are well integrated into IT strategies can potentially enhance the satisfaction level of business executives by ensuring that IT contributes more effectively towards achieving business strategies.

Furthermore, a BYOD policy that is well integrated into IT strategies can increase management satisfaction by ensuring that IT contributes more effectively to the achievement of business strategies. This can be measured by the level of satisfaction of managing directors with the contribution of IT to the achievement of business strategies, rated on a scale from 1 (not satisfied) to 5 (very satisfied).

Well-curated IT portfolio integration of BYOD policies can increase business satisfaction by aligning the IT infrastructure more closely with business needs and preferences. Satisfaction can be measured on a scale of 1 (not satisfied) to 5 (very satisfied) and serves as an indicator of the effectiveness of BYOD integration into the IT portfolio (see Table A.19).

In addition, regular updates to the IT portfolio, which include adjustments to the BYOD guidelines, help to ensure an up-to-date and responsive IT environment that adapts to changing business requirements and technological developments. The frequency of updates in the last 12 months is an important indicator of the dynamism and adaptability of the IT strategy.

Table A.19 Internal Processes—APO05

KPI and Formula	Relevance to BYOD
Level of business satisfaction with IT portfolio composition: Scale from 1 (not satisfied) to 5 (very satisfied)	A well-curated IT portfolio, inclusive of BYOD policies, can enhance business satisfaction by aligning the IT infrastructure more closely with business needs and preferences.
Frequency of update of the IT portfolio: Number of updates in the last 12 months	Regular updates to the IT portfolio to incorporate or adjust BYOD policies can ensure a fresh and responsive IT environment, adapting to evolving business requirements and technological advancements.

The introduction of BYOD strategies will increase the efficiency of relationship managers by enabling them to manage more relationships effectively. This will thus have a positive influence on the number of relationships managed per relationship manager, which would be measurable by corresponding KPIs (Table A.20). In a further step, stakeholder satisfaction with the relationship management could be improved by integrating flexible and customised IT solutions that offer BYOD strategies. This satisfaction can be measured on a scale of 1 to 5, with a higher value indicating greater satisfaction.

Table A.20 Internal Processes—APO08

KPI and Formula	Relevance to BYOD
Number of relationships managed per relationship manager: Number of relationships / Number of relationship managers	BYOD policies can potentially streamline processes, allowing relationship managers to handle more relationships efficiently, therefore having a positive impact on this KPI.
Stakeholder satisfaction with relationship management: Scale from 1 (not satisfied) to 5 (very satisfied)	Integrating BYOD strategies can possibly enhance stakeholder satisfaction by providing them with flexible and custom-tailored IT solutions, thereby increasing the efficiency of relationship management.

The integration of BYOD strategies can significantly reduce the number of complaints from stakeholders, as it enables a more efficient use of IT resources that better meets stakeholder expectations. Likewise, stakeholder satisfaction can be increased by incorporating BYOD guidelines, as a system is established that is better aligned with individual preferences and working habits, as shown in Table A.21.

Table A.21 Internal Processes—APO11

KPI and Formula	Relevance to BYOD
Number of stakeholder complaints: Number of complaints received in a period	A well-structured BYOD policy could potentially reduce the number of stakeholder complaints by ensuring a smoother and more efficient use of IT resources, thereby meeting stakeholders' expectations more accurately.
Stakeholder satisfaction with the quality management system: Scale from 1 (not satisfied) to 5 (very satisfied)	BYOD integration can facilitate a higher degree of satisfaction by providing a system that is more aligned with individual preferences and work habits, promoting a positive response from the stakeholders.

Regular risk management reviews, which also take BYOD policies into account, enable the organisation to stay informed of the risk situation and take timely action to mitigate the risks associated with BYOD. In addition, ensuring stakeholder satisfaction through effective risk management is crucial, especially in view of the potential risks associated with BYOD practices. An appropriate risk management strategy could create a harmonious balance between the flexibility offered by BYOD and the security of organisational data, as highlighted in Table A.22.

Implementing BYOD policies can increase the risk of security breaches. To ensure a secure environment for the use of personal devices for organisational tasks, it is therefore essential to carry out regular security tests that enable the timely identification and mitigation of security risks, see Table A.23. Furthermore, BYOD can be a controversial point in terms of IT security. Building robust security measures that adequately protect organisational data while enabling BYOD can lead to higher stakeholder satisfaction by balancing flexibility and security.

The introduction of BYOD strategies can foster the development of new IT services that in turn enable business process improvements by using personalised and familiar devices, which can lead to an increase in this KPI, according to Table A.24.

Table A.22 Internal Processes—APO12

KPI and Formula	Relevance to BYOD
Frequency of management review of risk management: Number of reviews in the last 12 months	Regular review of risk management, inclusive of BYOD policies, ensures that the organization is constantly aware of the risk posture and can take timely actions to mitigate risks associated with BYOD.
Satisfaction of stakeholders with risk management: Scale from 1 (not satisfied) to 5 (very satisfied)	Ensuring stakeholder satisfaction through effective risk management could be vital, especially considering the potential risks involved in BYOD practices. A proper risk management strategy could maintain a harmonious balance between flexibility offered by BYOD and security of organizational data.

Table A.23 Internal Processes—APO13

KPI and Formula	Relevance to BYOD
Frequency of security testing: Number of tests conducted in the last 12 months	BYOD policies inherently increase the risk of security breaches. Regular security testing can help in timely identification and mitigation of security risks, ensuring a safe environment for the utilization of personal devices for organizational tasks.
Stakeholder satisfaction with IT security: Scale from 1 (not satisfied) to 5 (very satisfied)	BYOD can be a contentious point when it comes to IT security. Establishing robust security measures that can adequately safeguard the organizational data while allowing BYOD can lead to higher stakeholder satisfaction by balancing flexibility and security.

Furthermore, aligning BYOD policies with new or improved IT services can increase stakeholder satisfaction by providing services that match the preferences and habits of individual users who use their own devices.

A carefully crafted BYOD approach can help reduce the number of incidents leading to data corruption or loss by establishing clear guidelines and security protocols to be followed when using personal devices for business purposes, as listed

Table A.24 Internal Processes—BAI01

KPI and Formula	Relevance to BYOD
Number of business process improvements enabled by new or improved IT services: Number of improvements in the last 12 months	Implementing BYOD strategies can foster the development of new IT services, which in turn can enable business process improvements by leveraging personalized and familiar devices, leading to an increase in this KPI.
Stakeholder satisfaction with new or improved IT services: Scale from 1 (not satisfied) to 5 (very satisfied)	Aligning BYOD policies with new or improved IT services can enhance stakeholder satisfaction by offering services that cater to the preferences and familiarities of individual users, utilizing their own devices.

Table A.25 Internal Processes—BAI03

KPI and Formula	Relevance to BYOD
Number of incidents causing data corruption or loss: Number of incidents in the last 12 months	A well-structured BYOD policy can help in reducing the number of incidents causing data corruption or loss by setting clear guidelines and security protocols to be followed when using personal devices for organizational purposes.
Percentage of stakeholders satisfied with the reliability of IT services: $\frac{\text{Number of satisfied stakeholders}}{\text{Total number of stakeholders}} \times 100\%$	Ensuring the reliability of IT services through a streamlined BYOD policy can enhance stakeholder satisfaction by providing dependable services through a variety of devices, meeting individual preferences and needs.

in Table A.25. Furthermore, ensuring IT service reliability through a tight BYOD policy can increase stakeholder satisfaction by providing reliable services over a variety of devices that meet individual preferences and needs.

As can be seen from the Table A.26, incorporating feedback from BYOD users into regular updates plays an important role in driving improvements in the system. This can promote the effectiveness and acceptance of the IT environment. In addition, the analysis indicates that changes to business processes may accompany the implementation of a BYOD strategy. Therefore, it is essential to ensure stakeholder

Table A.26 Internal Processes—BAI04

KPI and Formula	Relevance to BYOD
Frequency of updates and improvements based on stakeholder feedback: Number of updates in the last 12 months	Gathering feedback from BYOD users and incorporating it into regular updates can potentially lead to improvements in the system, enhancing the effectiveness and receptivity of the IT environment.
Stakeholder satisfaction with new or changed business processes: Scale from 1 (not satisfied) to 5 (very satisfied)	Implementing a BYOD strategy might involve changes in business processes; ensuring stakeholder satisfaction with these changes is crucial to maintaining a positive perception of the IT environment and facilitating smooth transitions.

satisfaction in order to maintain a positive perception of the IT environment and to enable smooth transitions.

The introduction of a BYOD strategy can initially lead to an increased number of user-reported problems. It is therefore essential to monitor this KPI closely after implementation in order to maintain a productive IT environment, as shown in Table A.27. Furthermore, the table shows that stakeholder satisfaction is a key indicator of the success of the integration of BYOD into business processes. Monitoring this KPI makes it possible to make the necessary adjustments to ensure successful integration.

As can be seen from Table A.28, implementing BYOD strategies will support innovation by allowing employees to use the devices they are most familiar with. This could have a positive impact on management satisfaction with IT support for innovation.

The table also indicates that BYOD implementation may potentially relieve IT staff of the administration of standardised company devices, allowing more time to be spent on innovation and learning, which would positively influence this KPI.

From the information presented in Table A.29, it can be seen that BYOD strategies will increase the satisfaction of business process owners by providing more flexible and personalised IT support, which promotes a more efficient way of working. Furthermore, it can be deduced that by aligning BYOD strategies with business strategies, a higher level of integration of IT and business processes could be achieved, potentially improving overall operations and efficiency.

Table A.27 Internal Processes—BAI07

KPI and Formula	Relevance to BYOD
Number of user reported issues after deployment: Number of issues reported in the first 3 months after deployment	The introduction of a BYOD strategy might lead to an increased number of user-reported issues initially. It is essential to monitor this KPI closely to resolve issues promptly and maintain a productive IT environment.
Stakeholder satisfaction with new or changed business processes: Scale from 1 (not satisfied) to 5 (very satisfied)	BYOD strategies often involve changes to existing business processes; hence, measuring stakeholder satisfaction is vital to gauge the success of the BYOD integration into business processes and to make necessary adjustments based on feedback.

Table A.28 Learning and Growth—APO07

KPI and Formula	Relevance to BYOD
Satisfaction of business executives with IT's support for innovation: Scale from 1 (not satisfied) to 5 (very satisfied)	Leveraging BYOD strategies can potentially foster innovation by allowing employees to use the devices they are most comfortable with, potentially enhancing productivity and nurturing innovation.
Percentage of IT personnel time used on innovation and learning: $\frac{\text{Time spent on innovation and learning}}{\text{Total IT personnel time}} \times 100\%$	Implementing BYOD can potentially free up IT personnel time from managing standardized company devices, allowing them to allocate more time to innovation and learning, thus contributing positively to this KPI.

The information in Table A.30 suggests that a well-managed BYOD policy could increase stakeholder satisfaction by transparently presenting IT costs, benefits, and risks, thus enabling informed decision-making and optimised resource allocation.

Furthermore, it becomes clear that a dynamic BYOD strategy could foster a more adaptive IT strategy, where frequent updates reflect a proactive approach to addressing changing business needs and technological landscapes.

According to Table A.31, an efficient BYOD strategy can boost stakeholder satisfaction through high IT performance that caters to the needs and preferences

Table A.29 Learning and Growth—APO14

KPI and Formula	Relevance to BYOD
Satisfaction of business process owners with the support of IT to business processes: Scale from 1 (not satisfied) to 5 (very satisfied)	Implementing BYOD strategies can enhance the satisfaction of business process owners by offering flexible and personalized IT support, facilitating a smoother workflow and potentially improving business processes.
Level of integration of IT processes with business processes: Scale from 1 (low integration) to 5 (high integration)	By aligning BYOD strategies with business strategies, a higher level of integration between IT and business processes can be achieved, potentially improving the overall workflow and efficiency.

Table A.30 Learning and Growth—EDM05

KPI and Formula	Relevance to BYOD
Satisfaction of stakeholders with the transparency of IT costs, benefits and risk: Scale from 1 (not satisfied) to 5 (very satisfied)	Stakeholder satisfaction can be improved with a well-managed BYOD policy that transparently outlines IT costs, benefits, and risks, allowing for informed decision-making and optimized resource allocation.
Frequency of updates to the IT strategy: Number of updates in the last 12 months	A dynamic BYOD strategy can foster a more adaptable IT strategy, with frequent updates reflecting a proactive approach to evolving business needs and technological landscapes.

of individual users. Furthermore, regular performance reporting, facilitated by a well-executed BYOD strategy, could ensure that stakeholders are continuously kept informed, building trust and fostering greater alignment between IT operations and organisational objectives.

In conclusion, it can be said that the selection and application of relevant COBIT KPIs is essential for the successful implementation of compliance in an IT management system, especially when BYOD strategies are taken into account. The KPIs mentioned make it possible to systematically evaluate and continuously monitor

Table A.31 Learning and Growth—MEA01

KPI and Formula	Relevance to BYOD
Level of stakeholder satisfaction with IT performance: Scale from 1 (not satisfied) to 5 (very satisfied)	An efficient BYOD strategy can enhance stakeholder satisfaction by promoting a high level of IT performance that is responsive to the needs and preferences of individual users.
Frequency of performance reporting to stakeholders: Number of reports per year	Regular performance reporting, which can be facilitated by a well-implemented BYOD strategy, ensures stakeholders are consistently updated, fostering trust and alignment between IT operations and organizational objectives.

both the efficiency and the effectiveness of IT processes. By incorporating BYOD-specific indicators, companies can optimally exploit the advantages of BYOD, such as increased employee satisfaction and improved flexibility, while also identifying and managing potential risks at an early stage. The use of COBIT KPIs provides a structured framework that supports the strategic alignment of IT with business objectives. Overall, they help the organisation to improve the governance and management of IT resources, including BYOD, and to align them with compliance requirements. This paves the way for greater organisational agility, better risk management and increased user satisfaction.

(4) Monitoring of current developments, as well as validation and verification
In the final phase of the implementation process of a BYOD concept, which is carried out in the context of the COBIT framework and the IT-BSC, the continuous monitoring and analysis of operational dynamics and developments takes on a central role. The implementation process should by no means be considered complete, but rather as a continuous, cyclical undertaking that requires regular evaluation and, if necessary, adaptation. In this phase, it is particularly important to install a robust monitoring and management system that captures both quantitative and qualitative data. The aim is to monitor the performance indicators, also known as KPIs, in real time in order to evaluate the efficiency, effectiveness and strategic alignment of the implemented BYOD strategies. In addition, this system enables a verification of the implemented strategies with regard to their compliance with the original goals and objectives, as well as a validation in the context of real working condi-

tions. This constant monitoring and feedback system is essential for the long-term viability and success of the BYOD concept. It not only ensures compliance with compliance standards and security guidelines, but also enables an agile response to technological changes and operational requirements. This supports and optimises the continuous alignment process between IT and business strategies within the COBIT framework and the IT-BSC. The IPM provides the structural basis for this monitoring system by linking performance indicators, strategic objectives and governance controls within a unified framework. It enables the systematic validation and verification of BYOD strategies by offering reference points for deviation analysis, goal conformity and traceability. Through its layered architecture, the IPM facilitates continuous feedback and adaptive control, ensuring that both operational agility and strategic consistency are maintained over time.

Continuous monitoring

In the continuous monitoring and development phase, the primary goal is to generate a comprehensive real-time picture of the system state. This includes the continuous collection and analysis of all relevant parameters and KPIs that have been carefully identified and defined in the previous implementation phases. This continuous monitoring enables an agile response to dynamic changes, discrepancies or deviations in the system. The systematic collection of data thus creates a basis for an evidence-based management approach. The integration of automated analysis tools plays a significant role in this phase. These technologies are able to process and interpret complex data sets in real time or almost in real time. In doing so, they can perform not only reactive but also proactive analyses. This means that possible trends, patterns and anomalies can be detected and interpreted at an early stage. Such insights are invaluable as they provide decision-makers with in-depth data and analysis, ensuring a higher degree of accuracy and reliability in decision-making.

Furthermore, these automated tools enable the creation of comprehensive reports. These can be prepared at different levels of granularity to provide both a macroscopic overview and microscopic insights into specific aspects of the system. Combining quantitative data and qualitative analysis, these reports can paint a holistic picture of the system's state, integrating both technical and business perspectives.

Validation and verification

In the final implementation phase of a BYOD system developed within the COBIT framework and an IT-BSC, continuous monitoring of system performance and effectiveness plays a key role. This monitoring serves as a starting point for the distinct but complementary processes of validation and verification. Validation acts as a quality assessment mechanism that checks the compliance of the implemented strategies with the assumed organisational goals. This is often achieved through a wide range of KPIs defined in the planning phase. Through systematic collection and analysis of data, it assesses whether the achieved results meet the defined objectives and requirements, thereby answering the question of whether 'the right thing has been done in the right way'. By contrast, verification focuses on the technical accuracy of the implementation. This process involves rigorous testing through various test mechanisms to ensure that the system meets the specified technical requirements. Thus, verification addresses the question of whether the system 'correctly implements the intended right thing'. Furthermore, the introduction of a maturity model represents a significant step in the continuous improvement of quality. Such a model provides a structured method for assessing the current development stage of the system and enables targeted, iterative adjustments to optimise performance.

The maturity model, firmly rooted in the COBIT framework, offers a structured approach to evaluating an organisation's current state of development in terms of the integration and alignment of its IT resources and strategies. The focus here is on assessing how far a company has progressed in developing its BYOD strategy and to what extent its IT BSC is effectively aligned with the COBIT 2019 framework. A core element of the maturity model is the assignment of different capability levels to the individual process activities examined as part of the COBIT Performance Management (CPM). This model is based on Capability Maturity Model Integration (CMMI) version 2.0 and comprises six defined levels, each representing a specific stage of development. The detailed breakdown of these levels enables companies to obtain an accurate overview of their current status and to formulate targeted strategies for further development. It fosters a culture of excellence and continuous improvement, with a focus on data-driven decision-making and proactive strategy adjustment. These processes provide a backbone for the long-term implementation of the BYOD concept, as they allow for continuous adaptation to the changing landscape while helping to maintain the strategic direction of the organisation.

Contribution to scientific research

This dissertation has made a significant scientific contribution by closing the gap between the COBIT framework, the IT-BSC and the rapidly developing field of BYOD initiatives. Through the extensive research work, an introductory model has been developed that enables companies to systematically and efficiently implement BYOD initiatives in the context of an IT-BSC and the COBIT framework. Central to this model is the development of the IPM, which serves as a structural and semantic integration layer. It bridges the methodological gap between governance (COBIT), strategic performance logic (IT-BSC) and BYOD-specific implementation elements, thereby enabling a traceable, scalable and evidence-based integration architecture. The following points highlight the key elements of this paper:

This paper makes a significant research contribution by developing a holistic methodology that simplifies and optimises the integration of BYOD initiatives, IT-BSC and the COBIT framework. It fills a gap in the existing literature, in which these components have mostly been treated in isolation. By linking these elements, the work opens up new multidisciplinary solutions and provides a better understanding of the complex interactions between these areas. The methodology is empirically sound and takes into account both the strategic and operational aspects of IT management. It incorporates the challenges of BYOD implementation as well as the strategic considerations provided by COBIT and IT-BSC. This leads to practice-oriented recommendations for action that support decision-making in modern IT strategies in an evidence-based way. The IPM reinforces this evidence-based approach by providing a unified model architecture for deriving, aligning and operationalising performance indicators. Its layered structure enables empirical validation and supports the continuous refinement of strategic goals, governance controls and measurement logic. This integrative approach is not only of academic value, but is also relevant for business practice. It provides a sound basis for developing recommendations for action and promotes a nuanced understanding of the dynamic interactions that occur when BYOD initiatives are introduced. This is particularly important in view of the growing complexity in corporate IT landscapes.

The empirical study conducted as part of this dissertation serves as a crucial tool for validating and expanding the theoretical findings. This is not just a purely scientific exercise, but an essential mechanism for testing and substantiating the practical applicability and relevance of the presented research hypotheses. This study goes far beyond simply confirming the original research hypotheses. While the validation of the hypotheses is an important scientific contribution in itself, it is above all the empirically gained insights that give the research additional depth and practical relevance. By collecting and analysing real data, nuanced perspectives on the challenges, opportunities and limitations of integrating BYOD into an IT-BSC system in the context of the COBIT framework have been gained.

Particularly noteworthy is the role of the empirical study as a feedback mechanism for theory development. It provides an evidence base on which the theoretical models and concepts can be further refined and adapted. This dynamic interaction between theory and empirical research is a hallmark of rigorous scientific research and increases the credibility and applicability of the entire work. The empirical findings also provide a wealth of specific, applicable insights that can be directly incorporated into the design of management guidelines and the further development of the COBIT framework and IT-BSC. They help to narrow the gap between scientific research and business practice by highlighting the factors that should be considered when implementing BYOD in order to optimise efficiency, effectiveness and strategic alignment. Overall, the empirical study not only represents an extension of scientific research, but also serves as a robust basis for practice-oriented recommendations and future scientific research in this complex and constantly evolving field.

The question of how to measure the success of implementing BYOD initiatives is one of the most significant challenges in the context of information technology management research. The difficulty of defining measurable criteria for evaluating the success of such initiatives not only makes empirical verifiability more difficult, but also practical implementation. This work addresses this complex issue and makes a substantial contribution to both science and practice by identifying and operationalising specific indicators. The developed KPIs are carefully designed to work in synergy with the existing metrics of the COBIT framework and the IT-BSC. This integration creates a robust and comprehensive basis for performance measurement. The KPIs enable standardised, objective measurement of the effectiveness, efficiency and strategic alignment of BYOD initiatives, while meeting the rigorous requirements of scientific validity and reliability.

Another key advantage of this approach is the interoperability of the KPIs with the overarching management systems. The identified performance indicators are designed to integrate seamlessly into the existing structures of the COBIT framework and the IT-BSC. This avoids redundancies and promotes the efficient use of resources. This synergetic integration helps to exploit the full potential of BYOD initiatives and create significant added value for the organisation. The design of specific KPIs for BYOD initiatives in this work thus not only provides an innovative scientific method for addressing the problem, but also a pragmatic guide for IT managers and decision-makers. Establishing such a performance measurement system increases transparency, minimises risks and improves organisational performance overall. This is a significant advance in the operationalisation of management systems in complex IT environments and thus provides a robust foundation for future research and practical applications. The IPM provides the conceptual backbone for this operationalisation by enabling the mapping of KPIs to both governance requirements and strategic performance goals. It ensures that the performance measurement system retains methodological coherence while being adaptable to varying organisational and technological contexts.

The practical applicability of the research results is an essential value, especially in a rapidly changing and complex field such as IT management. By providing structured and evidence-based guidelines, decision-makers are empowered to not only evaluate BYOD initiatives in theory, but also implement them effectively in practice. The unique challenges and opportunities arising from the combination ofm]yrrt IT-BSC, COBIT framework and BYOD are considered in an integrated strategy. These recommendations for action are not only operationalisable but also scalable, so that they can be applied in companies of different sizes and in different industries. This increases the universal applicability of the research results and underlines their relevance for both the scientific community and industry.

At a time when the effective use of technology is increasingly seen as a crucial competitive factor, this work offers much-needed guidance. Combining theoretical rigour and practical applicability, the study advances the existing research landscape while also providing immediate added value for business practice. The work therefore functions not only as an academic construct but also as an operationalisable tool that can help improve the efficiency, effectiveness and strategic alignment of IT organisations.

Through these various contributions, this dissertation has made a substantial contribution to research in the field of IT governance. It serves as a basis for further scientific research and offers practical benefits for companies that are looking for efficient and effective methods for integrating BYOD initiatives. The IPM developed in this dissertation constitutes a transferable scientific framework that can be adapted in future studies to investigate other forms of IT innovation integration. Its generalisable structure supports theory development, empirical testing and practical application in equal measure.

Recommendations for future research

The present thesis marks a significant advance in the research field of IT management, particularly in the integration of BYOD initiatives into an IT BSC in the context of the COBIT framework. It offers profound insights and practice-oriented guidelines, while laying a robust foundation for further research. This research field is characterised by inherent complexity and is subject to constant change, both technologically and organisationally. The work not only clarifies existing concepts, but also opens up the horizon for future research possibilities. Without already outlining specific next steps, it is clear that the research here is not complete. The complexity of the topic and the rapid development in the field of information technology provide fertile ground for future academic and practice-oriented research.

The research work has developed and evaluated a specific methodology for the integration of BYOD in IT-BSCs in the context of the COBIT framework. This focus raises the question of the extent to which the developed methodology can be applied and adapted beyond its current scope. In the course of this, a variety of research approaches are opening up that could critically question and further develop the transferability and flexibility of the methodology. On the one hand, there is the possibility of extending the methodology to other technology initiatives. An interesting starting point here could be the transferability to newer or different technologies such as cloud computing, Internet of Things (IoT) or blockchain. Can the improvements achieved through BYOD integration also be expected in the introduction of cloud structures or IoT systems? Or are specific modifications or extensions of the methodology necessary to ensure its relevance in these different technology areas?

On the other hand, it would be interesting to put the methodology into the context of other governance and management frameworks that are also applied in the IT sector. Frameworks such as Information Technology Infrastructure Library (ITIL), Project Management Body of Knowledge (PMBOK) or Agile could serve as further test fields. How seamlessly can the developed methodology be integrated into these frameworks? What synergies or points of friction arise in the process, and how could these be addressed to ensure effective performance measurement and control? Answering these questions has not only scientific but also practical implications. It could help to better understand the limitations of the current methodology and at the same time evaluate its applicability, flexibility and robustness in different technology and governance contexts. This would identify any necessary adjustments to the methodology that would ensure its broader applicability and effectiveness. Overall, these research approaches could help to test the universality of the developed methodology and thus underpin its relevance in both academia and practice.

The present dissertation focuses primarily on the short-term effects of incorporating BYOD into IT-BSCs, specifically in the context of the COBIT framework. Although this snapshot provides valuable insights into the immediate benefits and challenges of implementation, an important dimension remains largely uncharted: the evolution of these effects over time. In this regard, longitudinal studies could provide a crucial extension to the research design.

Longitudinal studies would make it possible to systematically capture changes in performance indicators and other relevant metrics over an extended period of time. Such studies could both evaluate the stability of the improvements achieved and identify potential long-term side effects or unforeseen consequences. For example, questions regarding the IT organisation's ability to adapt to technological changes or the long-term impact on the IT cost structure could be examined. Furthermore, longitudinal studies could provide a differentiated view of the dynamics between the various elements of the system—BYOD, IT-BSC and COBIT. This is particularly interesting when you consider that organisations operate in a constantly changing technological and regulatory environment. How does the integrated methodology respond to new COBIT versions or to changes in IT security requirements? What adjustments are needed to continuously optimise the methodology? Such a longitudinal analysis could not only substantiate the scientific quality of the developed methodology, but also provide practical guidance for the long-term strategic planning and management of IT resources. It would close an important gap between theory and the long-term applicability of research results.

In the context of the present research, although the efficiency of implementing BYOD initiatives was examined in the context of IT-BSCs and COBIT, the financial aspect was not fully considered. Future studies could focus on a detailed cost-benefit analysis to better understand and quantify the profitability of the integration. Such a comprehensive analysis could start by identifying the initial costs of implementation, which could include both hardware and software investments, employee training, and any expenses for external consultants. In addition, the ongoing operating costs, such as maintenance, support, and licence fees, should be determined. The next step would be to compare these costs with the benefits expected from the integration. To do this, KPIs from the IT-BSC could be used to measure time savings, productivity increases or improved resource utilisation, for example.

It would also be important to define the period over which these investments should pay off. By discounting future cash flows, a Net Present Value (NPV) of the BYOD initiative could be calculated, which can serve as a basis for decision-making by management. Last but not least, intangible benefits, such as increased employee satisfaction or improved adaptability to market changes, should also be included in the cost-benefit analysis. Although these may be difficult to quantify, they play an important role in the long-term competitiveness of the company. Such a detailed cost-benefit analysis would thus enable a more holistic view of the profitability of BYOD integration within the framework of an IT-BSC and COBIT and could serve as a basis for decisions on implementation in similar contexts. It would also make it possible to evaluate the economic efficiency of the developed methodology and could therefore be an important addition to the aspects already examined.

In summary, it is clear that research in this area still has numerous untapped areas. While the extension of the methodology to other technology initiatives and frameworks can test the universality and adaptability of the developed approaches, longitudinal studies offer the opportunity to better understand the temporal development of the effects. In addition, a detailed cost-benefit analysis could provide valuable insights into the economic viability of BYOD implementation within the framework of IT-BSCs and COBIT. But even aside from these specific considerations, the field of research offers further dimensions that have not yet been explored in detail and that are worth investigating. There is therefore plenty of scope for future research that could examine both the aspects highlighted here and those not yet discussed in more detail.

Bibliography

(ILO), I. L. O. (2023). The future of work in the digital age. Retrieved August 27, 2023, from https://www.ilo.org/global/topics/future-work/lang--en/index.htm

Andriessen, D. (2013). The impact of byod on organizations. *Journal of Organizational Computing and Electronic Commerce*, *23*(2), 113–136.

Andriole, S. J. (2012). Business impact of web 2.0 technologies. *Communications of the ACM*, *53*(12), 67–79.

Applegate, L. M., Austin, R. D., & McFarlan, F. W. (2002). *Corporate information strategy and management*. Boston: Mcgraw Hill.

Avanade. (2012). The mobile workforce: The future of work. *Avanade Research Series*.

Bailey, D. E. [Diana E.], & Kurland, N. B. (2002). A review of telework research: Findings, new directions, and lessons for the study of modern work. *Journal of Organizational Behavior*, *23*(4), 383–400.

Bainey, K. R. (2016). *Integrated it performance management*. Boca Raton, FL: CRC Press.

Ballgas, R. (2004). Byod: Bring your own device. *Media Computing Group*.

Baltzan, P. (2023). M: *Information systems* (7th ed.). New York, NY: McGraw-Hill Education.

Bartik, A. W., Cullen, Z. B., Glaeser, E. L., Luca, M., & Stanton, C. T. (2020). *What jobs are being done at home during the covid-19 crisis? evidence from firm-level surveys*. National Bureau of Economic Research.

Baschin, A. (2001). *Die balanced scorecard für ihren informationstechnologie-bereich*. Frankfurt/Main: Campus.

Bentley, M., O'Brien, J., & Smith, K. (2020). A review of the legal and regulatory implications of remote working. *Journal of Business Law*, *55*(6), 525–544. https://doi.org/10.1093/jbl/hak031

Bentley, T. A., Teo, S. K., McLeod, L., Tan, F., Bosua, R., & Gloet, M. (2016). The role of organisational support in teleworker wellbeing: A socio-technical systems approach. *Applied Ergonomics*, *52*, 207–215.

Bernhard, M. (2000). *Balanced scorecard in der it—welchen nutzen bringt uns die it?* Siegen: ECG Management.

Beynon-Davies, P. (2019). *Business information systems* (3rd ed.). London, UK: Red Globe Press.

Bick, A., Blandin, A., & Mertens, K. (2020). *Work from home after the covid-19 outbreak* (tech. rep. No. Working Paper No. 2017). Federal Reserve Bank of Dallas.

M. Groß, *Managing IT in the Age of BYOD and Remote Work*,
https://doi.org/10.1007/978-3-658-51216-3

Biron, M., & van Veldhoven, M. (2016). When control becomes a liability rather than an asset: Comparing home and office days among part-time teleworkers. *Journal of Organizational Behavior*, *37*(8), 1317–1337.

BITKOM. (2013). Byod in deutschen unternehmen: Status quo und trends. *BITKOM Studienbericht*. Retrieved August 27, 2023, from https://www.bitkom.org/sites/main/files/file/import/130304-LF-BYOD.pdf

Blankenhorn, H. (2005). *Den wertebeitrag der it im unternehmen ermitteln und steuern, in: Blomer, roland/ mann, hartmund/ bernhard,* martin g. (hrsg): Praktisches it-management. Düsseldorf: Symposion Publishing.

Bloom, N., Liang, J., Roberts, J., & Ying, Z. J. (2015). Does working from home work? evidence from a chinese experiment. *Quarterly Journal of Economics*, *130*(1), 165–218.

Boswell, W. R., & Olson-Buchanan, J. B. (2007). The use of communication technologies after hours: The role of work attitudes and work-life conflict. *Journal of Management*, *33*(4), 592–610.

Bourgeois, D. T., Smith, J. L., Wang, J., & Mortati, J. (2014). *Information systems for business and beyond*. Washington, DC: Saylor Foundation.

Brodin, M. (2016). Bring your own device (byod): An analysis of a future trend. In A. Marcus (Ed.), *Design, user experience, and usability: Technological contexts* (pp. 140–150). Springer.

Brun, R. (2008). Planen—messen—steuern: Die kernprozesse von it-governance und it-controlling. *Information Management und Controlling*, *23*, 60–68.

Brynjolfsson, E., Mitchell, T., & Rock, D. (2020). The productivity gains from remote work. *MIT Sloan Management Review*, *61*(3), 1–7. https://doi.org/10.1162/smr_r1000127

Buckley, R. (2012). How to cope with byod. *SC Magazine: For IT Security Professionals*, 23–26.

Bulgurcu, B., Cavusoglu, H., & Benbasat, I. (2010). Information security policy compliance: An empirical study of rationality-based beliefs and information security awareness. *MIS Quarterly*, *34*(3), 523–548.

Bundesamt, S. (2022). Arbeitnehmer im homeoffice. *Statistisches Bundesamt*, 10–15.

Calder, A. (2013). Is the byod movement worth the risks?. *Credit Control*, *34*(3), 65–70.

Carr, N. G. (2003). It doesn't matter. *Harvard Business Review*, *32*, 10–45.

Center, P. R. (2023). Americans' views on bring your own device (byod) policies. *Pew Research Center—Internet & Technology*. Retrieved July 12, 2023, from https://www.pewresearch.org/internet/2023/07/20/americans-views-on-bring-your-own-device-byod-policies/

Chen, L.-D., Chen, G., & Capistrano, E. (2013). Business–it alignment maturity of companies in china. *Information & Management*, *50*(1), 57–67.

Chen, S.-H., & Kuo, L.-Y. (2021). Telecommuting, spillover effect, and local environment: A case study for taiwan. *Sustainability*, *13*(2), 582.

Choudhury, P., Foroughi, C., & Larson, B. Z. (2021). Work-from-anywhere: The productivity effects of geographic flexibility. *Strategic Management Journal*, *42*(4), 655–683.

Cisco. (2021). Bring your own device. Retrieved July 25, 2023, from https://www.cisco.com/c/en/us/solutions/enterprise-networks/bring-your-own-device-byod/index.html

Commission, E. (2003). Commission recommendation of 6 may 2003 concerning the definition of micro, small and medium-sized enterprises (2003/361/ec). Retrieved

September 11, 2023, from https://eur-lex.europa.eu/legal-content/EN/TXT/?uri=CELEX %3A32003H0361

Darvish, H., Mohammadi, M., & Afsharpour, P. (2012). Studing the knowledge management—effect of promoting the balanced scorecard perspectives. *Economics Insights*, *64*, 9–23.

DeFilippis, E., Impink, S. M., Singell, M., Polzer, J. T., & Sadun, R. (2020). *Collaborating during coronavirus: The impact of covid-19 on the nature of work* (tech. rep. No. Working Paper 27612). NBER Working Paper Series.

Delloitte. (2016). Global mobile consumer survey: Us edition.

Deloitte. (2016). The future of work: A journey to 2025. Accessed 5 May 2025. Retrieved May 5, 2025, from https://www2.deloitte.com/insights/us/en/focus/technology-and-the-future-of-work.html

Destatis. (2019). Homeoffice: Wenig beschäftigte arbeiten überwiegend von zu hause. Retrieved July 25, 2023, from https://www.destatis.de/DE/Themen/Arbeit/Arbeitsmarkt/Homeoffice.html

Dillman, D. A. (2000). *Mail and internet surveys: The tailored design method*. John Wiley & Sons.

Division, U. N. S. (2023). International standard industrial classification of all economic activities (isic). Retrieved September 11, 2023, from https://unstats.un.org/unsd/classifications/Econ/

Duvall, E. M. (2005). Telework: A productivity paradox? *IEEE Internet Computing*, 9(6), 85–89.

Ehrmann, H. (2007). *Die balanced scorecard*. Leipzig: Kiehl.

Elghaly, A. (2018). Towards a comprehensive understanding of the different concepts related to the adoption of consumer it in the workplace. *Journal of Theoretical and Applied Information Technology*, *96*(18), 6141–6155.

Elmasri, R., & Navathe, S. B. (2015). *Fundamentals of database systems* (7th ed.). Boston, MA: Pearson.

Eurofound. (2020). Living, working and covid-19. Retrieved July 25, 2023, from https://www.eurofound.europa.eu/publications/report/2020/living-working-and-covid-19

Eurofound, & the International Labour Office. (2020). Living, working and covid-19. Luxembourg: Publications Office of the European Union.

Eurofound and the International Labour Office. (2017). *Working anytime, anywhere: The effects on the world of work*. Luxembourg: Publications Office of the European Union and ILO.

European Parliament and Council. (2016). Regulation (eu) 2016/679 of the european parliament and of the council of 27 april 2016 on the protection of natural persons with regard to the processing of personal data and on the free movement of such data, and repealing directive 95/46/ec (general data protection regulation).

Eurostat. (2023). Employed persons working from home as a percentage of the total employment, by sex, age and professional status. Online database. Retrieved May 5, 2025, from https://ec.europa.eu/eurostat/databrowser/view/lfsa_ehomp/default/table

Federal Statistical Office of Germany (Destatis). (2024). Almost one in four employed persons worked from home in 2023. Press release No. N032, 18 June 2024. Retrieved May 5, 2025, from https://www.destatis.de/DE/Presse/Pressemitteilungen/2024/06/PD24_N032_13.html

Felstead, A., & Henseke, G. (2017). Assessing the growth of remote working and its consequences for effort, well-being and work-life balance. *New Technology, Work and Employment*, 32(3), 195–212.

Fischer, A. (2012). The impact of cloud and byod computing on software compliance and audit. *Credit Control*, 60–62.

Fonner, K. L., & Roloff, M. E. (2010). Why teleworkers are more satisfied with their jobs than are office-based workers: When less contact is beneficial. *Journal of Applied Communication Research*, *38*(4), 336–361.

French, A. M., Guo, C., & Shim, J. P. (2014). Current status, issues, and future of bring your own device (byod). *CAIS*, 35(10).

Gajendran, R. S., & Harrison, D. A. (2007). The good, the bad, and the unknown about telecommuting: Meta-analysis of psychological mediators and individual consequences. *Journal of Applied Psychology*, *92*(6), 1524.

Gallaugher, J. (2023). *Information systems: A manager's guide to harnessing technology* (5th ed.). Boston, MA: FlatWorld.

Gartner. (2013). Gartner says most global enterprises will allow employees to use personal devices at work by 2016. *Gartner Press Release*.

Gartner. (2020). The future of work reinforces importance of byod. Retrieved July 25, 2023, from https://www.gartner.com/smarterwithgartner/the-future-of-work-reinforces-importance-of-byod/

Gartner. (2023). Market guide for bring your own device (byod) security. *Gartner Research*. Retrieved July 12, 2023, from https://www.gartner.com/doc/3987709/market-guide-bring-your-own-device-byod-security

Gaulke, M. (2002). *Management von operativen risiken*. Oldenbourg: Oldenbourg Wissenschaftsverlag.

Gaulke, M. (2020). *Praxiswissen cobit*. Heidelberg: dpunkt.verlag.

Ginovsky, J. (2012). "byod" quandary. *ABA Banking Journal*, April, 24–27.

Golden, T. D., & Veiga, J. F. (2005). The impact of extent of telecommuting on job satisfaction: Resolving inconsistent findings. *Journal of Management*, *31*(2), 301–318.

Golden, T. D., Veiga, J. F., & Dino, R. N. (2008). The impact of professional isolation on teleworker job performance and turnover intentions: Does time spent teleworking, interacting face-to-face, or having access to communication-enhancing technology matter? *Journal of Applied Psychology*, *93*(6), 1412.

Golden, T. D., Veiga, J., & Simsek, Z. (2006). Telecommuting's differential impact on work-family conflict: Is there no place like home? *Journal of Applied Psychology*, *91*(6), 1340.

Gollmann, D., Massacci, F., & Yautsiukhin, A. (2006). *Quality of protection: Security measurements and metrics*. Berlin: Springer.

Grembergen, W. V. (2000). The balanced scorecard and it governance. *Information Systems Control Journal, 2*.

Grembergen, W. V., & Haes, S. D. (2009). *Enterprise governance of information technology: Achieving alignment and value, featuring cobit* 5. Springer.

Grembergen, W. V., & Haes, S. D. (2018). Introduction to cobit 2019. In *Enterprise governance of information technology: Achieving alignment and value, featuring cobit 5* (pp. 57–69). Springer.

Groß, M. (2024). Integration of cobit 2019 and byod: An empirical analysis of performance measurement in the context of the balanced scorecard. *Power System Technology*, 48(1). Retrieved from https://powertechjournal.com/index.php/journal/article/view/524

Gupta, B., Seetharaman, A., & Raj, J. R. (2013). The usage and adoption of cloud computing by small and medium businesses. *International Journal of Information Management*, *33*(5), 861–874.

Haes, S. D., & Grembergen, W. V. (2005). *It governance and its mechanisms*. cf. pp. 23-25. Hershey, PA: Idea Group Publishing.

Haes, S. D., & Grembergen, W. V. (2015). *Enterprise governance of information technology: Achieving alignment and value, featuring cobit* 5. Springer.

Haes, S. D., & Grembergen, W. V. (2019). An exploratory study into it governance implementations and its impact on business/it alignment. *Information Systems Management*, *26*(2), 123–137.

Haeseler, H. R., & Hörmann, F. (2005). *Strategy maps—eine echte bereicherung? in: Seicht (2005), jahrbuch f*ür controlling und rechnungswesen. Dayton: LexisNexis.

Haider, G. (2000). *Unternehmensführung und informationstechnik*. Springer.

Harris, J., Ives, B., & Junglas, I. (2012). It consumerization: When gadgets turn into enterprise it tools. *MIS Quarterly Executive*, 11(3).

Harris, M. A., Patten, K., & Regan, E. (2018). The need for byod mobile device security awareness and training. *Proceedings of the EDSIG Conference*.

Henderson, T. (2012). Top tools for byod management. *networkworld*, Nov, 22–30.

Herath, T., & Rao, H. R. (2009). Protection motivation and deterrence: A framework for security policy compliance in organizations. *European Journal of Information Systems*, *18*(2), 106–125.

Hill, E. J., Miller, B. C., Weiner, S. P., & Colihan, J. (1998). Influences of the virtual office on aspects of work and work/life balance. *Personnel Psychology*, *51*(3), 667–683.

Hinds, P. J., & Bailey, D. E. [D. E.]. (2003). Out of sight, out of sync: Understanding conflict in distributed teams. *Organization Science*, *14*(6), 615–632.

Hjorth, D., & Peters, P. (2019). Entrepreneurship as craft. *Entrepreneurship Theory and Practice*, *43*(3), 507–525.

Horváth, P. (1997). *Balanced scorecard*. Stuttgart: Schäffer-Poeschel.

Hunt, J. (2012). Byod policy—what businesses need to consider. *Credit Control*, 33(5/6), 69–71.

IDC. (2012). Idc mobile enterprise survey. *IDC Research Report*.

Institute, I. G. (2011). *Cobit 5: A business framework for the governance and management of enterprise it*. IT Governance Institute.

Institute, P. (2020). The cost of insecure endpoints. *Ponemon Institute*.

Intel. (2009). Intel identifies growing trend of consumerization of it. Retrieved July 25, 2023, from https://newsroom.intel.com/editorials/intel-identifies-growing-trend-consumerization-it/

ISACA. (2019a). *Cobit 2019 framework: Introduction and methodology*. ISACA.

ISACA. (2019b). *Cobit 2019 framework: Introduction and methodology*. ISACA.

ISACA. (2019c). *Cobit 2019 implementation guide: Implementing and optimizing an information and technology governance solution*. ISACA.

ISC(2). (2023). Byod security guide. *ISC2 White Paper Series*. Retrieved July 12, 2023, from https://www.isc2.org/blogs/byod-security-guide

Kamleitner, J., & Langer, M. (2006). *Business it alignment mit itil, cobit, rup*. Bad Homburg: Serview Verlag.

Kaplan, R. S., & Norton, D. P. (1992). The balanced scorecard—measures that drives performance. *Harvard Business Review, Jan–Feb*(1), 71–79.

Kaplan, R. S., & Norton, D. P. (1996a). *The balanced scorecard*. Harvard Business Review Press.

Kaplan, R. S., & Norton, D. P. (1996b). Using the balanced scorecard as strategic management system. *Harvard Business Review*, Ja–Feb, 75–85.

Kaplan, R. S., & Norton, D. P. (2001). *The strategy-focused organization: How balanced scorecard companies thrive in the new* business environment. Harvard Business Review Press.

Kaplan, R. S., & Norton, D. P. (2004). *Strategy maps: Converting intangible assets into tangible outcomes*. Harvard Business Review Press.

Kearny, A. (2011). Byod: The next wave of mobile computing. *A.T. Kearny*.

Kelliher, C., & Anderson, D. (2010). Doing more with less? flexible working practices and the intensification of work. *Human Relations*, *63*(1), 83–106.

Kersten, H., & Klett, G. (2008). *Der it security manager*. Wiesbaden: Vieweg + Teubner.

Kersten, H., Reuter, J., & Schröder, K.-W. (2011). *It-sicherheitsmanagement nach iso 27001 und grundschutz*. Wiesbaden: Vieweg.

Keyes, J. (2013). *Bring your own devices (byod) survival guide*. New York: CRC Press.

Klotz, M. (2019, August). *It-compliance nach cobit®2019*. https://doi.org/10.13140/RG.2.2.34583.11687/1

Klußmann, N. (1997). *Lexikon der kommunikations- und informationstechnik*. Heidelberg: Hüthig,

Kniffin, K. M., Narayanan, J., Anseel, F., Antonakis, J., Ashford, S. P., Bakker, A. B., ... Troth, A. (2021). Covid-19 and the workplace: Implications, issues, and insights for future research and action. *American Psychologist*, *76*(1), 63.

Köffer, S. (2015). Byod-related aspects of value creation. In H.-J. Warnecke & A. Wegner (Eds.), *Understanding the implications of digitisation and automation in the context of industry 4.0* (pp. 177–192). https://doi.org/10.1007/978-3-658-07556-5_11

Kommission, E. (2022). Home office in the eu: Overview of the legal framework. *European Commission*, 12–15.

Kossek, E. E., Lautsch, B. A., & Eaton, S. C. (2006). Telecommuting, control, and boundary management: Correlates of policy use and practice, job control, and work–family effectiveness. *Journal of Vocational Behavior*, *68*(2), 347–367.

Krcmar, H. (2003). *Informationsmanagement*. Berlin: Springer.

Kumar, A., & Rahman, Z. (2020). Working from home during covid-19: Employees' perception and experiences. *Journal of Public Affairs*.

Kurland, N. B., & Bailey, D. E. [D. E.]. (1999). Telework: The advantages and challenges of working here, there, anywhere, and anytime. *Organizational Dynamics*, *28*(2), 53–68.

Kütz, M. (2002). *Balanced scorecard im it-bereich*. München: Symposium.

Kütz, M. (2009). *Kennzahlen in der it*. Heidelberg: dpunkt.verlag.

Living, working and covid-19. (2020). Luxembourg: Publications Office of the European Union.

Mann, S., & Holdsworth, L. (2003). The psychological impact of teleworking: Stress, emotions and health. *New Technology, Work and Employment*, *18*(3), 196–211.

Marr, B. (2010). *Balanced scorecards for the public sector*. London: Ark Group.

McAfee. (2020). The new byod: Best practices for a productive remote workforce. Retrieved July 25, 2023, from https://www.mcafee.com/enterprise/en-us/security-awareness/home-office/the-new-byod-best-practices-for-a-productive-remote-workforce.html

Microsoft. (2021). The next great disruption is hybrid work—are we ready? Retrieved July 25, 2023, from https://www.microsoft.com/en-us/worklab/work-trend-index/hybrid-work

Miller, K. (2012). "byod: From company-issued to employee-owned devices". *Network Security*, (6), 5–8.

Miller, K. W., Voas, J., & Hurlburt, G. F. (2012). Byod: Security and privacy considerations. *IT Professional*, *14*(5), 53–55.

Mirza, F., Weiss, C., & Jekel, R. (2012). "bring your own device" shakes up it departments. ATKearney.

Muller, A., Frey, S., & Väätäjä, H. (2019). Challenges and opportunities of byod policies in the workplace: An empirical investigation. *Proceedings of the 52nd Hawaii International Conference on System Sciences*.

Naranjo-Gil, D. (2012). The role of technology use in the performance effects of the balanced scorecard. *Journal of Applied Management Accounting Research*, *10*(1), 37.

Neely, A. (2007). *Business performance measurement: Unifying theory and integrating practice* (2nd ed.). Cambridge, UK: Cambridge University Press.

Nilles, J. M. (1975). Telecommunications and organizational decentralization. *IEEE Transactions on Communications*, *23*(10), 1142–1147.

on Trade, U. N. C., & Development. (2021). *World investment report 2021: Investing in a changing world*. UNCTAD.

Otley, D., & Emmanuel, C. (2013). *Performance measurement and management: A strategic approach to management accounting*. Boston, MA: Cengage Learning.

Pew Research Center. (2020). How the coronavirus has changed the way americans work. Based on surveys conducted during 2020, including Gallup data. Retrieved May 5, 2025, from https://www.pewresearch.org/internet/2020/12/09/how-the-coronavirus-has-changed-the-way-americans-work/

Pohlmann, N., & Blumberg, H. (2006). *Der it-sicherheitsleitfaden*. Heidelberg: mitp.

Raab-Steiner, M., & Benesch, W. (2010). *Informationssicherheitsmanagement: Konzepte, methoden und techniken*. Springer Vieweg.

Rappaport, A. (1986). *Creating shareholder value: The new standard for business performance*. New York, NY: The Free Press.

Risby, J. (2004). The balanced scorecard: A worldwide survey of management tools. *Balanced Scorecard Collaborative*.

Rodham, J. (2012). Get used to byod. *Backbone*, 12–14.

Schmid-Kleemann, M. (2003). *Balanced scorecard im it-controlling*. Zürich: Universität Zürich.

Schnell, R. (1991). *Methoden der empirischen sozialforschung*. Oldenbourg.

Schnell, R. et al. (2008). *Methoden der empirischen sozialforschung*. Oldenbourg.

Schooley, B., & Marien, C. (2020). Byod: An empirical study of employee apprehension and supportive organizational initiatives. *Journal of Computer Information Systems*, *60*(3), 233–242.

Silk, A. J. (1998). Balanced scorecard: A performance management tool for learning organizations. *Journal of Strategic Performance Measurement*, *2*(1), 13–22.

Siponen, M., Mahmood, M. A., & Pahnila, S. (2014). Employees' adherence to information security policies: An exploratory field study. *Information & Management*, *51*(2), 217–224.

Siponen, M., Willison, R., & Baskerville, R. (2012). Information security management standards: Problems and solutions. *Information & Management, 49*(5), 226–234.

Soomro, Z. A., Shah, M. A., & Ahmed, J. (2016). Information security management needs a more holistic approach: A literature review. *International Journal of Information Management, 36*(2), 215–225.

Speckbacher, G., Bischof, J., & Pfeiffer, T. (2003). A descriptive analysis on the implementation of balanced scorecards in german-speaking countries. *Management Accounting Research, 14*, 361–388.

Stanley, M. (2013). The future of mobile computing. *Morgan Stanley Blue Paper Series.*

Stanton, B. et al. (2015). *Security of mobile computing devices.* National Institute of Standards and Technology, NIST SP—800–124 Revision.

Stavrou, E., Panaousis, E., & Kandias, M. (2018). Security economics to inform behavior change: A systematic approach. *Behavior & Information Technology*, 37(10-11), 1037–1057.

Sullivan, C., & Staas, D. (2014). Exploring the legal implications of telecommuting. *Journal of Internet Law, 17*(11), 1–21.

Sury, U. (2005). It-governance. *Informatik Spektrum, 23*, 68–71.

Syntonic. (2016). 2016 employer report: Byod usage in the enterprise.

Tarantino, A. (2012). *Governance, risk, and compliance handbook for oracle applications.* Jones & Bartlett Learning.

van Bon, J. (2005). *Itil v3—das taschenbuch.* Niederlande: Van Haren Publishing.

Versteegen, G. (2003). *Risikomanagement in it-projekten.* Berlin: Springer.

Verweire, K., & Van den Berghe, L. (Eds.). (2004). *Integrated performance management: A guide to strategy implementation.* London, UK: SAGE Publications Ltd.

Violino, B. (2012). The byod security challenge. *Insurance Networking News, 15*(6), 29–31. Retrieved from http://search.ebscohost.com.ezproxy.wales.ac.uk:2048/login.aspx?direct=true&db=bth&AN=80233906&site=ehost-live&scope=site

Wang, R. (2020). Comparative study of byod (bring your own device) and cyod (choose your own device) in the context of security and privacy. In *2020 international conference on computing, networking and communications (icnc)* (pp. 517–521). IEEE.

Ward, J., & Peppard, J. (2002). *Strategic planning for information systems.* Chichester: John Wiley & Sons.

Weill, P., & Ross, J. W. (2004). *It governance: How top performers manage it decision rights for superior results.* Harvard Business Press.

Weiss, J., & Anderson, E. (2020). Managing employee compliance with information security policies: The critical role of top management and organizational culture. *Decision Sciences, 51*(4), 788–827.

Wiedemann, A. (2012). *Balanced scorecard als instrument des bankencontrollings.* Siegen: Uni Siegen.

Williams, S. (2005). The balanced scorecard: A survey of fortune 500 companies. *Strategy & Leadership, 33*(2), 4–10.

Willis, D. A., & Madsen, S. (2013). *Bring your own device: The facts and the future.* Gartner Research Report.

Wright, N., Dawson, M., & Omar, A. (2020). Cyber risk and the u.s. financial system: A pre-mortem analysis. *FRB of New York Staff Report*, (934).

Zumstein, D. (2005). *Balanced scorecard in der it.* Bern: Uni Bern.

MIX
Papier aus verantwortungsvollen Quellen
Paper from responsible sources
FSC® C105338

If you have any concerns about our products, you can contact us on
ProductSafety@springernature.com

In case Publisher is established outside the EU, the EU authorized representative is:
Springer Nature Customer Service Center GmbH
Europaplatz 3, 69115 Heidelberg, Germany

Printed by Libri Plureos GmbH
in Hamburg, Germany